From Wasteland to Wonder

easy ways we can help heal earth
in the sub/urban landscape

Basil Camu

From Wasteland to Wonder: Easy Ways We Can Help Heal Earth
in the Sub/Urban Landscape, 2nd Edition

ISBN 979-8-9900303-0-5 (print)
ISBN 979-8-9900303-2-9 (digital online)
Copyright © 2024, Basil Camu

All rights reserved. No part of this publication may be reproduced, stored in a retrieval system, or transmitted in any form or by any means without the prior written consent of the publisher, except by a reviewer, who may quote brief passages.

Printed in Canada.

Published by Leaf & Limb, 511 Nowell Road, Raleigh, NC 27601, USA
www.leaflimb.com

The views expressed in this publication are those of the author and do not necessarily reflect policies and/or official positions of Leaf & Limb or Project Pando. Mention of product names in this publication does not constitute endorsement by the author or Leaf & Limb or Project Pando.

To receive permission to reproduce any content, please email wonder@leaflimb.com.

To donate to Project Pando and support its mission to connect people with trees to help heal Earth please visit: www.leaflimb.com/pando.

Photo credits: cover and pages 6, 9, 10, 15, 18, 20, 22, 25, 26, 28, 30, 33, 34, 36, 39, 40, 41, 42, 46, 48, 49, 52, 54, 56, 58, 73, 88, 91, 112, 114, 124, 130, 137, 138, 141, 145, 155, 159, and 210 from iStock.com, 10 from Alamy, 202 and cover by Layne Lawson/Unsplash and all others by Tessa Williams/Leaf & Limb.

This book was written in loving dedication to this marvelous, pale blue dot that we call home.

It is also dedicated to my dearest friend Morgan who is equally marvelous.

table of contents

Why This Book is Worth Your Time — 6

This Book is My Act of Reciprocity — 12

Section 1: Four Fun Essays About Healthy Natural Systems — 16
1. Trees Build Soil — 18
2. Soil Stores Fresh Water & Trees Move It — 22
3. Trees Feed & Shelter Terrestrial Life — 26
4. Trees Pump CO_2 From the Atmosphere & Sequester It Within Life — 30

Section 2: Four Not-So-Fun Essays About Broken Natural Systems — 34
5. We Are Destroying Forests & Grasslands — 36
6. We Are Turning Soil into Dirt & Running Out of Fresh Water — 42
7. We Are Killing Life — 46
8. In Terms Of CO_2, We Are Returning to the Carboniferous Period — 52

Section 3: Fast & Easy Ways to Help Heal Earth — 56
9. Some Important Notes Before We Begin — 60
10. Start with Planting Trees—One of the Most Important Things We Can Do — 64
11. Save Existing Trees—They Rarely Need to Be Removed — 80
12. Perform Structural Pruning to Increase Strength—It's the Only Pruning That Matters — 96
13. A Very Short Diversion on Pruning Shrubs — 108
14. Promote Soil Bursting with Life — 112
15. More Easy Ways to Promote Outrageous Diversity! — 130

Section 4: More Powerful Ways to Help Heal Earth   142

    16. Lawns Are Ecological Disasters—Replace Them
        with Meadows from Seed   148
    17. Pocket Forests—A Better Way to Plant Trees   164

Section 5: Lead & Inspire Communities to Help Heal Earth   176

In Closing   202

Please Donate to Project Pando & Help Heal Earth   204

A Note of Gratitude   206

Appendix   210

References   212

why this book is worth your time

By the end of this book I hope to convince you of three points:

1. The way we currently manage the suburban and urban (henceforth *sub/urban*) landscape is creating a wasteland and harming the well-being of Earth.

2. The landscape paradigms and practices outlined in this book do the opposite—they help heal Earth.

3. When we work to help heal Earth, we save time and money because we are working with natural systems instead of against them.

When I began this journey, I joined my dad as his business partner in what was then called Leaf & Limb Tree Service. I did not know the first thing about trees—except how to cut them down. My goal was to grow and optimize the business model, increase revenue, and generate as much profit as possible. In short, my goal was to become rich by cutting down trees.

But along the way, I started learning more about the complexity of trees and soil. I came to understand and appreciate how they play an essential role in the well-being of life on this planet. We decided to transform Leaf & Limb into a company that cares for trees instead of one that cuts them down.

Through this change I came to clearly see what should have been obvious: **our current landscape paradigms and practices produce millions of acres of sub/urban wasteland that exacerbate some of our most serious environmental issues.** We pave over forests, use giant machines to scrape away soil, and turn thriving grasslands into dead lawns. Rain is unable to soak into the ground and instead rushes downhill, causing erosion and flooding. We repeatedly soak the land in toxic chemicals that kill life. There is little food for the migrating birds, butterflies, and pollinators that need it. Even when we attempt to replant trees we miss the mark—they generally have handicapped root systems, are improperly installed, and die prematurely. Worst yet, many species are from other parts of the world and create ecological disasters within their new ecosystems.

There is hope! The methods I outline in the coming pages do the exact opposite. They help heal Earth instead of causing harm. These methods also help save time and money, because we perform fewer tasks by working with natural systems instead of against them. Think about swimming with a water current versus swimming against it. The latter is our existing model. It takes effort to swim upstream—we use a lot of energy in exchange for little movement. What I teach in this book is swimming with the current, which means we use less energy and achieve greater results.

Here's the new game plan in a nutshell: increase photosynthesis and transform dirt back to soil. Properly plant native trees. Help them attain a long, healthy life. Preserve existing trees. Get rid of lawns in exchange for native meadows planted from seed. Stop using fertilizers and harmful chemicals. Do everything we can to increase the abundance and diversity of life within the sub/urban landscape.

Let me assure you that there is no catch and no sacrifice required. I am not going to ask you to do anything more difficult or unpleasant than what you are already doing (quite the opposite). All I ask is that you keep an open mind, because I'm going to dismantle many facets of our current landscape paradigms and practices. Please hold your ideas about the ways we currently care for trees, lawns, and sub/urban spaces lightly and leave room for new ones. We can think of our ideas like clothes—they do not define us.

Much like clothes, when our ideas become old and worn, we should trade them for new ones.

I'm saving the best for last. After we transformed Leaf & Limb from a traditional tree service into what it is now, I found that caring for trees, soil, and the well-being of Earth yields a more beautiful world than what I had experienced previously. My life is full of joy and purpose; joy because I experience so many moments of wonder, and purpose because I feel empowered to help solve big issues using the spaces where I live, work, and play. My hope is that what follows provides you with similar experiences.

Here is an overview of what to expect in the coming sections of this book:

Section 1: Four Fun Essays About Healthy Natural Systems
The essays in this section explain how the systems of photosynthesis and soil formation work and how they affect water, carbon, and all other life on land. Understanding these systems and relationships provides a knowledge base for everything that follows. These essays are meant to be entertaining and easy to understand.

Section 2: Four Not-So-Fun Essays About Broken Natural Systems
This section is a downer. My apologies in advance. In these essays I revisit the same systems from Section 1, but this time I illustrate how we are damaging them. These essays provide a foundation for why we need new paradigms and practices in the sub/urban landscape.

Section 3: Fast & Easy Ways to Help Heal Earth
This section provides tutorials and instructions for the easiest concepts that we can implement quickly on our properties to help heal Earth. This and the remaining sections are built on first-hand experience from me and my colleagues at Leaf & Limb and Project Pando since 2010.

Section 4: More Powerful Ways to Help Heal Earth
Here we learn about planting pocket forests and thickets from saplings, as well as meadows from seeds. By working with communities of plants instead of individual plants, we generate some unexpected benefits (including less maintenance as compared to the status quo) and increase our ability to help heal Earth by orders of magnitude. These actions also provide incredible beauty! A meadow in July is one of the loveliest things I have experienced.

Section 5: Lead & Inspire Communities to Help Heal Earth
For those who want to help shift paradigms even more, we can work with our communities to gather native seeds, raise them into trees, and give them away for free. The model outlined in this section not only makes native plants more widely available while bringing people together through a shared sense of purpose and community, but it also has the power to change hearts and minds—and paradigms by extension.

this book is my act of reciprocity

Robin Wall Kimmerer (author of *Braiding Sweetgrass*) proclaims, "Share. Give thanks for what you have been given. Give a gift, in reciprocity for what you have taken. Sustain the ones who sustain you and the Earth will last forever."

I love this concept and felt inspired when I first read it. **I decided to give away this book for free as my act of reciprocity, my tiny way of saying "thank you" for the incredible privilege of being alive.** I have experienced so much joy working on this book, and it brings me even more joy knowing that I can now share it with you in hopes that together we can help heal Earth.

The digital copy is fully free and the hard copy costs only the amount necessary to cover printing and distribution costs. I know many of you are generous people who will insist on paying something, perhaps as your own act of reciprocity. If that is you—and thank you in advance—you can do so in the form of a donation to our non-profit, Project Pando.

We at Leaf & Limb founded Project Pando in 2017. It is a community-driven effort where we collect seeds from wild, native trees and then raise those seeds into saplings, which we give away for free. We have grown and given away tens of thousands of native trees and shrubs. We have inspired people around the city, state, and country to replicate our work and begin growing trees for their own projects. Volunteers who knew nothing about trees, ranging from school kids to retirees, are now happily growing, planting, and tending to native trees throughout their communities. You will learn more about these efforts in Section 5 of this book where I provide the full model for Project Pando in the hopes that you and others will join, replicate, and build on our work.

Should you decide to give, I promise this: *every* **penny you donate—and I do mean literally every penny—will directly support our work at Project Pando, which aims to help heal Earth.**

You can donate using this QR code:

You can also donate by visiting **www.leaflimb.com/pando-donations**, by texting **"PANDO"** to **53555**, or by emailing **wonder@leaflimb.com**.

For those who prefer more traditional methods, you can also send a check to Project Pando, 511 Nowell Road in Raleigh, North Carolina, 27607. Please make payments out to "Project Pando."

QR Codes—What They Are & How to Use Them

QR codes allow me to provide you with videos and links that supplement the topics covered in this book without you having to type a tedious URL. To use a QR code, start by opening the camera app on your cell phone or tablet. Then point the camera at the QR code. You should see a window, bubble, or URL pop up on the screen of your device. Click that with your finger. It will take you to the intended video or webpage.

I have also listed all the links for these QR codes at **www.leaflimb.com/links** for those who prefer not to use QR codes or are not able to do so. The QR codes are not necessary; you can skip them altogether. They only serve to enhance the experience. I intentionally made sure that the core lessons of this book are all written so you can learn everything without QR codes.

For those who do use the QR codes, if ever you encounter a broken link or some other issue, please let me know by sending an email to **wonder@leaflimb.com**. Thank you!

this book is my act of reciprocity

Oh, and why the name Project Pando? Pando is a massive clonal colony of Quaking Aspens located in Utah. Each of the 50,000 trees in this colony is connected to one another by a single root system. Project Pando is built on the belief that—like Pando in Utah—we are all connected, helping one helps all, and there is strength in unity. By achieving good for all and being stewards of our shared resources, we attain a brighter future.

SECTION 1:
four fun essays about healthy natural systems

To understand the three central points of this book, we need some basic knowledge about how trees create soil, how soil holds water, how all three work in unison to create other life, and how these processes use carbon from the sky. These essays are meant to be entertaining and easy to understand. They will provide context for the issues I describe in Section 2 and the specific how-to topics that begin in Section 3.

Please note that I focus a great deal on trees in Sections 1 and 2 since I know them well. But much of what I write about trees is true for other plants and ecosystems. Lawns are the notable exception. They are more akin to sidewalks than they are to natural ecosystems.

Please also note that everything I write about in Section 1 is *far* more complicated than described. If you want to learn more, there are many books and resources available on all these topics. I will list some in the Appendix located at the end of this book.

Get ready—Earth is fascinating! Let's dive in.

CHAPTER 1

trees build soil

Our favorite star, affectionately referred to as the Sun, generates energy that travels 93 million miles to Planet Earth. It makes this journey in 500 seconds! Trees and other plants have remarkable cells that use the Sun's energy to change a mixture of water and carbon dioxide (called CO_2 for short) into oxygen and sugar. We call this process *photosynthesis*.

The sugar contains the carbon portion of the CO_2. Thanks to photosynthesis, carbon moves from floating freely in the atmosphere to being locked away in a stable state within the tree. This is an important feature called *carbon sequestration*, a topic we will revisit in more detail in Chapter 4.

Trees use this sugar for all sorts of things, including growth, reproduction, and defense. Much of the sugar is sent down to the root system and released as food for bacteria and fungi. Nematodes, protozoa, and others feed on this bacteria and fungi. Then earthworms and arthropods eat the nematodes and protozoa. These activities (and many others!) form a thriving, underground ecosystem. The majority of all life on land (known as *terrestrial life*) lives underground and participates in this ecosystem. **This living underground ecosystem is the very definition of healthy soil.** In one teaspoon of soil, there can be billions of bacteria, protozoa, nematodes, and other tiny life! In the absence of this living underground ecosystem, we find dirt, not soil. To better understand this difference, let's look at the history of how soil was formed from dirt.

We'll begin our journey by zipping hundreds of millions of years back in time. We would find a planet composed mostly of rocks surrounded by oceans. There was no soil, no plants, and very little terrestrial life back then. If it rained, the water flowed over the rocks and quickly swept to the oceans. Over time, rain, wind, waves, and a variety of other processes weathered rocks into smaller particles, called sand, silt, and clay. **These three are the definition of dirt.**

But then something amazing started happening! Lichens began the process of turning dirt (sand, silt, and clay) into soil (dirt plus a living underground ecosystem). Lichens formed from a symbiotic relationship between fungi and algae or cyanobacteria. The algae and

cyanobacteria could photosynthesize, which provided food for the lichen team. The other part of the lichen team—the fungi—used their teeny, tiny strands (called *hyphae*) to collect water in hard-to-reach places and to absorb nutrients by breaking down dirt with organic acids. Between the two organisms, the lichen team was able to generate food, stay hydrated, and absorb nutrients in what was an otherwise barren landscape of rocks and dirt.

Over time lichen multiplied and spread across the land. They dissolved rocks, freed nutrients, and soaked up carbon at an increasing rate. As all life does, each lichen eventually died and its remains provided an infusion of carbon and nutrients into what had previously only been dirt. This combination of dead lichens and dirt was better suited to hold rain for longer periods of time. As these pools of water became infused with carbon and nutrients became more common, the complexity of life increased. Lichens yielded to liverworts. Glassworts and club mosses emerged, followed by horsetails, ferns, and finally the trees, flowers, and grasses we know today.

In a few weeks on the Cosmic Calendar, photosynthesis played a key role in transforming land that was once dirt into a thriving ecosystem with deep soil. Where there are healthy plants and soil, there is also an abundance of fresh water.

The Cosmic Calendar

"Hundreds of millions of years" is difficult to comprehend. I find that a concept called the Cosmic Calendar (popularized by Carl Sagan) makes vast timespans easier to understand. The Cosmic Calendar places the Big Bang at the start of the calendar (January 1 at 12:01 AM) and today's date at the end of the calendar (December 31 at 11:59 PM).

Using this system, the Earth forms on September 14. By September 25, life on Earth (prokaryotes) arrives. Significant oxygen begins to fill the atmosphere on December 1. Land plants appear on December 20, dinosaurs on December 24, mammals on December 26, and birds on December 27. We humans do not even show up until 10:30 PM on December 31. The Industrial Revolution begins less than one second before midnight. Using this scale, the average human lifespan (70–80 years) is less than one-fifth of a second.

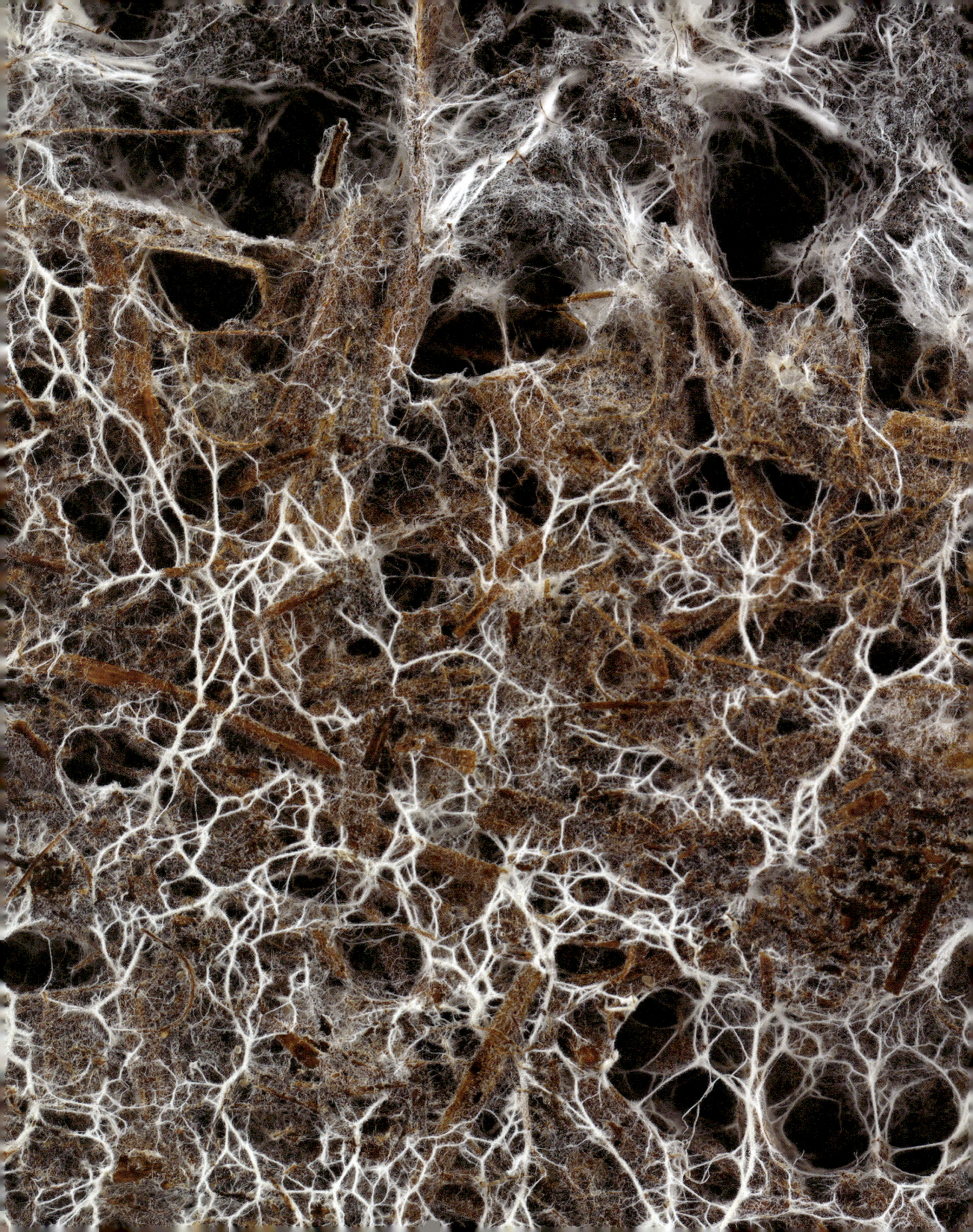

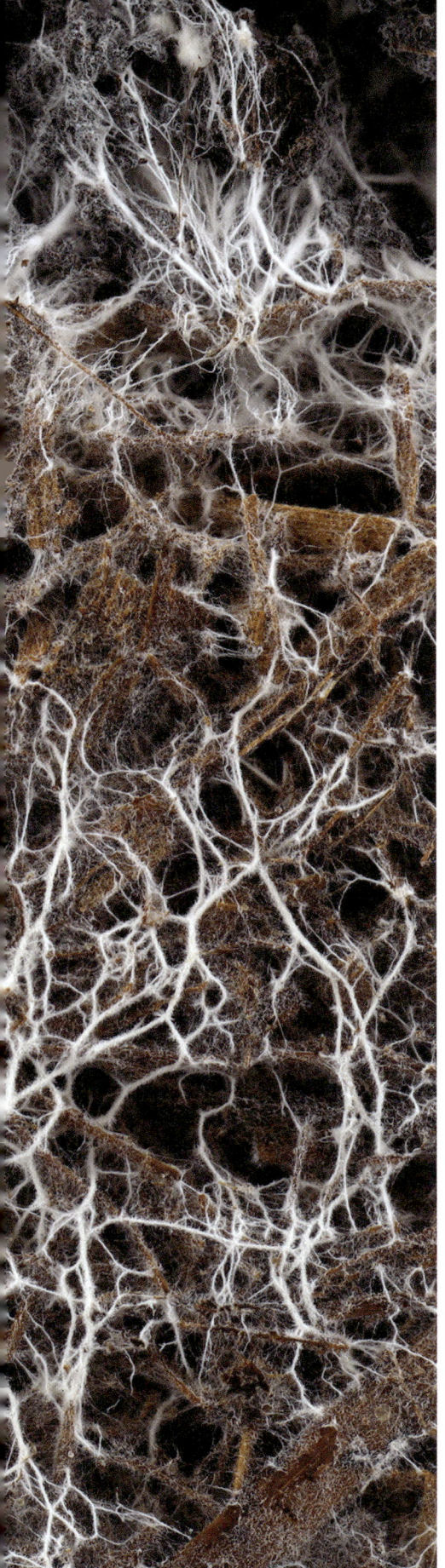

CHAPTER 2

soil stores fresh water & trees move it

Soil has structure, which means it has plenty of gaps between the dirt (particles of sand, silt, and clay) to hold air and water. It is helpful to think of soil as a sponge. Much like a sponge, it can hold water when there is rain and air when there is none. But how are these gaps—the soil structure—formed?

In short, life is what creates ideal soil structure. Bacteria, fungi, protozoa, nematodes, springtails, mites, ants, earthworms, and all other members of the soil ecosystem eat, poop, reproduce, and die. To do this they wriggle, crawl, and tunnel their way through dirt. Some are predators that eat others, and some are prey that hide from predators. Some eat *organic matter*, which is the dead remains of anything that was once living. Dead leaves are a good example. Some secrete slimes, glycoproteins, and other sticky substances. These and other activities produce soil structure in three primary ways:

1. Life moving in the soil—wriggling, crawling, and tunneling—produces gaps between particles of dirt.
2. Poop, dead bodies, and other organic matter form spacers between particles of dirt, producing gaps.
3. The sticky materials bind dirt together in clumps, which generates more gaps. We call these clumps *aggregates*.

If we could pull a cube of soil from the ground and closely examine it, we would find that roughly half of that cube is empty space created by these various activities. These gaps fill with water when it rains. During 1 inch of rainfall, approximately 27,000 gallons of water falls per acre. Soil can absorb nearly all of this rain. As water percolates into the soil, bacteria and fungi filter contaminants, pollutants, and heavy metals. Eventually clean, fresh water settles in giant storage areas underground called *aquifers*. These storage areas provide crucial hydration for terrestrial life.

Water's journey does not end there. When a tree has access to plenty of water stored in the soil and is basking under the warmth of the Sun, it sucks water through its roots, up the trunk, and into its leaves, where that water is used for photosynthesis. Well, *some* of it is used for photosynthesis. Most of it evaporates from the leaf into the atmosphere. This movement of water through the tree is called *transpiration*.

Transpiration generates a substantial amount of water movement. For example, a mature oak tree can transport over 40,000 gallons of water from soil to sky per year! By comparison, a typical swimming pool holds around 20,000 gallons of water. That is a lot of water moving from the soil into the atmosphere. This upward movement from transpiration generates an area of low pressure underneath in its wake. This low-pressure area sucks in air from nearby—some of which is filled with moisture from neighboring bodies of water or adjacent forests. Then the trees release volatile organic compounds (VOCs) into the sky, which interact with the moisture to generate rain. When the rain falls, it waters the trees, refills the soil, and the process repeats. This cycle spreads to other areas as long as sufficient forests and soil are present to facilitate it.

Trees are Also Air Conditioning Units

Transpiration also provides a cooling effect because the departing water carries heat energy from the soil, tree, and surrounding air (this is similar to when we sweat). We can think of trees as natural air-conditioning units since they help cool the surface of the planet. Between shading and transpiration, trees can help lower surface temperatures by 10°F to 45°F. Especially in cities where there are lots of buildings, roads, and other infrastructure that absorb and retain heat (called the *urban heat island effect*), trees can provide a counteractive cooling effect.

This helps illustrate some of what I'm attempting to describe:

Let's summarize, since this is a complicated process: trees help turn dirt into soil, which then acts as a sponge to hold water. Trees suck water from the sponge and release much of it into the sky, thanks to photosynthesis and transpiration. This release pulls in moisture from adjacent bodies of water and forests, which trees seed with VOCs to help create rain. This process then repeats and spreads to nearby forests, generating a steady supply of fresh water for terrestrial life.

Trees and soil are vital parts of Earth's irrigation system. **They help make fresh water readily available to the life that needs it.** Collectively, plants, soil, and water create the foundation for all other terrestrial life to flourish.

Fun Trivia to Impress Your Friends

Guess where the largest river in the world is located. Nope, not the Amazon. Not the Nile. Not the Yangtze. It's in the sky *above* the Amazon! Over 5 billion gallons of water flow up from the Amazon jungle into the sky via transpiration every day. Each tree acts like a little geyser by sending as much as 250 gallons of water per tree per day into the atmosphere. Then the trees send their VOCs into the sky and cause it to rain. The water then comes tumbling back down, helping support the lush jungles that grow in this area.

CHAPTER 3

trees feed & shelter terrestrial life

At a meta level, trees and other plants turn energy from the Sun into usable forms that fuel nearly all terrestrial life—including us humans. I want to start with humans because I'm fascinated by the depth to which we rely on plants.

We know that plants store and move fresh water, which is essential to all human life. Food—another basic need—also comes directly from plants or from something that consumes plants. For example, spinach is a plant that we eat, and grass feeds cows, which we also eat.

After food and water, our next basic need is shelter. We use wood, concrete, and steel to build our homes and office buildings. Wood comes from trees and both metal and concrete production rely heavily on fossil fuels, which also come from trees. Most fossil fuels are from the Carboniferous Period, when vast quantities of lush plant life died and over time formed deposits of coal, oil, and natural gas.

Speaking of which, as of 2022 nearly 82% of our global energy was powered by fossil fuels. We need energy to make electricity, power transportation, and operate industry. Energy production is at the center of our economy.

Production and consumption are also at the center of our economy. We use plant materials to make fabrics, textiles, art, clothing, tools, furniture, and so much more. Even plastic is derived from plants! After all, it is made from fossil fuels.

What about when we get sick? Roughly 25% of prescriptions dispensed in the United States are derived from plants, ranging from painkillers and weight-loss medications to treatments for Alzheimer's, Parkinson's, and cancer. Scientists believe that many more plant-based medicines have yet to be discovered.

Put this book down for a minute and look at all the objects around you. Think about how each object is made and where it comes from. **Many—if not most—will trace back either directly or indirectly to trees and other plants.** It's incredible!

This is not unique to humans. Plants form the foundation for all terrestrial food. Their leaves, twigs, stems, and bark feed beetles, worms, caterpillars, ants, cicadas, and all sorts of other insects, which in turn feed birds, bats, lizards, fish, opossums, and a litany of other insectivores and omnivores. Their roots and decaying parts feed robust populations of life in the soil. These in turn feed other life and on and on this goes, forming complex food webs. Plants and soil also provide shelter for terrestrial life. Tree hollows, branches for nesting, fields for bedding, grass shelters, burrows, and tunnels are but a few examples.

But not all plants are equal. Some plants provide more food and shelter than others. The ones that provide the most food and shelter for the local life that need it are called *native* species. Native tree species are those that have lived in a given ecosystem alongside many other local insects, birds, and mammals for timespans best measured on the Cosmic Calendar. Only with such time can caterpillars and other insects develop the adaptations necessary to overcome the trees' defenses and feed from their leaves. When this happens, insect populations increase and provide food for predatory birds and mammals. With time, highly specialized relationships and complex food webs develop. Here are three examples:

- Koalas only feed on leaves from eucalyptus trees in Australia.

- The Kirtland's warbler only nests in young jack pines, which grow in Canada.

- Red disa only grows in the Western Cape of South Africa and is pollinated exclusively by the Table Mountain pride butterfly.

Similar examples are endless.

Trees help feed, house, and support all terrestrial life, including us humans. Those that are native do this best for the greatest diversity of life. While doing so, they pull CO_2 from the atmosphere and sequester it.

When is a Species *Native* Versus *Non-Native*?

The general definition of *native* versus *non-native* centers on the degree to which a given species has co-evolved and developed specialized relationships with other species in its ecosystem. But it is hard to create an exact definition since our ecosystems have been fluctuating for ages and there are various baselines from which we could choose. Opinions vary widely. For example, a group of conservationists and scientists named the Ladder Group determined that the best baseline should be the time at which the most complete web of life existed. For them, this is the end of the Pleistocene Epoch, when glaciers receded and the planet warmed to produce the climate we know today. This is my favorite definition, but I'm not sure how to make use of it.

Here is a less perfect but more practical baseline that I often use: we can loosely define the North American ecology that existed before European arrival as being native within North America.

CHAPTER 4

trees pump co₂ from the atmosphere & sequester it within life

Carbon is a remarkable element. Carbon forms the foundational building blocks for all life on Earth, including proteins, carbohydrates, lipids, and nucleic acids. We can think of these as being LEGO bricks with the ability to form intricate life forms.

Recall that when trees perform photosynthesis, they use energy from the Sun to convert CO_2 and water into oxygen and sugar. The sugar is loaded with carbon that has been pulled from the atmosphere and is now sequestered within the plant. When the trees feed herbivores with their leaves and soil with their roots, they pass sequestered carbon from the plant to the consumer. Similarly, when consumers are eaten by predators, carbon moves between life forms. In this way, trees pump carbon from the atmosphere into terrestrial life and ecosystems as a whole.

Soil is a big recipient of sequestered carbon. Some estimate that it holds 80% of all carbon present within terrestrial ecosystems. We know that trees release carbon-loaded sugar from their roots to feed bacteria and fungi. Populations of bacteria and fungi grow and help feed below-ground predators such as protozoa and nematodes, who in turn feed springtails, who feed other predators, and so forth. Some do not hunt and instead eat organic matter. After consumption comes pooping, which also contains carbon, and serves as food for other members within the soil. Some die natural deaths and become organic matter. On and on this goes with dizzying complexity.

Above ground we find the same progression but with new species. Caterpillars and other insects consume leaves. Birds eat the insects and hawks eat the birds. Mice feed on acorns and coyotes hunt mice. Zebras munch on grass and lions munch on zebras. They all poop. Some reproduce. Some are never eaten and instead die natural deaths.

At every exchange below and above ground—whether from reproduction, predation, eating organic matter, pooping, or dying a natural death—carbon is passed between life to form growing populations. The net result is an accumulation of sequestered carbon from the atmosphere into the terrestrial ecosystem.

It is worth noting that the soil line does not serve as a barrier—ecosystems blend. For example, earthworms eat nematodes and birds eat earthworms. The bird poops and eventually dies. Both the poop and dead bird provide organic matter that bacteria below ground consume.

Terrestrial ecosystems are loaded with carbon. These are the original, vast storehouses of CO_2 from the atmosphere. If we go back in time to the early Carboniferous Period (millions of years before the dinosaurs), there were an estimated 1,500 parts per million (ppm) of CO_2 in the atmosphere, which is close to four times more than there is now. As the Carboniferous Period advanced, there was an explosion of life. CO_2 in the atmosphere began decreasing dramatically as forests pulled carbon from the sky and sequestered it into soil and other life. These plants did this in great quantities, creating thick beds of stable carbon in the ground (these formed the fossil fuels we rely on today). As a result of this transfer, CO_2 in the atmosphere plummeted, dropping as low as 200 ppm and ushering in an age of cold that lasted millions of years.

The pump driving the movement of carbon from the atmosphere to a sequestered state within life is photosynthesis. We can strengthen the pump and expand stores of sequestered carbon by increasing native plants, soil, fresh water availability, and the diversity of life. Or we can do the opposite, which has unfortunately been the norm.

trees pump co2 from the atmosphere & sequester it within life

Ocean Life and Carbon Sequestration

We have talked a lot about terrestrial life in this chapter. Ocean life also pulls CO_2 from the atmosphere. Here is one of my favorite case studies:

Like trees on land, phytoplankton perform photosynthesis, consuming CO_2 in the process. Zooplankton feed on phytoplankton and baleen whales eat zooplankton. Baleen whales include humpback whales, blue whales, and gray whales. These whales' bodies hold 33 tons of carbon on average! That is a lot of carbon being transferred from the atmosphere via planktonic creatures.

The story gets more interesting. These whales dive deep into the ocean to feed, obtaining nutrients from the depths. When they return to the surface, their nutrient-rich poop helps vast populations of phytoplankton grow and perform even more photosynthesis. Then the cycle repeats, but with larger populations. The net result is a growing population of phytoplankton, zooplankton, and whales, which means more and more carbon being pulled from the atmosphere and sequestered within oceanic life.

Unfortunately, over the past several hundred years we hunted many of these whales to near-extinction. Researchers estimate that if we could simply allow the population of Blue Whales in the southern hemisphere to return to their pre-whaling numbers, this would result in the sequestration of 3.6 million tons of atmospheric carbon, which is the equivalent of a temperate forest the size of Los Angeles.

There are many other fascinating case studies, such as the way in which otters protect kelp forests. When otters are allowed to thrive, they prevent sea urchins from killing kelp forests. Scientists have found that healthy kelp forests with otter protection hold 4 million more tons of atmospheric carbon than those without. That is a lot of extra carbon!

Carbon sequestration is central to ALL of life on land and sea.

SECTION 2:

four not-so-fun essays about broken natural systems

The essays in this section explain how we humans are damaging the systems outlined in Section 1. This will not be enjoyable to read, but it serves as a crucial foundation for this book: **these essays provide context for why we need the methods that I describe later in this book.** Namely, we are:

- Destroying forests and grasslands
- Turning soil back into dirt, which affects supplies of fresh water
- Killing the majority of life
- Releasing carbon back into the atmosphere in great quantities

Much like the previous section, I will simplify topics for the sake of making these essays easy to read and understand. There are many other serious issues that are inexorably woven through the fabric of these topics. Two examples are poverty and energy production. Consider poverty: for those doing their best to simply survive, how can they possibly worry about the health of this planet? They are trying to pay rent and feed their children at a time when both costs are rising steeply in comparison to wages for the average person. And what about energy production? These topics and many others are beyond the scope of this book. I have provided additional reading suggestions in the Appendix.

Lastly, **some hope!** I am not going to leave you in the lurch, I promise. The whole point of this book is to empower you to make appreciable, positive changes. These begin in Section 3.

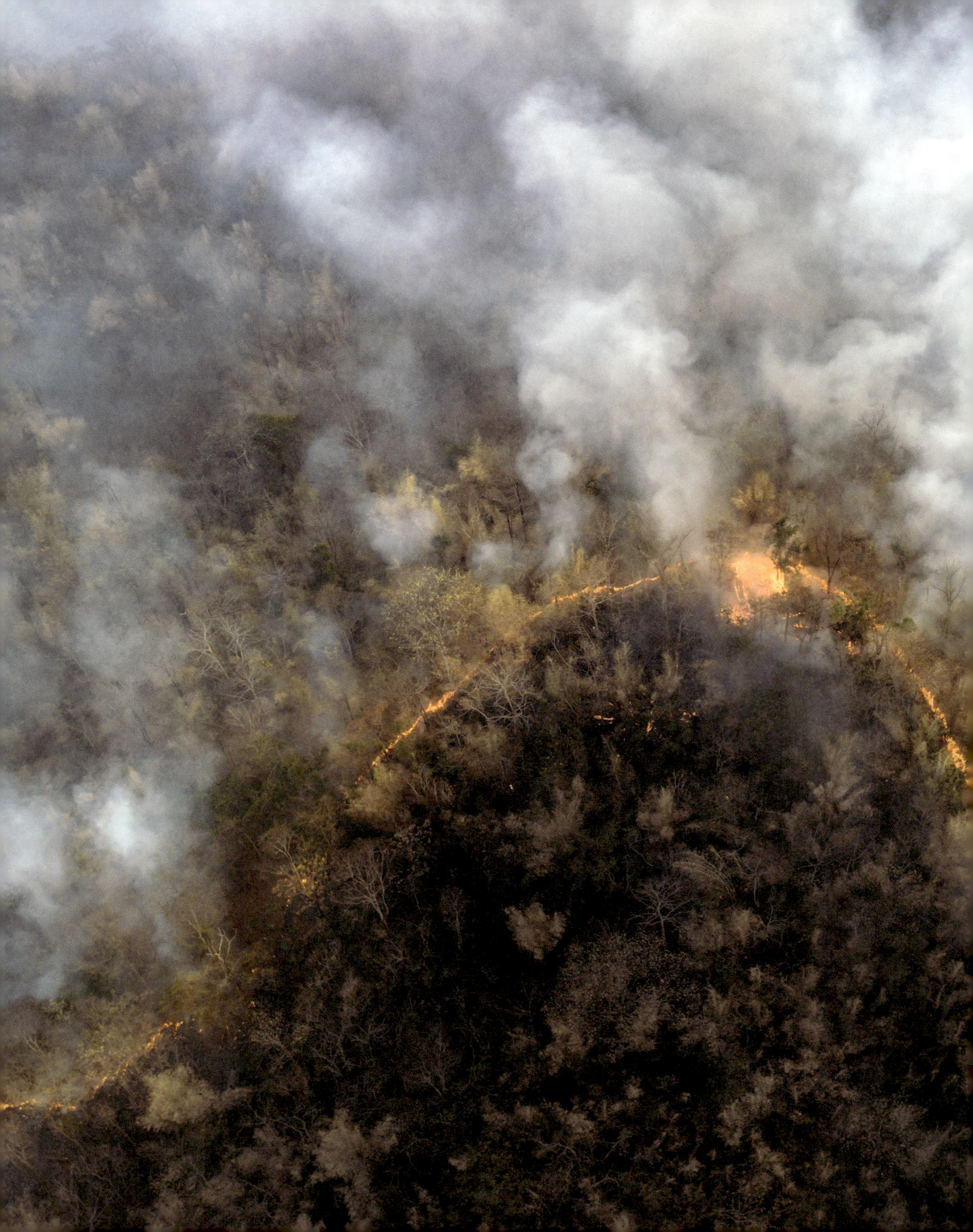

CHAPTER 5

we are destroying forests & grasslands

We humans have been destroying natural ecosystems ever since the rise of modern agriculture some 10,000 years ago. Once we learned how to cultivate plants and domesticate animals at scale, we began clearing land to make room for agriculture. Since then, we have destroyed approximately half of the world's forests and grasslands. Similar trends apply to other equally vital ecosystems, like mangroves and wetlands.

Although we have been cutting trees down since the rise of modern agriculture, there was a ceiling to how much damage humans could inflict, since for much of this time we had no machines and there were fewer people. But in the 1700s our rate of deforestation began escalating and continued to do so until the 1980s, when we reached peak global deforestation. Half of all the forests cut down in the past 10,000 years were removed in the past century.

Since then, the rate of deforestation has slowed, meaning the pace at which we cut down forests has decreased. But we are still cutting them down—from 1990 to 2020 we destroyed over 1 billion acres of forest. In recent years, we still cut down a football field worth of trees every two seconds. As tree populations continue to decline, some tree species are nearing extinction. Botanic Gardens Conservation International completed a project in 2021 called *The State of the World's Trees*, in which they found that a full one-third of all remaining tree species are teetering on the edge of existence.

A similar story has unfolded for grasslands. Consider the Tallgrass Prairies of North America, one of the most diverse ecosystems on Earth. At their peak, these prairies covered nearly 170 million acres, a vast grass sea stretching from Canada to the Gulf of Mexico. By 2003, around 87% of Tallgrass Prairies had been lost, with many of the surviving tracts in fragmented or degraded conditions. Today, the destruction continues—the National Park Service estimates that only 4% of these ecological treasures remain.

Agriculture is the biggest cause underlying this issue. We clear vast tracts of forests and grasslands to grow row crops and graze livestock. We use a shocking 50% of all habitable land (defined as land that is not covered by glaciers, beaches, or bare rock) for agriculture. More shockingly, we use 70% of all available fresh water on Earth to irrigate this agriculture, and half of that water is wasted due to evaporation and poor management practices.

That's not all. These farming operations drench their crops in fertilizers, which pollute waterways, kill life in lakes and oceans (we call these *dead zones*—there is one within the Gulf of Mexico that is the size of New Jersey!), create smog, and damage the ozone layer. The fertilizers and other misguided practices lead to the death of life in soil, resulting in dirt, which easily washes and blows away. In the United States, farming operations lose 20 tons of dirt

How We Cut Down Forests

Whenever we talk about this topic, I find it helpful to show how fast and effective we are at clearing forests. Long gone are the days of men with axes and saws. We have some very sophisticated and destructive machinery at our disposal.

per acre per year due to erosion alone. Over time, the land becomes barren and is abandoned. A study from Stanford University estimates that there are 1 billion acres of abandoned farmland across the globe, 99% of which have occurred in the last 100 years. **This land sits in ruin.**

The worst part? We clear all this land, waste all this fresh water, kill soil, and use myriad chemicals to grow our food only to waste it. In the US and other affluent countries 40% of all food produced is squandered. The global average is around 17%. Meanwhile, each day, 25,000 people, including more than 10,000 children, die from hunger.

Food in general—the way we grow it, transport it, prepare it, and waste it—

plays a large role in many of the issues we now face, including what some consider to be the most concerning metric: it contributes 19–29% of annual CO_2 emissions. We will address CO_2 in more detail in Chapter 8.

Let's turn our attention to the sub/urban landscape of the United States, where we have cleared forests and grasslands to grow a different type of crop: lawns. We seed, cut, fertilize, and irrigate a whopping 63,000 square miles of lawns, an area nearly the size of Georgia. We grow more lawns than corn and devote one-third of all residential water use to keep them hydrated. Yet they produce no food! We will discuss this in more detail in Chapter 16, where we learn how to replace lawns with gorgeous, native meadows.

We also cut down forests to harvest wood. When these are ancient, untouched ecosystems, which we call *primary* forests, the harm is irreparable. Because these ancient forests are thousands, if not millions, of years old (the Tarkine Rainforest in Tasmania has remained largely unchanged for 40 million years), they provide disproportionately more benefits in terms of soil, food, shelter, water, and carbon sequestration as compared to young forests. No money in the world can replace the Amazon, Tarkine, and the Congo Basin. Unfortunately, we are losing these ancient forests quickly; in 2022, we cut down over 10 million acres of tropical primary forest. This is an area larger than the state of Maryland!

The net result is not good. **In what is a mere two seconds on the Cosmic Calendar, we have badly damaged Earth's ability to perform photosynthesis.** Worse yet, these issues are not likely to get better any time soon. The human population is still growing and we are still cutting down trees to make way for agriculture, build sub/urban spaces, and harvest timber.

We know from Section 1 that photosynthesis is crucial to soil formation, fresh water availability, food and shelter for life, and carbon sequestration. Without trees and their photosynthesis superpowers, other systems begin to collapse. Indeed, we are seeing this with soil and fresh water availability.

More About Farming

The good news is that there are better ways to grow food. Regenerative agriculture is a method of growing food that aims to work with natural systems, bolster carbon sequestration, and boost the health of the soil ecosystem in general. There are other great systems as well, such as perennial agroforestry. While none are perfect, these alternative methods yield healthier outcomes. Here are some of my favorite resources for those interested in learning more:

- *Drawdown: The Most Comprehensive Plan Ever Proposed to Reverse Global Warming* by Paul Hawken.
- *Acres USA:* The industry publication for regenerative farming. I recommend their monthly magazine and incredible selection of books.
- *Rodale Institute:* Generally, a great source of information on these topics.
- *Growing a Revolution* by David R. Montgomery
- *Holistic Management: A Commonsense Revolution to Restore Our Environment* by Allan Savory

Finally, here is an outstanding presentation about perennial agroforestry:

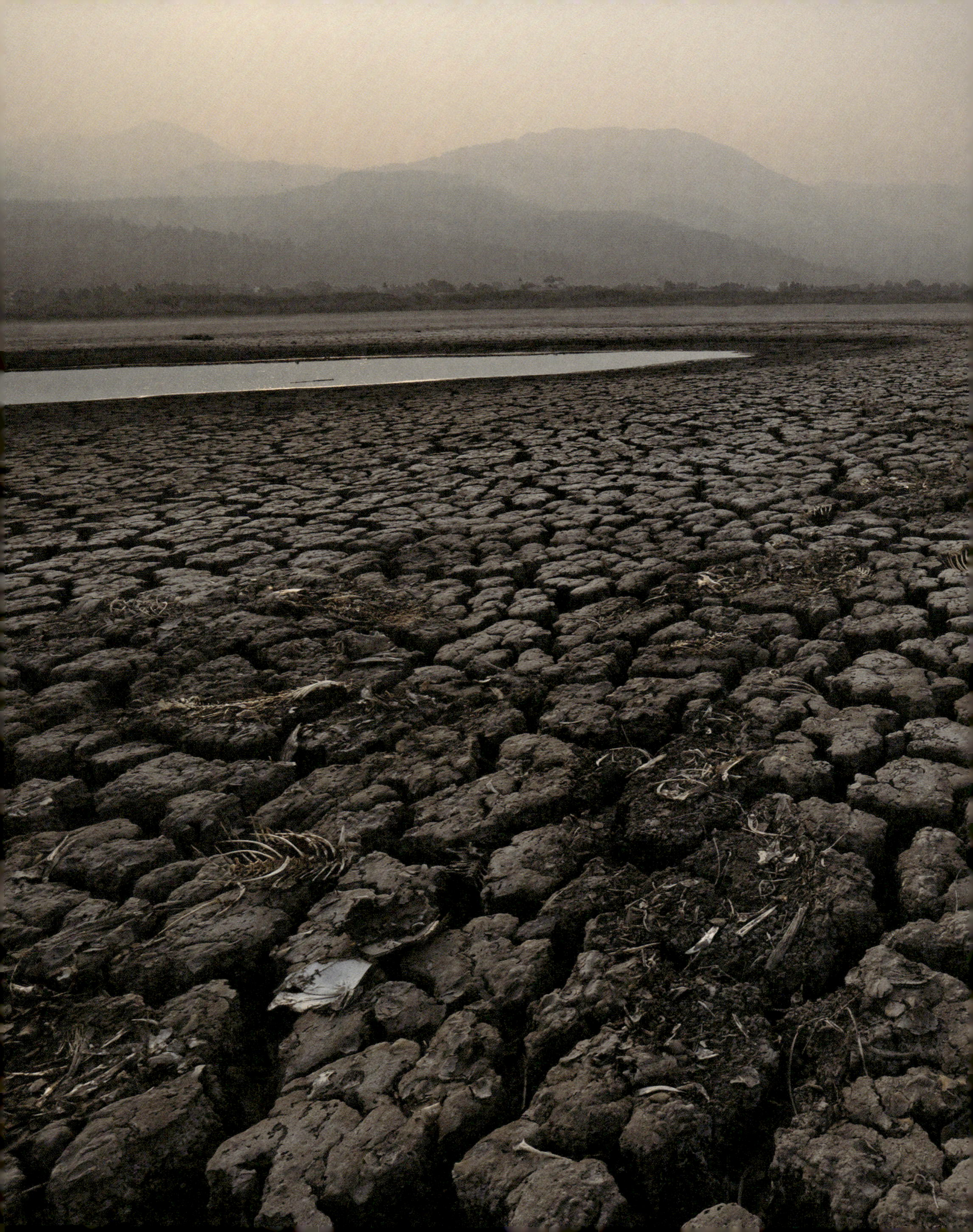

CHAPTER 6

we are turning soil into dirt & running out of fresh water

When we clear forests and grasslands for agriculture, development, and timber, the soil is either removed or it dies. According to the World Wildlife Fund, we have destroyed half of all soil on Earth in the past 150 years, which is roughly equivalent to the amount of forests and grasslands we have razed. Recall that we can think of soil as a sponge that holds water when it rains. Without this soil sponge, rain washes away instead of absorbing into the land and causes flooding. Over time, drought ensues.

Picture the following, something that is all too common in most sub/urban spaces today: we cut down trees, remove soil, and grade the land to build a shopping center. In this new space we find asphalt, sidewalks, buildings, mowed grass, and perhaps the occasional planted tree or shrub. There is nothing on this site that can hold water. Even the mowed grass is unable to do so—with its short stalks and tiny root system, it does virtually nothing to build soil.

In places like these, rain water rushes downhill, causing flooding in low-lying areas. The force and volume of this water loosens sediment, which causes erosion, clogs waterways, and harms the life living there.

Now imagine this happening across larger areas. Here in Wake County, North Carolina where I live, developers have cleared and paved over 11,000 acres of land in the past decade. One inch of rain across 11,000 acres yields 297 million gallons of water runoff (recall that 1 inch of rain yields approximately 27,000 gallons of water per acre). This sort of development is happening in many other counties across the state. Now routine rain events quickly turn into billions of gallons of water runoff, which causes serious flooding, especially near the coast. This is not unique to North Carolina. We see this happening all over the world.

The story gets worse. When this rain falls, it does little good for hydrating trees and refilling aquifers—there is no soil sponge to hold it. The rain washes back into the rivers and oceans and the cycle repeats. Without water in the soil and trees to pump that water into the atmosphere, conditions become hotter and drier. Water levels in aquifers begin to drop.

This generates high-pressure heat domes that make it hard for rain systems to enter this area. Only the big, fierce storms have the power necessary to breach these heat domes. The net result is less frequent, more intense rain and thunderstorms.

They dump large amounts of water in short periods of time. This water does not absorb into the land and instead washes downhill, leading to more intense floods. This cycle repeats and the water levels in the aquifers keep dropping.

A Demonstration of Soil Versus Dirt

This demonstration helps illustrate what happens to rain when it lands on soil versus dirt. Water is poured on both a pile of flour and a piece of bread. The water quickly runs off the flour and pools at the base of the pile. Nothing goes inside the flour. This is like rain running off dirt. In contrast, the bread soaks up all the water because it has gaps to hold it in place. Similarly, soil has gaps present and is able to soak up rain.

Meanwhile, we continue to pump water from the aquifers to drink, irrigate crops, and cool equipment used in energy production. None of these systems are efficient—we lose a substantial amount of water thanks to old and leaky infrastructure. The water levels in aquifers drop further.

Those trees and plants that are not able to grow deeper roots become increasingly thirsty and die. Streams and creeks disappear. A decline of all life becomes the norm. The land becomes barren and there is no water, leading to drought and widespread suffering. Allan Savory said it best when he stated, **"it's not drought that causes bare ground, it's bare ground that causes drought."**

This helps illustrate the points I'm trying to make:

[QR code]

According to E.O. Wilson, who is widely considered one of the greatest natural scientists of our time, "The world as a whole is already well into a water crisis. About eighteen countries, home to half the world's population, are draining their aquifers. In Hebei Province, in the heart of China's northern grain belt, the average water level in the deep aquifer is dropping nearly three meters a year. Underground water levels are falling so fast in the lowlands of rural India that in some localities drinking water must be trucked in."

Research based on NASA satellite data confirms this very point: of the 37 largest aquifers on Earth, 21 have surpassed tipping points and are now on their way to being depleted. Of these, 13 are considered highly stressed—or worse— threatening regional water security and resilience. As of 2016, an estimated 4 billion people—two-thirds of the global population—faced severe water scarcity for at least one month of the year. For half a billion, water scarcity was a year-round crisis. Recent reports indicate that the situation has continued to deteriorate.

Let's stop for a moment and envision ourselves in one of these situations. Imagine worrying about water for one month every year—or worse. Water is critical to our existence. **We talk a lot about the implications of running out of oil; how much worse would it be if we ran out of fresh water?**

Consider recent events: Cape Town, South Africa nearly ran out of water in 2018 and California has faced numerous serious water shortages in the past decade. News stories about droughts in East Asia, East Africa, Western Europe, and other parts of the world are becoming more numerous. This same trend is happening here in the United States—our major aquifers are running dry.

Photosynthesis, soil, and fresh water availability are all closely entwined. A decrease in one—particularly photosynthesis—results in a decrease for all. This places stress on multiple types of life, many of which are already under dire pressure from overhunting and habitat destruction.

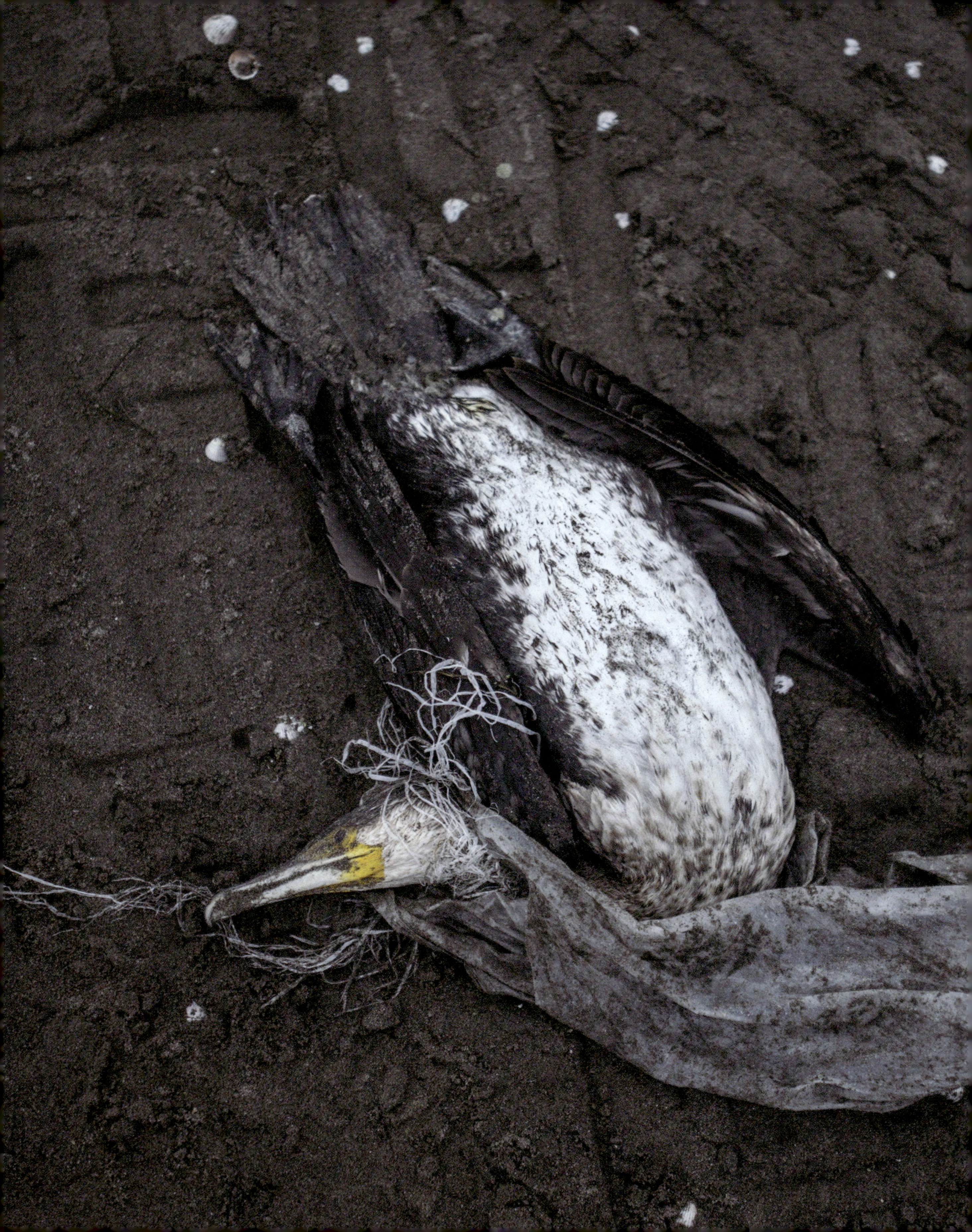

CHAPTER 7

we are killing life

From the moment *Homo sapiens* first burst out of Africa and began spreading across the planet in search of new food some 50,000 years ago, we hunted most megafauna to extinction, which created chaos for ecosystems across the planet. Within a few thousand years of the first humans entering North America, 75% of all large species—including mammoths, mastodons, giant sloths, American cheetahs, and American lions—were gone. Versions of this same story had previously transpired in Europe, Asia, and Australia. The only exception was Africa, where local species had co-evolved with us.

Here is another one of many examples from more recently: there were roughly 60 million bison in North America before the Europeans arrived. By the early 1900s there were fewer than 200 bison remaining. We humans hunted them to near extinction and did the same thing to grizzly bears, mountain lions, wolves, elk, pronghorn, beavers, and sea otters. Thankfully these species survived, but others (the passenger pigeon, great auk, Carolina parakeet, and ivory-billed woodpecker) were not so lucky.

I wish I could say these days were behind us. But they are not. Consider tuna. It is a big business, worth around $40 billion per year, and makes up an estimated one-quarter of global seafood trade. Here in the United States we eat over 600 million pounds of canned tuna every year (those numbers do not include sushi or filets)! This results in overfishing of tuna that has decimated their populations. Fishing pressure drove the population of Pacific bluefin tuna to right under 3% of its historic size. Not only are we pushing tuna to the edge of extinction, but we are also harming and killing other sea creatures in the process. As an example, longline fishing, one of the techniques used to catch tuna, kills an estimated 250,000 loggerhead turtles and leatherback turtles annually, both of which are critically endangered. The fishing industry calls this collateral damage "bycatch," and throws it back in the ocean to rot. Estimates suggest that bycatch amounts to a shocking 38 million tons of sea creatures and 40% of all fish caught every year. Thanks to bycatch and overfishing in general, we have reduced fish populations by anywhere from 50 to 90%, depending on the species. **All this because we like to eat tuna.**

Many of the species described above—including tuna—are known as *keystone* species. A keystone species is one that has low functional redundancy, meaning if it disappears from its ecosystem there are no other species that can fill that specific niche. They hold entire ecosystems intact. When they die, so too does the life that relies on them. By killing megafauna and other keystone species, we have indirectly harmed and killed many other species that relied on them for survival.

Consider a case study in Yellowstone National Park involving the gray wolf, which is a keystone species in that region. By the mid-1900s, gray wolves had mostly been hunted to extinction in the lower 48 states of the US. Intensive surveying of Yellowstone National Park from 1975 to 1977 failed to find a single wolf. But thanks to the Endangered Species Act of 1973 (one of the most important laws in history in terms of conservation), awareness about the importance of wolves increased. As a result, in the mid-1990s the Fish & Wildlife Service began reintroducing wolves back into Yellowstone. The changes that ensued were profound. The wolves hunted elk, which had a cascading effect on the health of plants. Without such heavy, unrestrained elk predation, various plant species were able to rebound, especially willows, aspen, cottonwood, and berry-producing shrubs. Wolf kills provided scavenge opportunities for eagles and ravens. Their populations grew. Berries from the bushes fed a growing number of bears and supported the resurgence of six different species of songbirds. Wood from willows, aspens, and cottonwoods helped the beavers and enabled their populations to rebound.

The beavers created new dams, thus changing the path along which the streams flowed. Water flow slowed and stream sediment decreased. Populations of trout and other fish rebounded. Slowing water also meant that more water percolated into the land, which benefited trees, and thus herbivores. As bird, beaver, trout, and herbivore populations increased, so too did populations of predators. More kills released more nutrients for plants. Plant life surged and with it so did populations of insects, more birds, and new herbivores. Species that had not been seen in the area for many years reappeared. Entire terrestrial and aquatic ecosystems began to heal. Overall soil fertility increased and life continued to explode, in both diversity and abundance. All this because a keystone species—the gray wolf—was reintroduced into its native habitat.

This only scratches the surface of the full effects, most of which are not yet known. Researchers are still learning about new outcomes and connections. This makes me think of the quote by Frank Edwin Egler: **"Nature is not more complex than we think, it is more complex than we CAN think."**

Here is more about this case study:

Not only have we obliterated life directly through hunting and indirectly through the eradication of keystone species, but we have also done so through habitat destruction. All terrestrial life needs forests and grasslands to live their lives. When we destroy these places—as we have been doing over the past 10,000 years—we destroy their ability to feed, find shelter, and reproduce. There are many ways we destroy habitat. One is by completely clearing an ecosystem using bulldozers and other large machinery. We also destroy habitats when we split them apart. This is called *fragmentation*, and it happens when we build roads, railroads, fences, and other structures that cut through tracts of land and divide ecosystems indiscriminately. This happens across the planet. Here are some real-life examples:

Most life needs uninterrupted wild space in which to live and travel. Consider the red wolf, which used to thrive here in North Carolina and across the southeastern United States. They need as many as 80 square miles to survive. There are very few places in North Carolina with enough space to allow for such range. As a result, red wolves must cross highways, travel around cities, and find a way under fences or go around them. They must also avoid being shot by farmers. Sadly, red wolves have not been able to survive such conditions. As of October 2023, there are currently 11 known red wolves remaining in the wild in North Carolina.

There is another highly damaging form of habitat destruction, which is the introduction of something called an *invasive* species. Invasive species are non-native species that cause widespread harm and destruction when introduced to a new ecosystem. Here is a recent example:

Before 1900, the American chestnut was a common native species in North America, particularly in the Appalachian Mountains, where it provided food and shelter for many insects, birds, and mammals. They were referred to as the redwoods of the East Coast due to their incredible size and maturity. In 1904, some folks brought a Japanese chestnut tree to the United States. Unbeknownst to them, this tree carried a tiny fungal pathogen called chestnut blight. Within the year, experts found this pathogen in American chestnut trees in the Bronx Zoo. It was fully lethal; the American chestnut had not evolved any defense that could withstand this fungus. Within 35 years, it swept across the country and decimated huge population of American chestnuts, killing somewhere around 4 billion trees. Populations of plants, insects, birds, and mammals that relied closely on the American chestnut all suffered as a result. Some species—such as the chestnut ermine moth and the phleophagan chestnut moth—went fully extinct. The accidental introduction of the invasive chestnut blight caused incomprehensible damage to life and ecosystems across the US.

During our expansion across the globe we carried seeds, rats, insects, and germs, to name a few. Some of these had profound impacts on the new ecosystems into which we entered. Especially today, with

The Danger of Shifting Baseline Syndrome

Each generation is born with a new baseline for what is normal and only sees a little change during its lifetime. We damage Earth a little more with each passing cohort. Because we only get to see a small part of the bigger story, we struggle to comprehend how much overall destruction we humans have caused. Ecosystems that look normal to us today would horrify our ancestors. Meanwhile, the generations march by and the damage continues. This is known as the Shifting Baseline Syndrome and serves as a very real impediment to recognizing and correcting our role in the degradation of Earth.

The World Wildlife Fund's *Living Planet Report 2018* published the following data: **we've seen a 60% decline in the population size of birds, reptiles, mammals, fish, and amphibians (on average) in the past 40 years.** In 2004 the International Union for Conservation of Nature (IUCN) reported that the current rates of extinction for birds, mammals, and amphibians were at least 48 times greater than natural extinction rates. A widely cited paper published in the *Proceedings of the National Academy of Sciences* calls this massive loss of life a "biological annihilation" that represents a "frightening assault on the foundations of human civilization."

In what amounts to mere minutes on the Cosmic Calendar, we humans have killed an unimaginable amount of life through hunting and habitat destruction. According to Paul Martin, an expert on this topic, virtually all animal extinctions in the past 50,000 years were caused by humans. We are pushing life on this planet to the brink of existence.

increased global trade comes the increased movement of potential new invasive species. Burmese pythons in the Everglades, emerald ash borer, fire ants, zebra mussels, kudzu, feral swine, European starlings, and Asian carp are a few from a long list of highly invasive species that have created ecological disasters here in the United States. This is happening all over the world at an increasing pace.

Sadly, there is no end in sight. We cut down and fragment forests and grasslands to make way for new agriculture, neighborhoods, and development every day. With that comes the eradication of more keystone species, soil loss, and diminishing fresh water. Continued globalization perpetuates the introduction of more invasive species that wreak havoc. Collectively, this results in more and more carbon being released into the atmosphere.

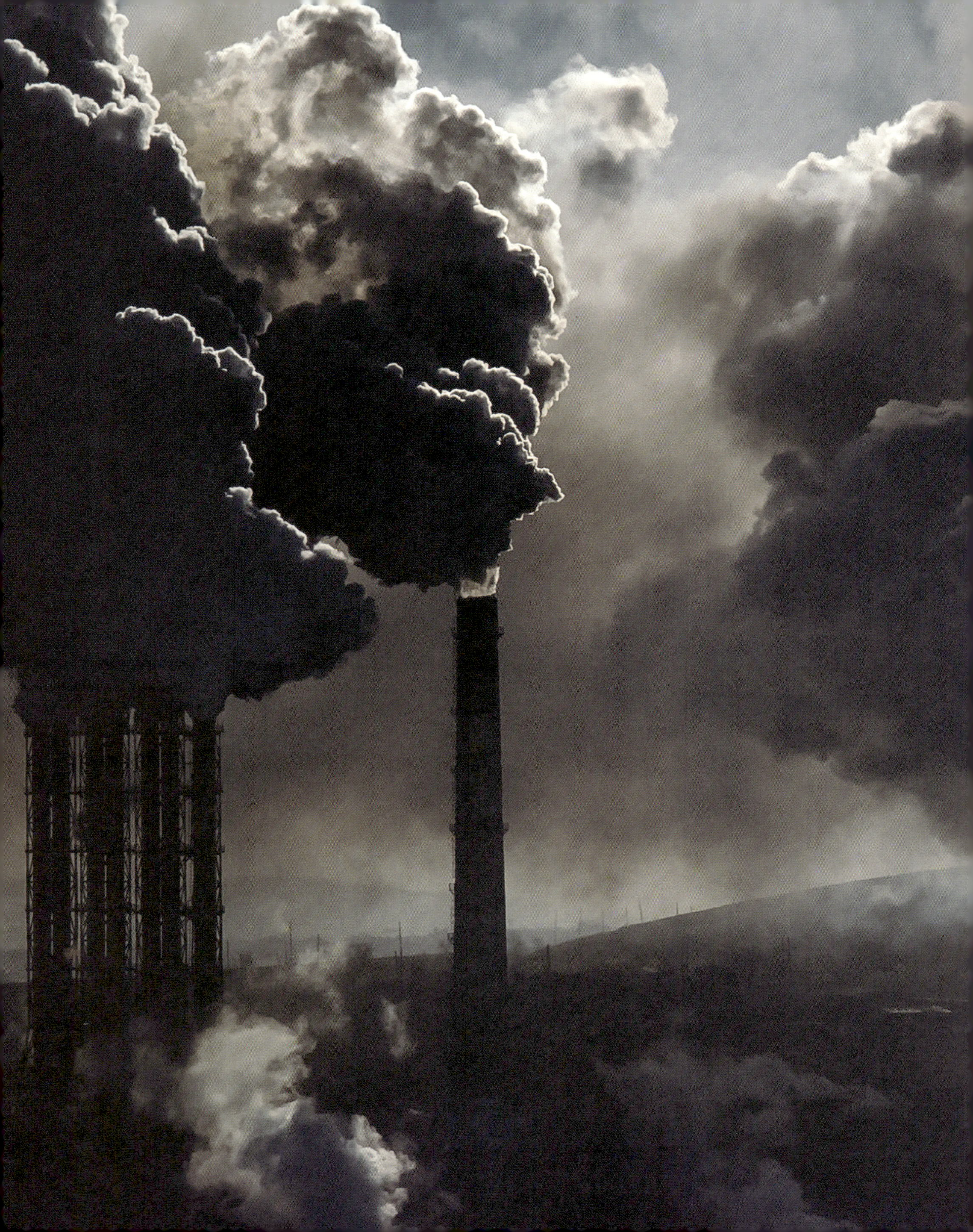

CHAPTER 8

in terms of co₂, we are returning to the carboniferous period

Since 1750, we have increased carbon in the atmosphere by around 50%. We measure atmospheric CO_2 in parts per million (ppm). Using core samples of ice and trees, we can accurately measure historical levels of CO_2 in the atmosphere. From these data, we know that 250 years ago the amount of CO_2 in the atmosphere was around 280 ppm.

When Charles David Keeling first started measuring atmospheric CO_2 levels at the Mauna Loa Volcano back in the 1950s, the atmospheric CO_2 was at 313 ppm, around 13% higher than it had been in the mid-1700s. Seventy years later, we are already at 417 ppm. This is the highest it has been in at least 14 million years. To make matters worse, this number is likely going to rise at an accelerating rate since oceans have been absorbing tremendous amounts of CO_2 from the atmosphere. At some point they will reach their limit.

It is no coincidence that this dramatic rise has occurred during the period in which we have cut down half of forests and grasslands, turned half of soil back to dirt, and killed life in droves. Recall that photosynthesis is the pump driving the movement of carbon from the atmosphere to a sequestered state within plants, soil, and other life. The pump grows stronger with more native plants, soil, and fresh water. The amount of sequestered carbon increases with growing populations and diversity of life. Yet we are damaging all parts of this system.

In addition, we are also pumping carbon into the atmosphere as we burn a tremendous amount of coal, oil, and natural gas to produce electricity. We learned in Chapter 4 that most of these fossil fuels were formed by plants during the Carboniferous Period. By mining and burning fossil fuels at an increasing rate, we release the carbon captured during that period and undo millions of years of photosynthesis.

Given that we are damaging the natural systems responsible for sequestering carbon while simultaneously emitting record levels of carbon previously captured by these same natural systems across millions of years, it should come as no surprise that CO_2 levels in the atmosphere are skyrocketing. Many scientists think we will hit 500 ppm within the next 30 years. Perhaps we will even hit 1,500 ppm at some point, which was the norm during the Carboniferous Period.

CO_2 levels in the atmosphere provide us with a loud warning. They signal frightening human ignorance, an enormous loss of life, and critical damage to some of Earth's most powerful natural systems. Nassim Taleb wrote the following in Black Swan: "The position I suggest should be based both on ignorance and on deference to the wisdom of Mother Nature, since it is older than us, hence wiser than us, and has been proven much smarter than scientists. **We do not understand enough about Mother Nature to mess with her.**" Luckily, it's not too late to fix these issues. There is so much we can do to help heal Earth where we live, work, and play.

in terms of co₂, we are returning to the carboniferous period

A Technical Dive into CO_2, Longwave Radiation, and Global Warming

I like to think of Earth as a greenhouse that hurtles through space at 67,000 miles per hour. Whoever coined the phrase "life moves fast" was spot on! Much like a greenhouse typically has plastic or glass that helps hold in heat, so too does this planet—except it is an atmosphere made up of nitrogen (N), oxygen (O_2), carbon dioxide (CO_2), methane, ozone, and several other gases that we collectively call *greenhouse gases*.

When the Sun shines its warm energy onto this planet, about 50% of the energy makes it to the surface of Earth. This energy, much of which is visible to us as light, is called *shortwave radiation* due to its relatively short wavelength. The Earth absorbs this shortwave radiation and then reradiates it back out toward the atmosphere. This reradiated energy has an increased wavelength and is now called *longwave radiation*.

Here is the kicker, the point that really matters: **it turns out that our atmosphere is NOT transparent to longwave radiation in the same way that it is to shortwave radiation.** This longwave radiation does not simply pass back through the atmosphere. Instead, the gases absorb it, heat up, and radiate energy back down toward the Earth's surface, which warms the planet. This incredible process is part of what makes Earth habitable. Without it, Earth's surface temperature would plummet to around -2°F.

Here are two ways we affect this system. First, more CO_2, methane, etc. in the atmosphere increases the heating effect. Second, fewer trees, more development, and a more barren landscape in general lead to a warmer surface, which increases the amount of longwave radiation emitted from Earth back into the atmosphere. This also increases the heating effect.

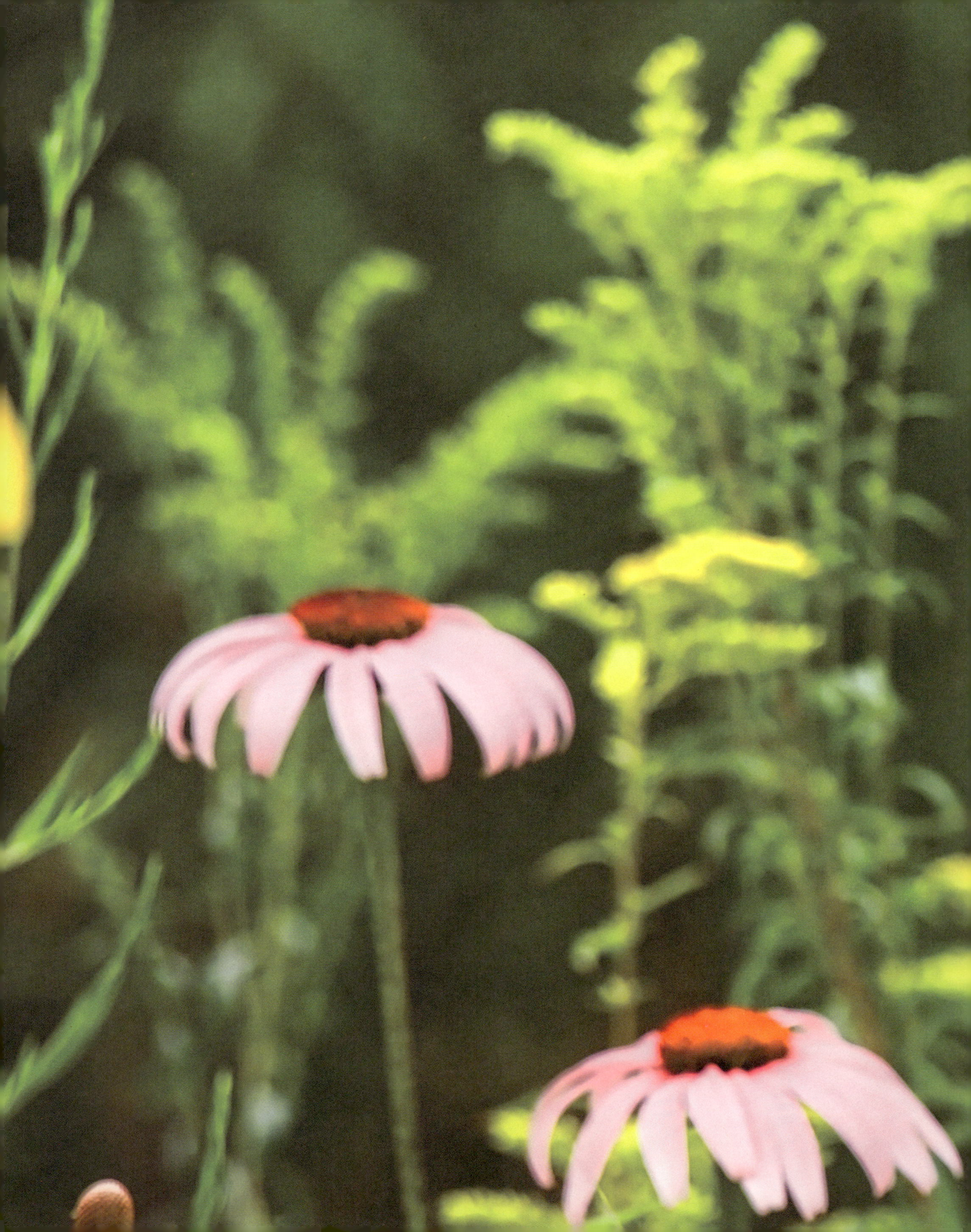

SECTION 3

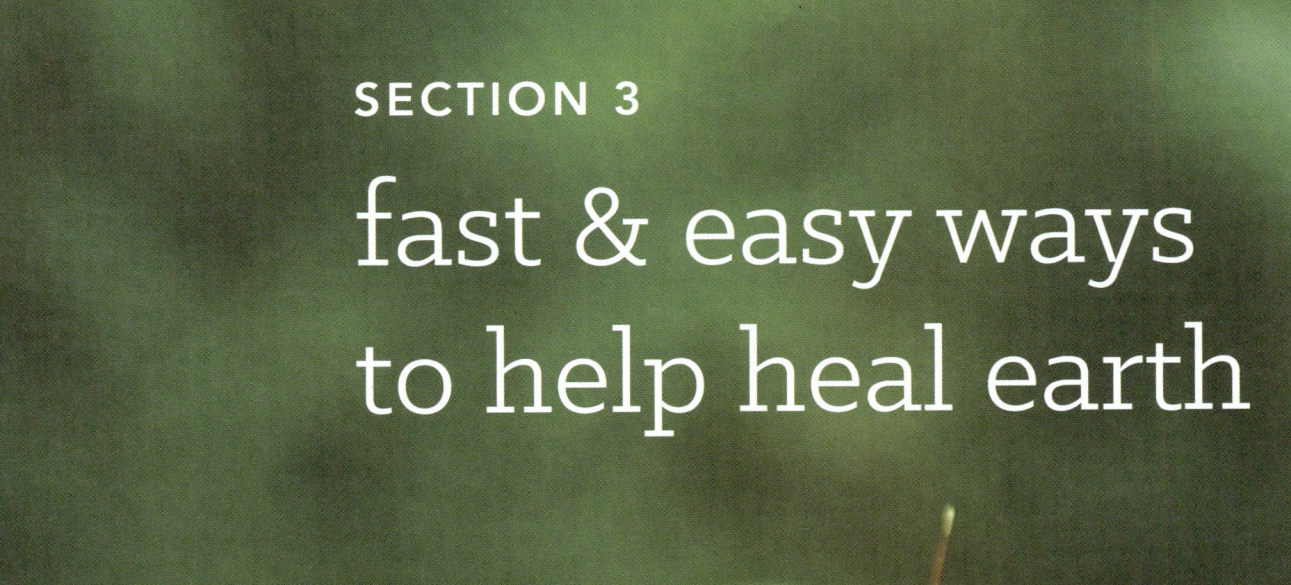

fast & easy ways to help heal earth

The stage is set. We now have enough background information to understand how the systems of photosynthesis and soil formation work, and how they affect water availability, carbon sequestration, and all other life on land. We also understand how we are damaging these systems and causing incredible harm to other life and Earth as a whole. Now what?

It's time for hope and action! Let's learn new landscape paradigms and practices that help heal Earth by addressing the issues we read about in the previous section. The new approach is simple: increase photosynthesis and build soil. Plant native trees, flowers, and grasses. Help them attain a long, healthy life.

Preserve existing and mature trees. Get rid of lawns. Stop using fertilizers and harmful chemicals. **Do everything we can to increase the diversity and abundance of life.** From here on, I'm going to use the term *outrageous diversity* (a term from Michael Phillips, author of *Mycorrhizal Planet*) when referring to the diversity and abundance of life.

We can use the land where we live, work, and play to foster powerful natural systems and help heal Earth. These systems have been tried and true for millennia. More native trees and flowers means more photosynthesis, which means more soil, more water, more life, and less CO_2 in the atmosphere.

Indeed, there are great case studies demonstrating this point.

Here are two of my favorites:

1. Yacouba Sawadogo is a farmer from Burkina Faso who transformed a section of the Sahara into forest and positively impacted the lives of many members of his community. A film called *The Man Who Stopped the Desert* was made about this work.

2. John Liu worked with the Chinese government and the local population to turn a dry, exhausted wasteland called Loess Plateau (an area the size of the Netherlands) into a green oasis. Here is a case study about this project:

I hope this section and those that follow bring you more free time, more joy, and the satisfaction that comes with making positive change. It's a triple win and it all starts with the ground under our feet.

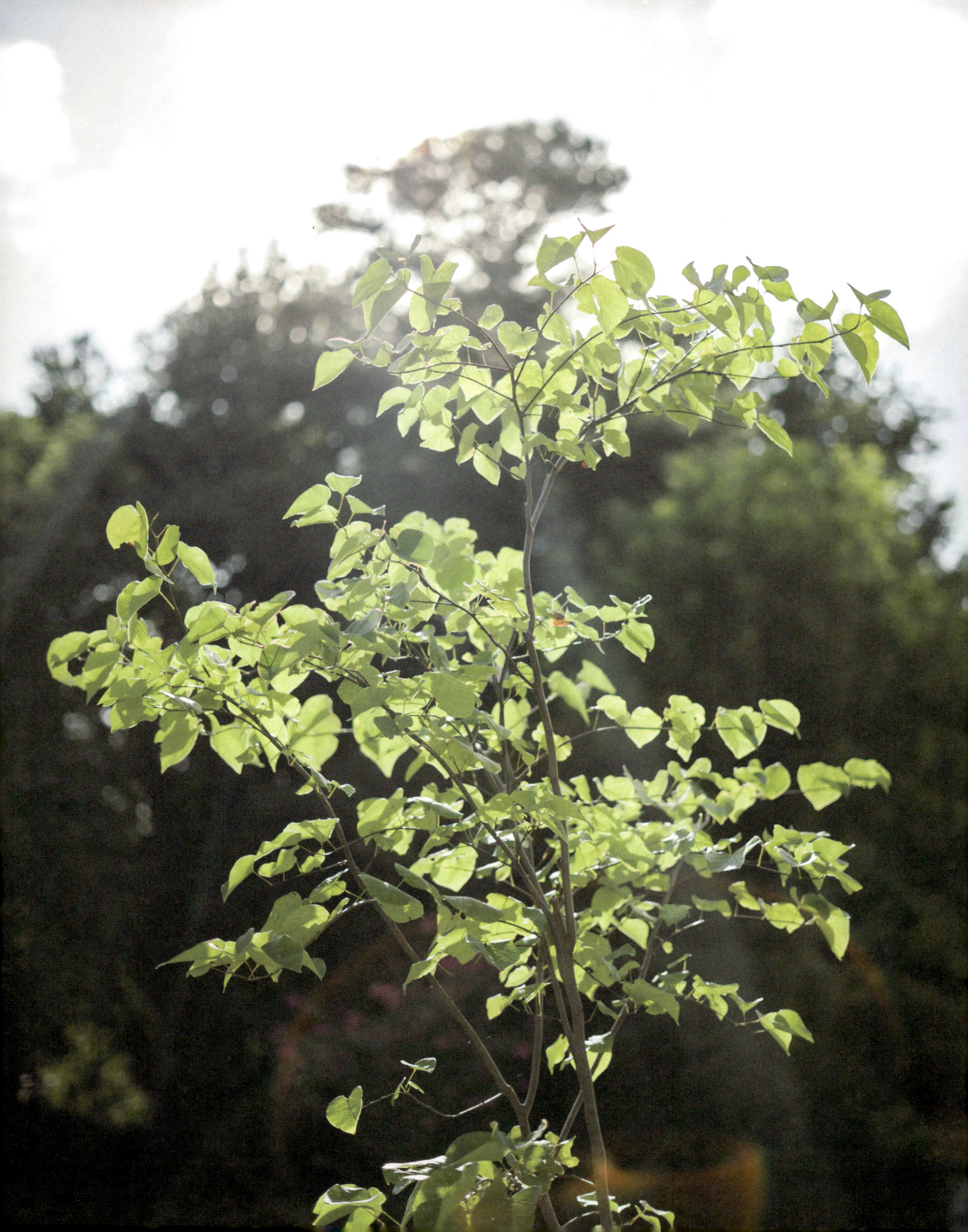

CHAPTER 9

some important notes before we begin

In the remaining sections of this book, I'm going to teach you what I have learned during my career. Some instructions will be very easy (e.g., leaving fallen leaves under a tree) and some will be more complicated (e.g., how to plant native meadows). I have attempted to start with the easiest options and work toward more complicated ones as the book progresses. Before we begin, here are some important notes:

Rooted in Real Work

Everything that comes next is based on the cumulative knowledge and experience we have built at Leaf & Limb and Project Pando. We are a team of highly credentialed tree experts who care for trees because we love this planet. We also focus a great deal on building healthy soil, creating meadows with native flowers and grasses, and encouraging life to return to the sub/urban landscape. We are gardeners, mushroom foragers, bird watchers, ecological do-gooders, hikers, ecology nerds, and general lovers of life. All this to say, everything in this book has been tested in the real-world arena. It is essentially a collection and synthesis of the things we do every day with clients, volunteers, and the surrounding community. The ideas in this book work.

This does not mean we know everything; we don't. Working with trees, soil, and natural systems is a humbling experience because there is so much to learn. Five lifetimes would not be enough to absorb it all.

Guiding Frameworks

One of our guiding frameworks at Leaf & Limb is **when in doubt, look to ecosystems for guidance.** Many of the approaches in this book originate from what we observe in the forests and fields around us. Another related framework is this: **life was doing fine without humans for a long time.** This is not to say that humans are not great! Rather, it is to remind us that many of our actions in the sub/urban landscape are unnecessary.

Some Information Must Be Regionally Filtered

The information in this book is based primarily on my experiences working in Raleigh, North Carolina and the surrounding cities (Durham, Chapel Hill,

Cary, Apex, and others). If you live in a different region, you will need to make adjustments based on when your seasons start and stop. Please note that I do not refer to seasons like Winter, Spring, and Summer. Instead, I refer to the only two seasons that matter for plants and soil: the growing season and dormant season.

We can sync our seasons through soil temperature. As a rule of thumb, 50°F is the magic number. This temperature roughly correlates to important seasonal changes, buds growing, leaves falling, insects emerging, birds migrating, and many others. When the soil temperature heats to 50°F on average, this marks the approximate beginning of the growing season. When it cools back to 50°F on average, this marks the approximate beginning of the dormant season. We should measure soil temperature by placing a soil temperature probe approximately 4 inches below the surface of the soil. Or we can find information about current soil temperatures online from our local weather groups and universities.

Do not worry about being super exact. I'm intentionally keeping this loose because the truth is working with plants offers a *lot* of leeway. This is not like baking a cake, which requires precision. It's more like making a fun salad with our favorite vegetables and toppings—it is ok and encouraged to be inexact and experimental.

The 80/20 Rule

One of the biggest challenges of writing this book was figuring out how to walk the line between giving enough information necessary to perform a task without creating information overload, since so many of these topics are very dense. I decided to go with the 80/20 Rule. I attempt to provide you with 20% of the actions required to obtain 80% of the desired results in an effort to keep this book enjoyable and easy to implement.

There is a lot more to be learned about every single topic featured in this book. For those interested, there are additional books, articles, and resources available in the Appendix and via various QR codes throughout the book.

Signs Are Game Changers

Many of the practices put forth in this book run contrary to cultural norms and traditional landscape paradigms. Some may raise eyebrows from passersby, generate complaints from neighbors, and attract the attention of HOA and municipal inspectors. One remedy is the use of educational signs. I have found that I can turn anything—even a brush pile—into something that attracts positive attention and engagement if I place a sign nearby. I recommend a sign with a pleasing design and QR code linking to an online article, video, etc. Not everybody knows how to use a QR code, so it is important to provide very clear instructions on how to use it. Here is an

some important notes before we begin

example of one we use at Leaf & Limb that works quite well:

and internal training at Leaf & Limb. They depict a variety of production quality and characters. The videos do not always perfectly align with what is written here. If in doubt, defer to the content in the book. If you decide to use a video tutorial, my recommendation is to treat it as a supplement to the text, not an alternative. The text has more precise information.

A Note Regarding How-To Videos

I have included many how-to videos in Sections 3, 4, and 5. I included these because I think it is generally easier to learn from videos than it is to learn from written text. Some are videos from other experts. Most are videos we made for the sake of educating clients, volunteers,

Feedback Please

Please send me feedback! Your insights and ideas could pave the way for a better, revised edition in the future. I would love to hear where you were confused and struggled. I would also love to hear about the moments that provided you with inspiration or an "ah-ha!" You can reach me at **wonder@leaflimb.com**.

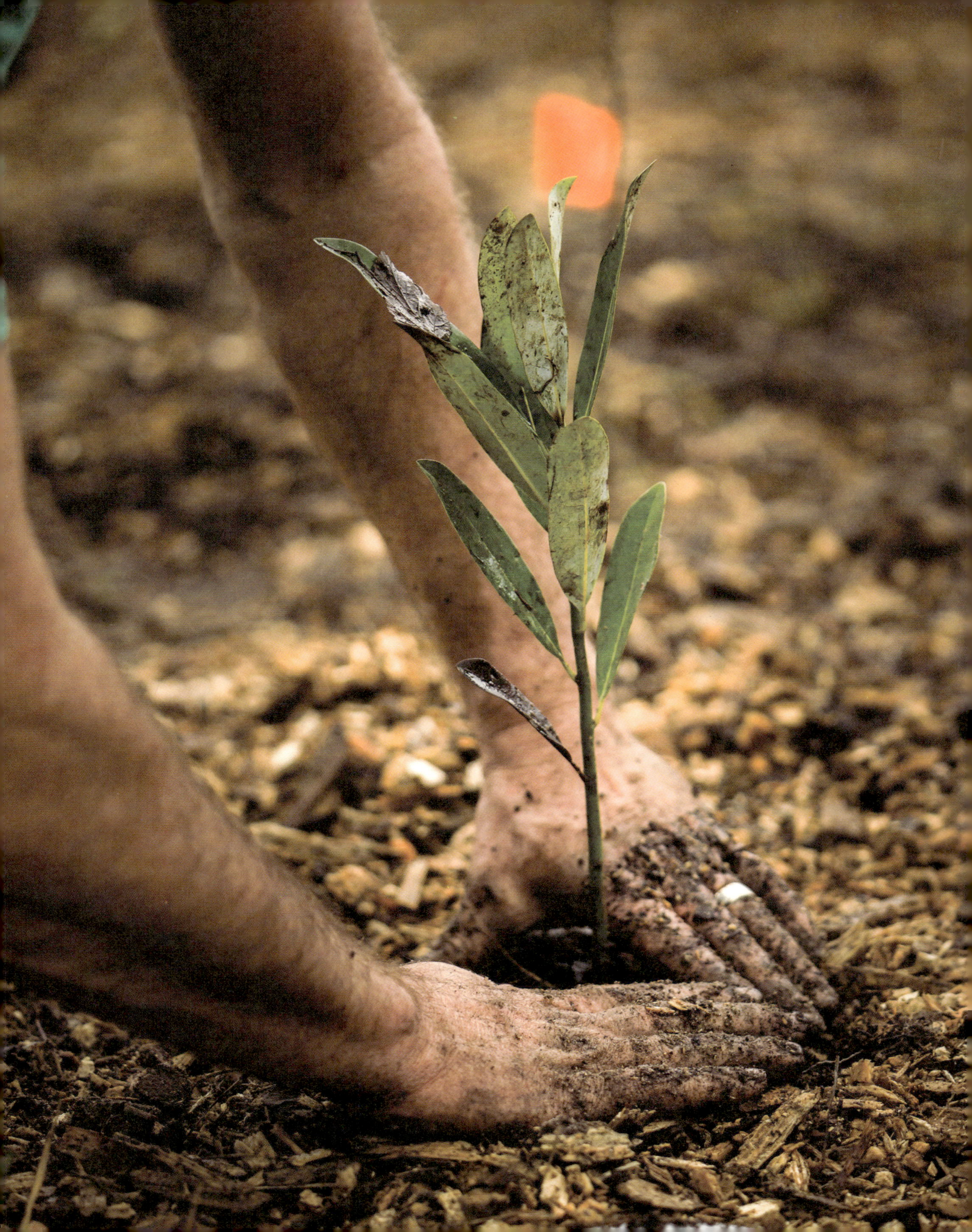

CHAPTER 10

start with planting trees—one of the most important things we can do

What better place to start than with planting trees?! By now we know the incredible role that they play in Earth's natural systems. They are the foundation for soil, water, sequestering carbon, and all terrestrial life.

But hang tight—we are not going to learn how to plant the typical trees that we would normally buy from a nursery, which are trees growing in containers (called *containerized* trees) and trees dug from fields (called *balled and burlapped* trees). These two will henceforth be referred to as *traditional nursery trees*. They are heavy, expensive, and difficult to properly plant.

Instead, we are going to learn how to plant saplings. They are cheap and very easy to plant—a tree of this size can be planted in three minutes or less. Better yet, they usually live longer, healthier lives as compared to traditional nursery trees.

First, What Is a Sapling?

Saplings are young trees, usually in the range of 1–3 years old, and are typically between 1–3 feet in height. We can grow them (more about this in Section 5 of this book), dig them up, or purchase them. If the latter, saplings are typically sold as *bare root*, which means they do not have any soil around their roots and are not

How to Plant Traditional Nursery Trees

I recognize that for some projects planting traditional nursery trees is the only option. When this is the case, it is crucial that they are planted properly or else they will die prematurely. This requires carefully following very specific steps. Here is a comprehensive video guide for installing containerized trees that includes all of these specific steps. The process for planting balled and burlapped trees is the same, except we must also remove all burlap and the top half of the wire basket from the root ball.

potted in containers. The best place to buy them is a local native nursery if that option exists. If not, they ship easily, which means we can order them from online stores and a variety of other organizations like Arbor Day Foundation and our state forest service. Especially with native plant nurseries being far less common than traditional nurseries, this greatly expands our ability to access native trees and shrubs. This is the beginning—let's explore all the other reasons why saplings are better than traditional nursery trees.

Saplings Are Easy to Plant

We can plant 20 or more saplings in an hour, which is about the same time it takes to plant one traditional nursery tree, pending the exact size. The work itself is easy because we are using small plants that require tiny holes. The planting process requires almost no technical expertise. So long as the trunk and roots are in approximately the right place, the plant will adapt. It is very hard to improperly plant a sapling.

Planting traditional nursery trees, on the other hand, is hard work. They are heavy and challenging to transport. The labor required to dig the holes is physically demanding. The planting itself leaves little room for error; we must meet a high technical standard. As a result, the majority of all traditional nursery trees planted in the sub/urban landscape have been installed improperly, which leads to sickly trees dying premature deaths. A USDA study analyzing tree life expectancy in sub/urban areas found that the typical street tree lifespan is 19–28 years, far shorter than what it should be. An oak in the wild can live over 1,000 years. They are not even considered to be mature until they reach 300 years of age.

Saplings Establish Quickly with Little Help

Saplings generally need little to no time to *establish*, which can be defined as the point when growth returns to pre-transplant levels. Saplings usually establish during the first growing season and generally need little to no supplemental watering.

Pending the size of the tree, how it was planted, site conditions, growing zone, maintenance practices, and whether the tree is watered or not, it can take years for a traditional nursery tree to establish. In perfect conditions with regular watering, it will generally take a tree with a trunk

Support for Tree Planting Efforts

In addition to planting trees, perhaps you would also like to support organizations that do the same? Before you send any money or resources, here are some things to evaluate and consider when choosing the organization:

1. Make sure the plants they use are native to their region.

2. Make sure they avoid harming an existing ecosystem. For example, we should not replace a native grassland with a native forest; we need both. Ditto for wetlands, mangrove swamps, and many others.

3. Make sure they are not planting *monocrops*, which is the practice of growing a single species. Natural forests have many native species.

4. Make sure they are not planting trees for biofuel operations, which means the trees will be harvested for fuel, or harmful farming operations, like palm oil plantations.

5. Make sure they do not use planting efforts as a justification for removing a mature forest. Unfortunately, this happens.

6. The best planting efforts are closely aligned with the local communities who live in and rely on those spaces. Incorporating local knowledge, efforts, and buy-in often increases the resilience, longevity, and impact of planting efforts.

7. The best tree-planting efforts also give attention to the longevity and long-term health of the trees. Tree-planting is great, but we need those trees to live and thrive beyond our lifetime.

8. Finally, we must be wary of *greenwashing*, which occurs when an organization markets itself as environmentally friendly or sustainable, when in fact it is not. It's a gimmick intended to mislead consumers who prefer to buy goods and services from environmentally-conscious brands.

diameter size of 2 inches one to two years to establish. Because conditions are rarely perfect, a tree of this size will typically take two to four years to establish. Bigger trees will take longer.

Watering requirements for traditional nursery trees will depend a lot on when, where, and how the trees were planted. Regardless of the details, the amount of watering required for these larger trees will always be substantially more than for saplings. Bigger plants need more water than smaller ones.

The net result is that while a traditional nursery tree may look bigger on the day it is installed, it is likely to be outpaced by a younger sapling over the five-to-10-years time horizon. Although it seems counterintuitive, by planting a sapling we will actually have a larger tree faster. We will also save time and effort on watering.

Saplings Are Cheap

Saplings usually cost $3 to $7 per plant if we buy them (or free if we collect them outside). In contrast, most standard traditional nursery trees cost $40 to $90 each, with prized species like Japanese maples costing $200 to $300. Larger trees cost far more.

After purchase, we need to transport these trees. For saplings that is easy. But for traditional nursery trees, we either need a spacious vehicle, pickup truck, trailer, or will have to hire somebody to help. This adds effort and expense.

Saplings Have a Smaller Carbon Footprint

Carbon footprint is the term used to describe all the fossil fuel required for a given activity. In the case of growing a tree, this includes energy for powering machinery, irrigation, fertilizer production, staff driving to/from work, transportation of supplies to and from the nursery, and so much more. It adds up quickly for a nursery operation (this is true for most businesses, Leaf & Limb included). The fact that it only takes one or two years to grow a sapling compared to three to five years for an average traditional nursery tree reduces the carbon footprint substantially.

Most Important: Saplings Have Ideal Root Structure

The health and structure of a tree's root system plays a key role in its longevity and health. A healthy root system is one that radiates straight out from the base of the trunk and extends to well beyond the edge of the canopy. It is full of small feeder roots, which help keep the tree healthy, and various types of large structural roots, which help keep the tree stable. Here are some examples of what these root systems look like:

Saplings typically have ideal root systems. Even when they are less-than-ideal, they are generally young enough to be able to overcome early defects. It's a different story for traditional nursery trees. Let's look at both types in more detail:

Balled and burlapped trees are grown in a field. When the time comes for the tree to be sold, an operator uses a large machine to dig it out of the ground. This spade cuts away the majority of the tree's root system, leaving only the 2–3 feet of roots immediately surrounding the trunk. This is a small fraction of the tree's full root system. The tree will spend years repairing this damage. It may or may not succeed over the coming decades.

Containerized trees are grown in pots. As they develop, roots grow in circles around the inside of the pot. Well-developed tree roots should not form circles; this leads to critical root defects at a young age. Not only that, but due to traditional growing practices, the nurseries often bury what is known as the *root collar*. The root collar is the base of the trunk where it flares out and becomes the root system. When it is buried, roots will grow around the trunk and strangle it. These strangling roots harm the tree's health and often lead to premature death. These issues must be corrected before planting, which means cutting away root mass. It is normal to remove anywhere from 10% to 50% of the roots of a typical containerized plant.

69

As with the balled and burlapped trees, it takes time to overcome this loss. Even with the best pruning, there is no way to fully undo the damage of growing in a container, which often leads to health and structural issues that plague the tree for its whole life.

What's the Catch? Pushback Against Small Trees

Why do most individuals and organizations opt to plant traditional nursery trees instead of saplings? Part of this is simply due to a lack of knowledge. Another part is convenience—it's easy to drive to a local nursery and buy a plant. Based on my experience, however, the primary reason is the desire for the instant gratification of a larger tree, regardless of the long-term implications.

That said, there is one downside to saplings that will require attention: saplings are more fragile than larger trees. We must keep them safe from lawnmowers, string trimmers, and passersby. It is a lot easier to accidentally mow down a young sapling as compared to a tree with a 2-inch diameter trunk.

Luckily this issue of fragility is easy to solve—far easier than the various problems generated by traditional nursery trees. We can protect these saplings in a variety of ways, including with tree guards, various cages, and fencing. I will explain how later in this chapter.

How to Plant Saplings

Next let's learn the process for planting saplings!

Step 1: Assess the Growing Site Conditions

Before we begin, we must first choose the right species for the given location. Otherwise, the tree may be doomed. Consider a tree growing underneath powerlines. It needs to be a species with a short maximum height or else the utility company will remove it (or severely prune it). Here are some questions we should consider. But first, a video tutorial for those interested:

Here are the factors to evaluate before we begin:

1. What is our goal with this tree or shrub? For example, is our goal to provide food and shelter for birds? Provide shade? Or maybe our goal is functional (e.g., privacy screening, soaking up water in a low-lying area, or holding soil stable)? There are many possible goals. If the goal is simply to get more native trees in the ground, then great! Proceed to the next steps.

2. How much sun will this plant receive during the various seasons? To check sun conditions, you can either make observations or use a sun tracker app on your phone or tablet. I list some of my favorite apps in the Appendix.

3. What are the overhead space constraints? Are there limits to how tall or wide this tree or shrub should grow?

4. What are the soil constraints for the roots? Is there sufficient soil in which to grow?

5. What are the basic soil moisture conditions? We do not have to get technical. We mostly need to determine if the soil is extra dry, extra wet, or somewhere in between.

There could be other miscellaneous factors to consider, such as speed of growth desired, budget constraints, and so on—but there is no need to overthink any of this.

Step 2: Choose the Right Native Species Based on Site Conditions

Once we have determined our goals and site conditions, it is time to choose our favorite native tree and shrub species. Let's quickly define some terms before we continue:

- **Native plant:** For the sake of this book, native is defined as the plants that offer the most benefits to the widest diversity of local life within the ecosystem in which they all co-evolved. This will generally be plants that grew within a given local ecosystem before the arrival of Europeans to that given local area. This definition works well for North, Central, and South America. It will not work as well in other areas, like Europe.

- **Near-native plant:** This means it is native to an adjacent or nearby ecosystem. Perhaps not as good to local life as a true native, these are still better than non-native options. Near-natives may represent a necessary compromise between fulfilling a certain need, such as being tolerant to growing conditions

71

next to a street, while still attempting to provide some food and shelter for life that needs it.

- **Non-native plant:** This is a species introduced from another ecosystem that has not had enough time to co-evolve with local life in the ecosystem in which it now participates. Non-native plants provide less food, shelter, or other benefits as compared to native plants. Non-native plants are not necessarily invasive (more about this next), but they do represent an opportunity cost—that space could be occupied by something that benefits more local life. For example, Asian varieties of azaleas and camellias are quite popular across much of the Southeastern United States. They do not invade ecosystems, but they have little ecological value. They could be replaced with plants that provide more food and shelter to local life that needs it.

- **Invasive plant:** This is a non-native plant that outcompetes native plant species for valuable resources. These species harm ecosystems, leading to a decrease in the abundance and diversity of life—the very opposite of what we hope to achieve. **Invasive species are not inherently bad.** They are wonderful in their native ecosystems. It is our fault they were moved to this new ecosystem and caused destruction.

For those who have little-to-no experience picking native species, the easiest and fastest option is to contact a local or on-line native nursery and ask them for their favorite recommendations given the site conditions.

Roots, Pipes, Foundations, and Sidewalks

When deciding where to plant trees and what species to pick, folks often express concern about tree roots growing into their foundations, pipes, and damaging sidewalks. The good news is that we generally do not need to worry about these issues. Roots have no interest in growing into our foundation or pipes. Sidewalks and driveways (often referred to as *hardscapes*) are more susceptible to root damage. Luckily, if this does become an issue, we have good solutions that we'll discuss in the next chapter. In the meantime, here is a fun video to learn more:

For those who would like to take a deeper dive, here are my general recommendations for how to choose the right native species:

- Start by finding local native plant societies and organizations. They often provide an abundance of resources and expertise available for free. Where I live, we are fortunate to have the North Carolina Native Plant Society.

- Reach out to local garden clubs. Some offer resources and ideas for native plants.

- There are many online plant databases and resources that provide information regarding local native plants. For example, NC State University offers a plant database called the "North Carolina Extension Gardener Plant Toolbox." I will list others in the Appendix.

- There are numerous social media groups, subreddits on Reddit, and Meetups that focus on native plants. Some are purely online and others offer an in-person learning component.

- Search for classes and resources related to native species at local arboretums, botanical gardens, and nurseries.

- Sign up for newsletters from the organizations that provide ongoing education about native plants. For example, each newsletter from North Carolina Wildlife Federation teaches readers about native and invasive plants and insects.

- Last but certainly not least, refer to books and publications. There are many great options available. I will list some in the Appendix.

Plant Oaks – A Keystone Species

Oaks are often keystone species in their ecosystems and provide a great deal of food and shelter to an incredible breadth of life. Let's use the white oak as an example. Their leaves feed around 1,000 different types of caterpillars and various other insects, which in turn feed countless local and migratory birds. Their acorns are full of protein, fat, and carbohydrates—all of which are essential food for over 100 different types of vertebrates, including raccoons, deer, and chipmunks. They provide homes for bats, birds, bees, and countless others.

They also serve as food and habitat for micro-ecosystems in the bark, moss, roots, and so forth. Consider one gram of moss, which is approximately a handful. It contains 132,000 tardigrades, 150,000 protozoa, 800 rotifers, 3,000 springtails, 400 mites, 500 nematodes, 200 fly larvae, and many other species, each with their unique roles and specializations within the moss ecosystem.

Unfortunately, according to Morton Arboretum's *The Red List of Oaks 2020*, 217 of all 430 oak species are of conservation concern and 89 species are endangered or critically endangered. We can help alleviate this issue by planting native oaks.

Step 3: Time to Plant the Saplings!

By far the best time to plant trees and shrubs is during the dormant season. This will give them plenty of time to acclimate and begin growing some new roots. Those roots will help the saplings survive and thrive when the growing season returns. Plants installed during the dormant season generally have a higher rate of long-term survival and require little-to-no watering during the growing season.

If we have a mild dormant season with little snow, we can plant any time during this season. For those of us in the Southeast, we have a wide planting window that typically runs from November through February. If our area receives lots of snow and has deep frosts due to very cold weather, I recommend planting late in the dormant season, as soil temperatures unthaw and begin to approach 40°F on average.

This does not mean we cannot plant during the growing season; we can. But we either have to water frequently or accept increased tree mortality.

Now it's time to plant the saplings! **Our overall goal is to ensure the sapling's roots are in the ground, pointing down, and the trunk is above ground.** Here is the video tutorial showing the basic process for planting saplings:

1. There are many tools we can use to dig, including a hand trowel, a Hori Hori knife, a flat shovel, or a normal shovel. My favorite option is a shovel with a square, straight blade that is often called a *nursery spade* or *garden spade*. I also recommend a tool called a *dibble bar* as a possible option for those planting lots of saplings.

2. Using our tool of choice, the next step is to create a wedge in the soil big enough to insert the sapling's roots. We do so by driving the tool into the ground and pushing it as deep as it will go. Then we push it forward to create a wedge in the ground. Sometimes we may need to repeat this process several times to widen or deepen the wedge. However we do it, the goal is to make sure the wedge is deep enough to hold the roots.

3. Then we place the sapling's roots in the wedge. Make sure all the roots are in the soil. We must also do our best to ensure the roots are all pointing down. If the tips of the roots are not pointing down, and instead bend to the side or up toward the sky, we call these *J-hooks*. We need to avoid creating J-hooks if possible.

4. Once the plant is in place, close the wedge and pack the soil around the sapling's roots.

5. Add arborist wood chips (see Chapter 14 for more information about arborist wood chips) around the new sapling. Aim for a depth of 1–3 inches.

6. Here are two other options to consider:

    a. If we want to help inhibit weed growth, place some cardboard around the sapling under the arborist wood chips. Position it as close to the sapling as possible and extend it out to 1–3 feet from the trunk.

    b. If we have leaf mold (partially rotted leaves) or leaf compost (fully rotted leaves), we can add those as well. We can place them in the hole, under the arborist wood chips, or both.

That's it! We have now planted our sapling.

Care for Our New Tree

Saplings are very hardy and do not need much to thrive. Even when they wilt and appear to die, are accidentally cut down, or are eaten by deer, they often re-sprout. Here are some general care tips that we can follow:

Watering

With saplings, watering is generally not necessary. But perhaps we want to give our saplings some extra love or perhaps conditions are very dry and the saplings are struggling. In either case we can provide them with some water by using a hose to give each tree a 90-second splash every two to three days. If there are many saplings, we can set up a sprinkler or some sort of temporary irrigation of our choosing. Do not install permanent irrigation such as underground sprinkler systems. We want to stop watering as soon as possible so the trees can learn to survive on their own. This makes them more resilient and means we avoid wasting a precious resource.

We should water during the evening since it will remain in the soil for longer. If we water in the morning or afternoon, the water will evaporate quickly. Some say watering in the evening can create rot and fungal issues. This is of little concern for native saplings (and most plants, in my experience).

Arborist Wood Chips

Add fresh arborist wood chips each year. As the tree matures and grows larger, we should aim for a depth of 3–6 inches. This provides amazing health benefits for our tree. Avoid placing arborist wood chips on the root collar. Burying the root collar leads to strangling roots that damage the health of the tree and often lead to premature death. If possible, the arborist wood chips should extend out to the edge of the canopy, at a minimum. Further is better.

Tree Guards

We may need to install protection around each sapling (or group of saplings) to keep it safe from string trimmers, deer predation, rabbits, and so forth. There are all sorts of good options we can make or buy. My favorite go-to option is this:

Buy a roll of chicken wire (or sturdy equivalent) that is 4 feet wide. Cut out sections that are approximately 5 feet long. For each section, connect the ends to each other using scrap wire or a zip tie. Then place this hoop—which should have a 4-foot height with 1.5-foot opening—around the tree. Hold the hoop steady by placing sod stakes across the bottom of the hoop and pushing them into the ground. Please note that if you want a wider opening, you can increase the length of the chicken wire. The dimensions are flexible.

Here is the final, most crucial note: we must remove this hoop once the tree is large enough to survive on its own, which may take three to seven years. If we forget to remove this guard, it will kill the tree later. If there is any doubt about whether this tree guard will be removed in the future, we should either avoid using it or buy one that will pop off as the tree grows.

Structural Pruning

Structural pruning is essential to the long-term structural strength of the tree. I will cover this topic in depth in Chapter 12.

Planting Seeds Is Even Easier Than Saplings!

Another great option for growing native trees is to directly plant seeds in the ground where we want the trees to grow. This method mimics what happens naturally in the forest. Per usual, we'll start with a video tutorial:

Here are the written instructions:

1. Choose a place to plant the seeds. If there is grass or other vegetation growing there, mow it down as low as possible.

2. Create a tree guard made of chicken wire and pin it in place.

3. Scatter the seeds inside the circle.

4. Add a thick layer of leaves or leaf mold on top of the seeds.

5. Fill the bottom of the circle with 6 inches of arborist wood chips.

Whatever grows will grow. Whatever outcompetes the other seeds will be the winner. Or we can select the winners by cutting competing saplings as we see fit.

Best of all, we have the tree guard in place to keep the winning saplings from being damaged by mowing devices, deer, and other hazards. Remember to remove the hoop in three to seven years so it does not kill the tree later.

Whatever you decide to plant, don't forget the best part: watching it grow! There is nothing I love more than watching little saplings mature into large trees humming with insect and bird life. It is absolutely amazing!

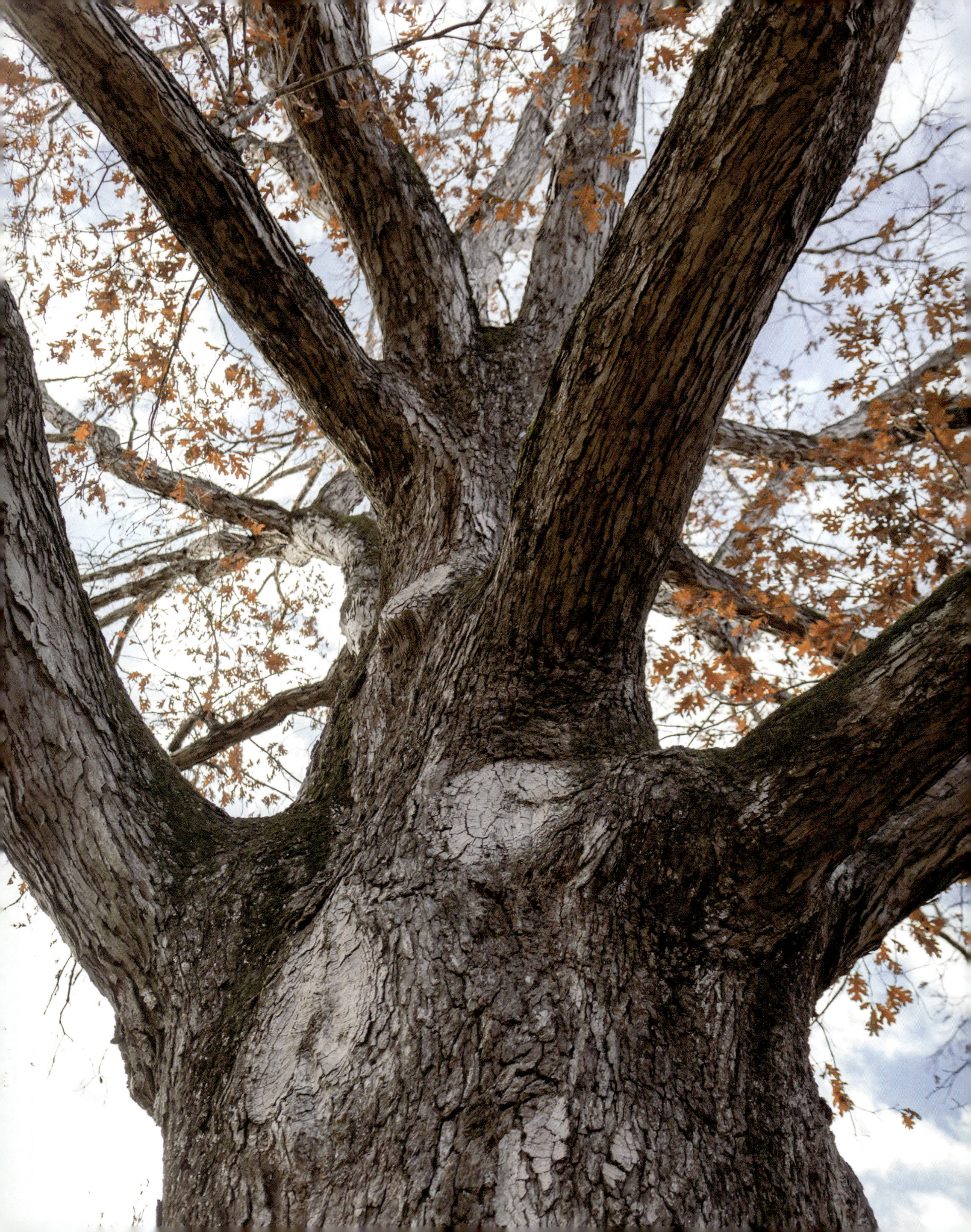

CHAPTER 11

save existing trees—they rarely need to be removed

We have talked a lot about planting new trees, but what about saving existing trees? By saving an existing tree we preserve all the benefits generated by that tree—soil, water, carbon, and outrageous diversity. We also save the money we might have spent on removing it. Was it Benjamin Franklin who said, "a tree saved is a tree earned?"

In my professional career I have observed that trees are often removed based on issues that either do not exist or could be easily solved without removal. These decisions are usually made due to a lack of knowledge about trees and alternative options. In this chapter my goal is to provide the information necessary to make better-informed decisions about whether a tree needs to be removed. **We will discuss three main topics:**

1. Trees we generally shouldn't worry about
2. Trees we should potentially worry about
3. How to inspect a tree for potential issues

Before we begin, let me give some disclaimers: trees are highly dynamic, living organisms that vary greatly by species, location, weather conditions, and more. My knowledge of trees is mostly limited to the ecosystems here in the Piedmont of North Carolina. It's not possible for me to describe or anticipate every condition or event that could possibly lead to health decline, structural failure, or death of a tree. I cannot guarantee that trees will be healthy or safe. Therefore, take all of this chapter with a grain of salt—if in doubt, please hire a trained professional with one or multiple of the following credentials: ISA Certified Arborist, ISA Tree Risk Assessment Qualification (TRAQ), ISA Board Certified Master Arborist, and ASCA Registered Consulting Arborist.

Make sure this professional aligns with the values put forth in this book. For example, find a professional from a company that emphasizes the importance of trees on their website and does not feature or glorify tree removal. Better yet, choose one that does not even offer tree removal services if this option exists. Tree removal projects are expensive and generate a great deal of revenue for most tree service companies. It can be hard for a professional to walk away from a removal opportunity, especially if work is slow or if they need to meet a target (I'm speaking from past experience from when Leaf & Limb used to remove trees).

Trees We Generally Shouldn't Worry About

After many years of working in the tree service industry, I have heard many unfounded fears and misinformation when it comes to trees and the supposed need to cut them down. Here are the concerns I hear most often and why they are not generally concerning.

"I saw my tree swaying in the wind (or a storm) and I'm worried it's going to fall on my house!"

Tree movement is a good thing! They are supposed to move. As they move, trees grow stronger by developing something called *response growth*. Think about how we humans work our bodies to build muscle: we lift things, push things, and move around. Although the physiology is very different, the concept is the same: when trees move in the wind they grow stronger. In addition, trees have all sorts of amazing structural features that allow them to withstand high winds, such as leaves that reconfigure into cones to minimize drag, a high twistiness-to-bendiness ratio

Mature Trees Provide Exponentially More Benefits

Mature trees, which can be loosely defined as those that have reached their full size in the sub/urban landscape, have 100 times more leaf and root mass as compared to a young tree. Imagine all those extra leaves to feed insects, twigs to house their young, branches for birds to build nests, bark on which moss can colonize, and crevices where bacteria can thrive. Then there are the many rotting branches, hollows, and nooks that serve as homes for woodpeckers, nesting sites for bats and migrating birds, food for fungi, and pools of water for salamanders and tree frogs. Below-ground is similar to above-ground; we find exponentially more roots that support a much larger community of bacteria, fungi, earthworms, and other members of this ecosystem as compared to young trees.

With their bigger trunks, denser crown of leaves, and more expansive root systems, mature trees create more soil, hold and move more water, sequester more carbon, and support more diversity. **These benefits can only be replaced with the time it takes for a tree to grow.** No amount of money in the world can transform a 10-year-old oak to a 350-year-old oak. Mature trees are invaluable.

save existing trees

in the trunk, and tensile buttressing, to name a few.

In the face of a hurricane, tornado, or major wind event all bets are off, even for the strongest and most healthy trees. But even if we have no trees on our property, that storm system can still drop trees and branches from other sites onto our house or building. I have personally witnessed this on multiple occasions during various storms here in North Carolina. All this to say, there is no reason to remove a tree because of the possibility of extreme weather and most certainly no reason to remove a tree because it sways in the wind.

"The tree is too close to my house. I'm afraid it will fall and cause damage— and maybe kill someone!"

Live trees have springy branches full of leaves that act as sails when they fall. They tend to fall more slowly and land with less impact, creating less damage. Buildings rarely collapse; roofs are strong and are designed to protect those living and working below. In my experience, the most serious damage occurs when live trees puncture the roof and rain enters that hole, creating internal water damage. Dead trees are different—they fall with force. If these are located near a building or house and could cause harm, they should be removed.

For those worried that a tree will fall and kill someone we love, the chances of this happening are extremely low. To put the risk into perspective, a review of mortality data in the United States found that nationwide there were 407 deaths from wind-related tree failure during the 13-year period from 1995 to 2007. At the individual level, that comes out to about a one in 690,000 chance each year. Compare this to your chances of dying in a motor vehicle accident (one in 9,000) and by drowning (one in 76,000). These risks are far greater, yet many of us think little of driving multiple times every day (or relaxing in and around water).

"That tree is HUGE! It scares me so much—it needs to be cut down."

The huge trees are generally the oldest trees. They have survived many years and weathered many storms. They have developed great strength and resilience in the face of many challenges. These are usually the safest trees we should fear *the least*. This assumes they have not been damaged or disturbed recently. An example of this would be a construction project nearby that caused damage to the tree's root system. This warrants closer inspection—more on this soon.

"I need to remove the tree because its roots are cracking my pipes, damaging my foundation, raising my sidewalk, or ruining my parking lot."

Roots in pipes, foundations, or lifting hardscapes often lead people to remove the offending tree. But this is usually unnecessary, resulting in wasted money and the loss of a healthy tree. Let's start with pipes and foundations.

Tree roots seek food and water. They have no interest in foundations and pipes. Tree

Some Fun Facts About Trees!

Trees are amazing and worth saving! We have learned so many reasons why this is true. Here are some more. Enjoy!

roots are like melted cheese; they ooze through and around objects, looking for the path of least resistance. They have no punching power. When roots encounter pipes and foundations that have no cracks, they turn and grow around or alongside these structures.

But if they encounter pipes and foundations with cracks, they often enter in search of water and other basic needs. These cracks usually occur due to improper installation, age, or settling. When plumbers, inspectors, and other technicians find roots in the pipe or foundation, they usually blame the root because they mistake correlation with causation. This basic mistake in logic has happened so often that trees now have a bad reputation for damaging pipes and other infrastructure, though they often play no part whatsoever in the damage. The solution is to prune the root and replace the pipe or fix the foundation, not to remove the tree. This will save us a lot of money on unnecessary tree removal costs.

With sidewalks and hardscapes in general, roots do tend to cause more issues. But there are many solutions that allow us to address the issue and preserve the tree. Here are some ideas:

- We can install root barriers on the outer edge of the hardscape to prevent roots from growing underneath. This is typically a proactive solution we must implement before the roots reach the hardscape.

- If a root is already causing an issue, we can prune the root and use a pavement grinder to sand down the portion of the hardscape that has been lifted. We may also be able to slide a root barrier in place to prevent future intrusions.

- There are companies that use subsurface injections of foam and epoxy to lift and level the hardscape. This can be a cheap, easy way to level a hardscape while leaving the tree and its roots intact.

- For sidewalks specifically, consider pouring an ADA-compliant rubber overlay or equivalent (there are many options) on top of the lifted portion.

- Maybe the hardscape is old and needs to be replaced? Resurface the area taking care not to damage the roots. We can do this by instructing our contractor to use a jackhammer and hand tools only and to avoid using heavy equipment near the roots. This will limit damage to the root system. Resurfacing allows us the opportunity to add more gravel and level the surface while leaving the roots intact.

The list goes on. I recommend exploring these and other options before making the decision to remove the tree. Here is a great resources for those interested in more:

And let's not forget one last option: do nothing. I realize that at times there may be city or HOA requirements to address the issues. We should also consider the needs of the elderly, pregnant, folks who rely on wheelchairs, and so forth. But if these are not a concern, consider leaving things as-is.

"I want to thin out some trees to increase the health of the largest trees."

It is normal for trees to grow in dense stands. This is typical in forests. Trees are stronger and healthier in groups than they are as individuals. In groups, their roots interlock and increase their holding power within the soil. They are less likely to blow over. From a safety and health aspect, thinning trees creates issues. It does not solve them. Better to ignore the situation and let the trees sort things out among themselves.

"I need to remove the tree because it is at the end of its lifespan."

A tree does not reach the end of its lifespan unless it has a fatal health issue or a structural defect that could cause it to fall and create harm to those nearby. Does this tree have such an issue? Could the issue be addressed by improving its structure or health? We will learn how to do these things in Chapters 12 and 14. In the absence of an issue, trees live a very long time. Maples can grow to be 400 years old in the wild. Some pine species here in North Carolina can reach ages of 200 to 500 years. There are oaks in the UK that are over 1,000 years old.

The point of all of these examples is that there is either nothing to worry about or there are better, cheaper solutions available than removing the tree. Now let's talk about trees we should potentially worry about.

New Life from Dead Trees

Dead trees (sometimes called *snags*) are a hub of life for dozens of species of birds and mammals, to say nothing of the countless insects, fungi, and bacteria that call them home. When a tree dies, its remains provide a new chapter of life for many others and boost outrageous diversity. Therefore, if we can leave a dead tree in place without creating a safety hazard, we should do so.

Still not convinced? Some of these snag-dependent residents create positive outcomes on our property. Here are two examples:

- Woodpeckers build homes in dead trees and then dine on Southern pine beetles, ambrosia beetles, and other beetles from nearby live trees. This helps protect these live trees from being harmed by beetles.

- Bats roost in dead trees and then happily eat mosquitoes. This is great for those living nearby—bats provide free mosquito control services!

Trees We Should Potentially Worry About

I want to immediately state that if we have one of the situations described next this does **not** mean we need to remove the tree. It means we should pay extra attention to that tree and consider calling a trained professional for additional advice. This assumes that the tree could harm people or property. If it is in the woods, or in an area where it will not cause harm if it falls, we have nothing to worry about. Leave it for the birds and other life that love dying and dead trees.

New Wind Exposure

When building new neighborhoods, shopping centers, and so forth, developers often clear-cut part of the forest. As a result, trees that were once sheltered in the heart of the forest are now exposed to new wind forces they have never encountered. They have not developed the necessary response growth to withstand these new winds. This makes them susceptible to what is known as *windthrow*, which is a fancy term for being blown over. It will take many years, perhaps over a decade, for these trees to adapt to their new conditions. If all goes well, they will move in the wind without falling and become stronger as they do so. But until then, they should be inspected every six to 12 months since they are more likely to fall than trees that have experienced consistent wind forces for the duration of their lives.

Construction Near Trees

Any time construction, digging, trenching, or disturbance of any kind (we'll call these *construction* for ease of reading) happens underneath the canopy of the tree, there is cause for concern. Construction often leads to smashed and cut roots, a decline in tree health and stability, and damage to the soil ecosystem. To learn more we need to get technical:

The area underneath the canopy near the trunk is particularly important, since there is a high concentration of roots located here. We will call this the *critical root zone*

(CRZ). I define the minimum CRZ as a circle having a radius equal to the diameter of the trunk measured at 54 inches above the ground (this is called *diameter at breast height* or DBH) × 18, as measured from the outside of the tree trunk. For example, if we have a trunk that is 12 inches DBH, the CRZ is calculated as follows: 12 inches × 18 = 216 inches or 18 feet. Thus, the CRZ is a circle with a radius of 18 feet, as measured from the outside edge of the trunk. I prefer a CRZ equal to the edge of the canopy, if possible, since more healthy roots are better for the tree. But this is not feasible for all construction projects.

There is another important zone, which we will call the *structural root zone* (SRZ). This is a circle whose radius measures DBH × 6 as measured from the outside edge of the trunk. Using the same example as before, this would be 12 inches × 6 = 72 inches or 6 feet. So the SRZ in this scenario is a circle with a radius of 6 feet as measured from the outside edge of the trunk. Please note that the definition of SRZ may vary by expert. Some go so far as to say that SRZ is equal to DBH × 3, which would be 36 inches in this example. I prefer to err on the conservative side.

The most dangerous disturbance is that which bisects the SRZ. According to best practices in the tree service industry, bisecting the SRZ leads to an increased likelihood that this tree has been structurally destabilized. It's much like removing a leg (or two) from a table. To be fair, this standard is not always accurate—it can vary based on where the majority of root growth is located and how deep the cut was made.

For construction outside of the SRZ but still within the CRZ, the primary concern is damage to tree health, not necessarily structural stability. The damage can often be remedied through a soil improvement process, especially if it affects less than 25% of the CRZ. For this process, we may need to hire a professional because these are not common tools. Here are specifications for this process:

1. Add 1–2 inches of leaf mold or leaf compost on the affected area or underneath the entire canopy.

2. Use an air knife powered by compressed air to turn this material into the soil.

3. Use the air knife to stir the soil to a depth of 8–12 inches.

4. When everything is done, cover the entire area with 3–6 inches of arborist wood chips.

5. If this occurs during the growing season, drench the root zone in water.

NOTE: If a professional or the tools are not available, proceed with adding the leaf mold/compost and arborist wood chips. These will help.

Once the soil improvement is done, we should continue doing everything possible to rehabilitate the soil within the CRZ of the tree, such as adding compost

Preserving Mature Trees During Construction

The issues related to construction can be avoided with advance planning and preparation before the project begins. Here are some tips:

- Avoid disturbing the CRZ. Set up tree protection fencing to prevent people, machines, and supplies from entering the CRZ. Better yet, stage the fences underneath the outer edge of the canopy to protect even more roots and soil—this will increase the probability that the tree survives and thrives after construction.

- Do not rely on orange plastic fencing as an adequate barrier; it rarely stops anybody. I strongly recommend chain link panels that are placed on stands and connected to each other via wire ties. Ironically, the shade of the few remaining trees are often the most sought-after rest areas on a construction site.

- Add 12 inches of arborist wood chips within the protected area. These will help disperse possible impacts and build soil.

- If additional protection is necessary, lay sheets of ¾-inch plywood on top of the arborist wood chips to absorb even more impacts.

- Provide supplemental watering (10 to 20 gallons of water per inch of trunk diameter per week) and monthly infusions of compost or compost tea to further boost health.

- If the CRZ must be disturbed, avoid trenching, grade changes, digging, and root cuts of any kind.

- If cuts must be made, they must not affect more than 25% of the CRZ and should not affect the SRZ in any way. Use air tools to open channels and use sharp saws and pruning tools to cut the roots in advance of the construction equipment. Excavators, trenchers, and other heavy equipment will tear and rip roots, which causes far more damage than clean cuts. When done, cover the exposed roots with soil so they do not dry out; and clearly mark the area where the operator should dig to avoid further damage to remaining roots. I recommend speaking with each equipment operator directly to add further clarity about where to dig and where to avoid digging.

- For big projects, boring underneath the root system is another possible option, though this will require boring pits and machinery.

These tips are a helpful start, but there are often other factors to consider. For anything beyond this information I recommend calling a qualified professional to help.

tea and replenishing arborist wood chips, all of which we will discuss in more detail in Chapter 14. In addition, the tree should be inspected every six to 12 months for no less than five years, but ideally 10.

It is worth noting that even in the absence of specific construction damage, this approach is often very effective at boosting the health of a tree, especially if that tree has not received care in the past. The sub/urban landscape is generally a tough place for a tree to grow!

Lifting Root Plate

Sometimes a leaning tree is growing toward the sun and is perfectly stable. This is usually the case. But sometimes a leaning tree is slowly falling over, which can be dangerous if there are people or structures underneath. We can discern the latter by inspecting the area next to the trunk on the opposite side of the lean. Are we able to see soil and roots lifting? Are there roots bulging out of the ground? Does the soil feel extra spongy under our feet? These are all signs that the tree may be falling. We must make sure we have a clear visual on this area.

I recall one specific example where I thought a leaning tree was stable. The ground on the opposite side of the lean felt firm and I could not see or feel any bulging roots. But English ivy was growing here and obstructing my view. To be extra sure, I removed all the ivy. I was shocked to find three large structural roots bowing out of the ground. I had been unable to feel them through the ivy. I traced these roots directly to the base of the trunk and was able to immediately determine that this tree was in imminent danger of falling. Because there was a house nearby, I advised that this tree needed to be removed (and gave the homeowner a handful of native saplings to replant in place of this tree).

Invasive Pests

There are a variety of invasive insects and diseases that kill trees and are challenging or impossible to stop. Some that come to mind are emerald ash borer, Dutch elm disease, Asian ambrosia beetles, chestnut blight, and beech bark disease. The species will vary considerably by region. Some of them can be deterred through a combination of preventative measures (e.g., trunk injections to impede emerald ash borer) and ensuring the target tree has excellent health. But once an invasive pest infests or infects a tree, the best options are often to either remove the tree or let it rot in place.

Invasive Trees

Invasive trees damage local ecosystems. They should be removed and replaced with native species. Research on mid-Atlantic ecosystems has found that native plants support 35 times more caterpillar biomass (total weight of the caterpillars) and three times more caterpillar species than non-native plants.

How to Inspect a Tree for Potential Issues

Let's briefly dive into the process for evaluating a tree. I want to emphasize that this next section is not a thorough tutorial. It covers the basics. Most of the things I outline next can be treated or addressed without needing to remove the tree. Before we dive into the details, here is a basic tutorial:

Canopy

Let's start at the top of the tree and work our way down. If we see upper branches dying, starting from their outer tips, this is a common and obvious sign that the tree is declining in health. This can occur throughout the entire canopy or within a concentrated portion of the canopy. This decline in health is often related to the tree being rooted in dirt, not soil. We can fix this using the soil improvement process outlined earlier in this chapter and the practices in Chapter 14.

It's important to note that branch death starting from their tips is very different from branches dying in the lower and interior portions of the canopy. Dead branches in the lower and interior canopy are normal and nothing to worry about. They are being shaded out by upper and outer branches.

Here are some other things to look for in the canopy:

- A lack of leaves when there should be leaves.

- Foliage falling before the dormant season begins.

- A deciduous tree holding on to dead leaves when they should have dropped.

- Foliage turning unusual colors at unexpected times.

- Insects defoliating more than 20% of the canopy. Keep in mind that some insect damage is good, normal, and to be expected. After all, insects and herbivores need to feed from trees and other plants.

- A low density of leaves as compared to other trees of the same species.

- Branches that protrude from the edge of the canopy further than other branches. These could be at higher-than-usual risk of splitting. They should be pruned to reduce length (more on this in Chapter 12, where we discuss structural pruning).

Trunk

The next area to examine is the trunk. Here are some possible issues to look for:

- Peeling bark, cracking bark, or other damage along the trunk which is not typical for that species. Ditto for abnormal colors and texture. Ignore lichen and moss. They are totally normal and nothing to worry about.

- Large holes, hollows, and columns of decay. See the sidebar for more information on this topic.

- Ooze, discharge, fine sawdust, or liquid seeping from the trunk.

- The smell of fermentation wafting from a specific location on the trunk.

- A strip of exposed wood running up the length of the trunk, which could be a sign of a recent lightning strike. Trees can often recover from lightning strikes.

- A new lean where there never used to be one. The tree could be slowly tipping over.

- Multiple trunks with a tight V-shape at the point of origin. These types of trunks are more likely to split over the long term and should be addressed through structural pruning if possible.

- A root collar buried under arborist wood chips, mulch, or dirt. We

Hollows & Decay Are Not Often an Issue

Hollows and areas of decay are often a normal part of tree maturation. The trick is discerning when a hollow is significant versus not. A good rule of thumb is that any time the trunk has a hollow or cavity that is greater than one-third of the overall circumference, we may need to be concerned. In other words, if a cavity or decay affects more than one-third of the trunk's outer portion, this warrants closer inspection and analysis. Any less than this is generally no cause for concern.

know from the previous chapter that a buried root collar will kill a tree. If we cannot see a prominent flare at the base of the trunk, or if it looks like a telephone pole that disappears straight into the ground, we know the root collar is buried—it must be excavated and exposed ASAP.

Roots

Roots are a very important part of the tree. They make up as much mass as the canopy, meaning that the weight of roots underground is equal to the weight of branches above ground. That said, the structure of the roots is different from the branches. In the sub/urban landscape, roots usually only grow about 2 feet down into the ground (main structural roots sometimes grow to a depth of 3 feet) and they extend beyond the edge of the branches, typically at least three times as far. These roots form a wide, flat plate underneath the tree.

Here are some thing to examine:

- Dirt versus soil. This is one of the most common underlying health issues we see for trees in the sub/urban landscape. It leads to a decline in health, which makes the tree more susceptible to other issues, like pest attacks. An easy way to check for dirt versus soil is with the Screwdriver Test (see the sidebar). We can fix this using the soil improvement process outlined earlier in this chapter and using the practices described in Chapter 14.

- Watch for mushrooms growing at the base of the trunk or on the nearby roots. Most are harmless, but there are a handful that could be signs of something more serious, like extensive root decay.

- Construction, trenches, digging, and other disturbance in the area underneath the canopy of the tree. As we discussed earlier, these can impact the health and the stability of the tree, pending the extent and severity.

- Single or multiple roots lifting out of the ground. This could indicate the tree is slowly tipping, as we discussed earlier.

- Soil that is consistently oversaturated when it had previously been dry. This could be due to a water leak, site change, or some other variable. This can injure or kill a tree that is not used to this sort of saturation. We should determine where this water is coming from and address the issue.

If we find a potential issue in the canopy, on the trunk, with the roots, or in the growing area, it may be necessary to call a trained professional for closer analysis. Generally speaking, most of these issues can be solved through care plans that should include some form of attention to the structure of the tree and the soil in which it grows, at a minimum.

I also want to emphasize that all of this assumes that the tree could harm people or property. If it is in the woods, or in an area where it will not cause harm if it falls, we have nothing to worry about. Leave it for the birds and other life that love dying and dead trees.

Let's discuss tree structure next.

The Screwdriver Test

The screwdriver test is a fast, easy option that gives us a reasonable barometer for the health of the soil (or lack thereof). It is a test I use frequently. Here is how to perform it:

Go find a screwdriver that is at least 12 inches long. Attempt to push it in the ground without using a great deal of force. If we can easily push it down 10 inches or more, this is soil. If it will only go down 5 to 10 inches, it's debatable as to whether this is soil or dirt, but it could still be improved. If the screwdriver goes down 5 inches or less, then this is dirt, not soil. Dirt is all too common in the sub/urban landscape but can be fixed, as we will learn in Chapter 14. This video contains a real-world application of the screwdriver test:

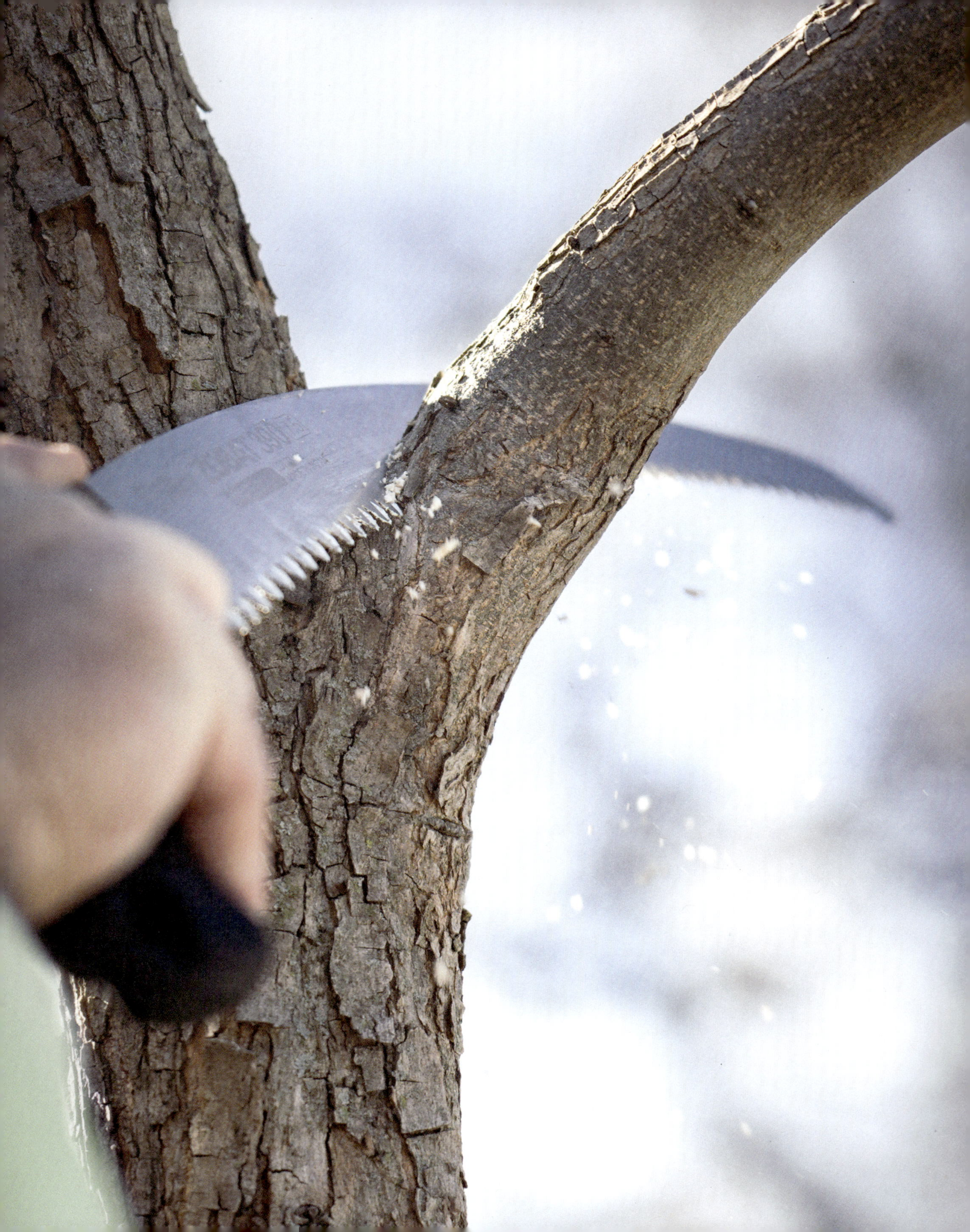

CHAPTER 12

perform structural pruning to increase strength—it's the only pruning that matters

If we want to help heal Earth, planting and saving trees is important. But we cannot stop there—we also want to help those trees live as long as possible. To achieve maximum longevity for trees in the sub/urban landscape, the two most important things we must do are maximize their strength and health. Aside from avoiding harm, like construction in the CRZ, the best ways to do this are pruning to create ideal structure and improving the health of the soil in which they grow.

Ideal structure and healthy soil are the juggernauts of tree longevity in the sub/urban landscape. Let's start with structure and then we will focus on soil in Chapter 14. Having poor structure increases a tree's susceptibility to being split or toppled during storms and high wind events. When this happens, it often mortally wounds or kills the tree and often causes property damage. We can reduce this issue through the act of structural pruning, which is the only type of pruning that matters in terms of caring for trees and helping them live long lives in the sub/urban landscape. There are other types of pruning, such as creating clearance from a nearby building, removing dead branches, and generating more space between the ground and the lowest part of the canopy (this is often called *raising the canopy*). These and other practices may achieve utilitarian and aesthetic objectives, but they do not increase the longevity of the tree. In some cases, they can actually create harm, especially when improper pruning cuts are utilized.

Structural Pruning—What Is it?

Picture that we are standing in a forest. The trees are crowded closely together. Within this environment, trees must grow tall and straight in order to reach sunlight. They must be efficient with branch growth, which means most of the branches are spaced apart from one another, and the diameter of each branch is significantly less than that of the trunk. These trees have an ideal structure that makes them strong and resilient in the face of heavy winds. This is the natural environment for most trees. In contrast, imagine a tree growing in the sub/urban landscape (or maybe you can look out your window to see one right now). Most trees growing in sub/urban spaces have too much room to grow and do not have to compete with other trees for sunlight. This is not a natural environment for most trees. They grow many trunks and long branches that are often crowded together. They do not have ideal structure and are likely to break during storms and heavy winds. If this happens, the falling branch or tree could damage homes, buildings, and cars. The tree will either die or begin declining from these new wounds, which results in the loss of a tree and money spent on removal and replacement. All of these are outcomes we want to avoid.

The good news is that we can avoid these negative outcomes through structural pruning, which mimics the competition a tree would experience in the forest. We use pruning cuts to train the tree to develop a tall, central trunk with small, well-spaced branches. In a way, this is using pruning cuts to biologically program a tree. Of course, we cannot control it or tell it what to do, but we can certainly influence how it grows.

By providing our tree with structural pruning, we reduce the possibility of it splitting or failing in various ways. It keeps our property safer and ensures the tree lives a longer, healthier life. **It is for these reasons that I rank structural pruning as one of the top two most important ways to care for trees in the sub/urban landscape.**

Improper Pruning Kills Trees!

Most pruning performed in the sub/urban landscape harms and kills trees. The issue I see most often is improper pruning cuts that lead to rot in the trunk, which harms its health, makes it more hazardous, and ultimately leads to its early demise. This is a slow process. It can take a decade or two, at which point it is hard to remember where and how the issue began. I wish these improper cuts were limited to inexperienced homeowners, but unfortunately most tree services and landscapers do the same.

Another practice I see is something called *topping*. This occurs when the top of a tree is removed. Topping is even more harmful than improper pruning cuts, especially for large shade trees like oaks and maples. Even if the tree survives, it will have multiple weakly-attached new trunks that are more likely to split, fall, and create damage. It will be structurally unsafe.

The concept of structural pruning is often confusing at first. This video helps clarify the important points:

Before I teach how to perform structural pruning, let's quickly divert into a bit of tree biology, which sets the stage for how and why we perform the cuts.

A Bit of Basic Tree Biology

Tree bark serves as an outer layer of defense to keep harmful wood-decay fungi from entering the tree. Once the bark is gone, which happens with any pruning cut, the inner wood is exposed and wood-decay fungi are able to enter the tree. Once they enter, they digest the moist, live wood and cause it to rot. If the tree cannot stop this attack, the fungi will spread, causing further rot, holes, and hollows. These may lead to falling branches, splitting trunks, and death of the tree.

In the forest, trees naturally perform self-pruning—the fancy term for this is *cladoptosis*. They do this in a way that prevents wood-decay fungi from killing the tree. When a branch is weak or not generating enough food, the tree will begin slowly shedding that branch by cutting off its supply of fluid and nutrients.

The branch begins rotting and eventually falls. The tree grows over the area where the branch was attached to the trunk and creates a permanent wall of bark that blocks invading wood-decay fungi (as with everything in this book, I'm simplifying this process for ease of readability).

This defense process is driven by something called the *branch collar*. The branch collar is located at the base of a branch where it meets the trunk (or a larger branch). The branch collar consists of overlapping layers of tissue that create a strong attachment point with the trunk. There are thin barriers called *protection zones* between the layers of tissue that help prevent wood decay fungi from entering the trunk. This is a tad technical—the point is that the branch collar plays an essential role in protecting trees from wood-decay fungi during cladoptosis and after.

By carefully studying how trees naturally prune themselves in the forest through cladoptosis, we arrive at a crucial point: **Do not damage the branch collar when pruning.** If the branch collar is damaged or removed during pruning, the tree will struggle to protect itself from harmful wood-decay fungi and may die. In the process, it will be more likely to break and cause damage. Next let's learn how to make a proper pruning cut.

Cut #1: A Proper Pruning Cut That Does Not Damage the Branch Collar

Before we begin, I want to acknowledge that the idea of pruning may feel overwhelming, especially when compared to the simplicity of planting a sapling or choosing not to remove a mature tree. I want to put your mind at ease: we will be working with young trees where it's ok to make mistakes because they are very resilient. We will focus on small branches using basic tools and simple processes. This is a fun and engaging process with visible positive outcomes!

We will need the following tools:

- **Bypass pruners**: use these for cuts on branches that are less than ⅓-inch in diameter.
- **Loppers**: use these to make cuts on branches from ⅓-inch to 1 inch in diameter.
- **Hand saw**: use this to make cuts on branches 1 inch in diameter and larger.
- **Optional:** Pole saw and pole loppers. These are great for cutting branches out of reach.

Let me add two important warnings before we dive in:

- **Wear personal protective equipment** required for each tool. I recommend eye and hand protection at a minimum. Wear a helmet when cutting branches overhead.
- **Work from the ground on safe, flat surfaces only**. Do not work from roofs, ladders, and other sloped and unstable surfaces without professional training and safety equipment. These are dangerous places.

To begin, we must first identify the branch collar. The branch collar is a bulge at the base of the branch where it meets the trunk (or a larger branch). With practice it will become easy to locate the branch collar. Whenever we make a pruning cut, the goal is to make the cut immediately adjacent to the outside of the branch collar. We do not want to remove or damage the branch collar, but we also do not want to cut too far away from the branch collar. Both make it hard or impossible for the tree to create protection against wood-decay fungi.

For branches less than 1 inch in diameter, we use bypass pruners or loppers to make the cut outside of the bulge, on the side furthest from the trunk (or larger branch). For any branch that is larger than 1 inch in diameter, we should use a hand saw to make the pruning cut. But be careful! These saws are sharp. Make sure hands, arms, and legs are not behind the direction of the cut—we do not want to accidentally slice our body after the saw breaks through the final bit of wood. It hurts!

When we use a hand saw we encounter a new issue: as we are cutting the branch, it could fall and peel bark from the underside of the branch collar and the trunk below where the branch attaches. This creates a serious wound that leaves the tree susceptible to attack from wood-decay fungi. We must avoid this or risk killing the tree. To do so, we perform something called the *3-Cut Method*.

Here is how to perform the 3-Cut Method. Before making the cut, let me first show what this looks like in video format.

We make the first cut under the branch to keep it from peeling bark from the underside. This cut should be made approximately 2–3 inches from the branch collar. With the first cut in place, we move our hand saw beyond this cut, to approximately 4–5 inches from the branch collar. Make this second cut starting from the top of the branch. Please note that the goal of these first two cuts is to reduce the weight of the branch without peeling bark, thereby freeing us to make a very precise final cut. The third and final cut must be made immediately adjacent to the outside of the branch collar. Do not damage the branch collar. Using a sharp saw will help make a great cut.

Congratulations! Now we know how to make a proper pruning cut. Let's learn one more type of cut before we dive into structural pruning.

Cut #2: A Reduction Cut

A *reduction cut* is one where we reduce the end of a main branch back to a smaller, side branch (the fancy term is a *side lateral*). That remaining side branch should be at least one-third of the diameter of the main branch so that it can sustain life for the remainder of the branch.

For small branches less than 1 inch in diameter, use bypass pruners or loppers to make the cut. For any branch larger than 1 inch in diameter, use the 3-Cut Method. Again, the goal with the first two cuts is to reduce the weight of the branch,

TRUNK AND BRANCH

FIRST CUT

SECOND CUT

FINAL CUT

MAIN BRANCH AND SIDE BRANCH

FIRST CUT

SECOND CUT

FINAL CUT

thereby freeing us to make a very precise final cut without having to worry about peeling bark. For reduction cuts, the third and final cut must be made at a 45° angle to the side branch and should not damage the branch collar of the side branch. This video helps explain this point:

How to Perform Structural Pruning

Now that we know how to perform these pruning cuts, let's learn how to apply them to perform structural pruning.

The best time to start this process is when trees are young, which I'm arbitrarily defining as anything between 1 and 10 years old, or thereabouts. It's easy to mold young trees as they grow and they are generally very resilient in terms of withstanding mistakes. The concepts we learn in this chapter can also be applied to large and mature trees, often to great effect, though we need new tools and techniques that require many years of professional training and are far beyond the scope of this book.

In terms of timing, the best time to prune is during the dormant season. For a young tree, which is the focus of this chapter, we should not remove more than 40% of its live growth. For older trees the limits would be less, generally in the range of 25% for medium-aged trees and 10% for mature trees. This can be adjusted according to the health of the tree; healthier trees can withstand more pruning and unhealthy trees can withstand less. Whenever we are in doubt, cut less versus more. We cannot reattach a branch once it's cut, but we can always prune more next year.

These are the three basic steps for structural pruning:

1. MOST IMPORTANT: Encourage one dominant, upright trunk.

2. Remove *bad branches*, which are those that:
   a. have a diameter greater than 50% of the diameter of the trunk.
   b. form angles less than 45° with the trunk.

3. Create vertical and horizontal spacing between branches.

Step 1: Make Cuts to Encourage One Dominant, Upright Trunk

Let's focus on the first step: encourage one dominant, upright trunk. Before we begin, here is a video demonstrating this work:

Begin by carefully assessing the tree. Identify the healthiest, most upright trunk—we can do this by tracing an imaginary line from the base of the tree up the biggest trunk, all the way to the point at which it ends at the top of the canopy. This will be our future dominant, upright trunk.

Are there other trunks present? Are there branches that are taller than our desired trunk? If yes, remove these first using one of the two types of pruning cuts. A competing trunk may not have a clearly defined branch collar. Even if we fail to

Leave Dead Branches When Possible

Much like dead trees, dead branches are a big boon to life. Dead branches provide nesting sites for birds, food for fungi and beetles, and homes for raccoons, to name a few. If we can leave dead branches in place without creating a safety hazard to people and property below, we should. Dead branches will not harm the overall health of the tree. Quite the opposite, in fact—by increasing outrageous diversity, they actually boost the overall health of the tree.

make a perfect pruning cut, young trees are highly resilient and will likely recover. This is not true for older and more mature trees, especially those in poor health. Using these cuts, we can essentially tell the tree to stop putting growth into other trunks and branches that are competing for height dominance and instead focus growth within what we have deemed to be the main trunk.

If these actions have resulted in 40% of live growth being removed, do not continue. Give the tree one year to recover and begin the process again. If we have not reached 40%, proceed to the next step.

Step 2: Remove Bad Branches

The next step is to use pruning cuts to remove two types of branches: those that have a diameter greater than 50% of the diameter of the trunk and those that form angles less than 45° with the trunk (the ideal branch forms a 90° angle with the trunk). These branches often have weak attachments to the tree and are the ones that tend to break as the tree matures. Find these branches and remove them or reduce them using the pruning cuts we learned earlier.

If these actions have resulted in 40% of live growth being removed, do not continue. Give the tree one year to recover and begin the process again starting at Step 1. If we have not reached 40%, proceed to the next step.

Step 3: Create Vertical and Horizontal Spacing Between Branches

When two or more branches originate adjacent to each other within a vertical or horizontal plane (meaning up/down the trunk or around the circumference of the trunk), they will grow into each other and compete for the same space. Especially as the tree ages and the branches become larger, these have a higher-than-average likelihood of breaking.

In this third step we want to prune to avoid this future scenario. The goal is to prune such that we create both vertical and horizontal spacing between branches.

Before making any cuts, take a moment to evaluate the entirety of the tree and form a plan. Make note or physically mark branches that we think should be removed. When choosing between branches on the same vertical or horizontal plane, always choose to remove the largest of the options. It is counterintuitive, but removing the larger branch helps reduce the possibility that this branch grows to a diameter of greater than 50% of the trunk (i.e., the bad branch we eliminated in the last step).

Begin making cuts and remember not to remove more than 40% of live growth in total (factoring in all previous steps).

Congratulations! We have structurally pruned a tree and helped it become more structurally stable and better able to live a longer life.

For those wanting to learn more about this topic, Dr. Ed Gilman is the preeminent expert on structural pruning. I highly recommend all his books, online articles, and videos.

Step 4: Repeat Structural Pruning Annually

I recommend repeating this process for as long as we are able. At some point, it is likely that the tree will be too tall for us to continue and we will need to hire a trained professional (see the sidebar for help on choosing the right service provider).

Here is a general structural pruning cycle I recommend:

- Structural pruning every year for the first 15 years. If this is not feasible, move to every other year.

- Continue every two to three years during the next 15 years of the tree's life.

- If this is not feasible, every three to five years is acceptable, though not ideal. In this instance, perform at least four pruning cycles across 20 years.

- Beyond this, perform structural pruning on an as-needed basis (e.g., to reduce branches growing into pockets of sunlight above the roof).

For trees that are already mature and have never received structural pruning, it's not too late. Although we cannot make as much of an impact as when we start early, we can still improve a mature tree's strength and safety, thus providing it with many additional decades of life. In this instance, I recommend hiring a trained professional to perform structural pruning every two to four years for at least six pruning cycles.

Before we discuss soil, let's take a quick pruning-related diversion.

Guidance for Choosing a Structural Pruning Service Provider

As I mentioned earlier, all these concepts apply to older and larger trees. But for these, we must also be able to safely use a chainsaw, climb trees, and employ rigging systems to control the descent of cut branches. This is no small feat and requires years of professional training. We should hire a professional service provider to perform these tasks.

Unfortunately, most tree service providers are not trained on how to perform proper pruning, much less structural pruning. Luckily some are—the trick is finding them. Here are some quick tips for identifying a qualified professional to perform structural pruning on our mature trees:

- Test their knowledge. Any trained professional should know everything described in this chapter and more. If they cannot describe branch collars, how to make proper pruning cuts, and how to perform structural pruning, do not consider using them.

- Ask them how they ascend the tree. Some folks use devices attached to their feet that allow them to spike into the trunk to ascend the tree. These are called *climbing spikes*, *spikes*, or *gaffs*. These cause harm to the tree and should never be used when pruning. This is a sure sign of an untrained professional. We should only hire pruning professionals that ascend the tree on ropes without spikes.

- Ask them about the role of a health evaluation before performing structural pruning (the healthier the tree, the more it can withstand in terms of pruning) and how they go about assessing the health of a tree. Common answers should include evaluating the conditions of the surrounding soil, how well previous pruning cuts have healed, and the density and color of leaves or buds in the canopy.

- Last but not least, do the same with the folks who arrive to perform the pruning. They may not be as knowledgeable as those that sold the work, but they must know how to identify branch collars, make proper pruning cuts, and perform structural pruning, at a minimum. Also, make sure they do not use climbing spikes.

One other variable worth mentioning: structural pruning in older trees typically entails fewer large cuts and more reduction cuts on small branches that are less than 6 inches in diameter. Mature trees are less resilient and cannot withstand the sort of pruning that young trees can tolerate.

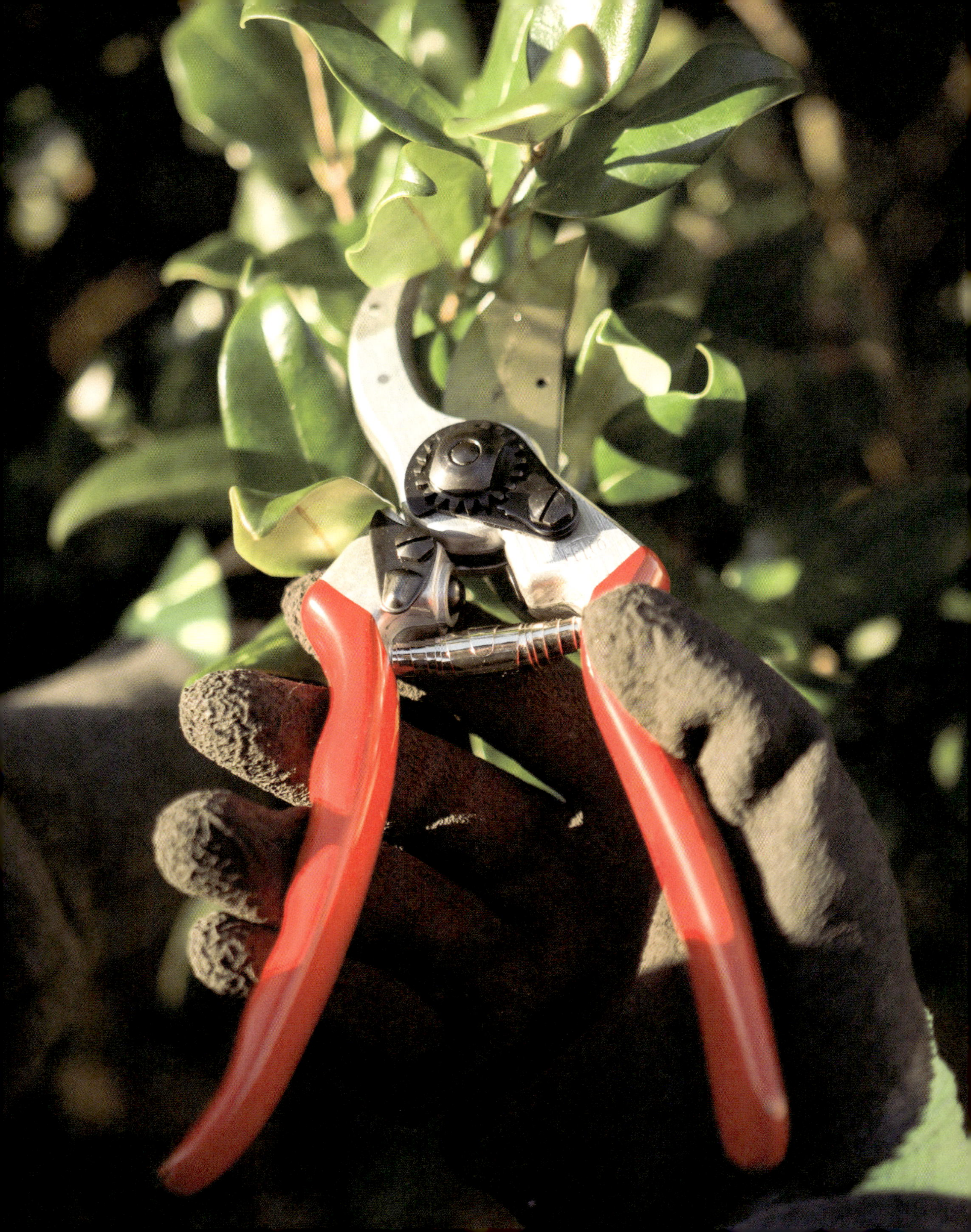

CHAPTER 13

a very short diversion on pruning shrubs

I hesitate to even include this chapter in this book. But shrub pruning occupies a great deal of energy and focus within the traditional sub/urban landscape. I decided this chapter provides enough positive outcomes (reduced time/effort, reduced CO_2 emissions, healthier plants) to be worth a quick discussion. My compromise to myself is that I will keep this chapter very short and sweet.

The best shrub pruning plan starts with selecting the right species for the given location. For example, if we want to use a shrub to fill a 6-foot space under a window, we should plant a native species with a maximum height of 6 feet. Do this and we will never have to prune at all!

But in most scenarios, the shrubs are already in place. If a species is too large for its location, we can either remove it and replace it with an appropriately sized native species or perform pruning, knowing we will always have to invest time and resources into battling the plant's DNA-driven growth objectives.

Assuming we choose to proceed with pruning, we should avoid doing so with hedge trimmers. They are generally the wrong tool because they make it hard to control what or how we are cutting. Indiscriminate cuts lead to an explosion in new growth, which we call the *Hydra Effect*. This is the opposite of our desired outcome. Now we must shear the shrubs again. This pattern repeats through the growing season, creating a maintenance trap. This is why shrubs sheared with hedge trimmers often have to be cut four to six times (or more) per growing season.

Gas-Powered Tools Harm Our Health

If the hedge trimmers are gas-powered, then there is another negative effect: we breathe in harmful pollution. Gas-powered tools emit exhaust containing toxic pollutants that can lead to respiratory illness, cancer, stroke, and cardiovascular disease, to name a handful. One gas-powered tool can emit more of these pollutants than a full-size pickup truck! This is nasty stuff we do not want to breathe. The exhaust also adds loads of CO_2 to the atmosphere.

Then we have the matter of plant health. Hedge trimmers cause extensive damage to plants by creating split and jagged ends on branches and leaves. The shrub uses valuable resources to attempt to heal these wounds, as well as to fuel each Hydra Effect. This depletion of resources leads to increased plant stress, a decline in health, and possibly death, especially in the event of a drought or pest outbreak.

Luckily, we have an alternative, which is pruning using bypass pruners and loppers (I will refer to this as *hand pruning*). Hand pruning allows us to be more careful about where we make cuts, which means branches can properly heal. In addition, we eliminate the Hydra Effect, which saves valuable resources for the shrub. Less damage and more available resources mean the shrub can divert energy towards growing, defending itself from pests, and generally being healthy.

Hand pruning also saves time. Hedge trimmers are often viewed as necessary because they are supposedly faster and more efficient than hand pruning, but this is not true. Hand pruning must only be performed once per year or every other year compared to multiple times per year when using hedge trimmers. If we measure time spent on this task across a full year, we spend less time hand pruning.

Hand pruning is so easy! Let's learn how to do it. First, the video tutorial:

To begin, we will need the same tools and protective equipment we outlined in the previous chapter about structural pruning. We should also follow the same safety guidelines. All the biology and concepts related to structural pruning apply to shrubs, but with some caveats:

- Shrubs are more forgiving than trees.

- It is often hard to find a branch collar. That is ok—make the cut in the general vicinity.

- It is often impossible to get the tip of the bypass pruners or loppers between the small branches of a shrub. This is ok. Make the cut as close to the ideal target as possible.

- We typically do not need a 3-Cut Method since the branches are tiny and we have no risk of tearing. Pruning is performed with bypass pruners, and occasionally with help from the loppers.

For shrub pruning, we will use two basic cuts that are similar to the ones we used for structural pruning, but with slight differences:

- **Removal cut:** remove the entire branch at its point of origin, which will either be at the main trunk or at another branch.

- **Reduction cut:** make the pruning cut back to *any* side branch.

Now that we know how to make the basic pruning cuts, it is time to apply them. Before we begin, we must set a goal. For trees our goal is to increase their strength. But shrubs do not need this. Our shrub pruning goals will generally be based on aesthetics.

The most common goal is to reduce height, reduce width, and tighten the form. To achieve this goal, we should stand 10 feet away from the shrub and stare at it while slightly blurring our eyes and softening our visual focus. What branches are sticking out most? We can pick the five most obvious choices and prune them back to within the interior of the shrub using one of our shrub pruning cuts. Typically, 30 cuts in total will achieve this goal for most shrubs. However, if we want to further tighten the form, we can perform 50 cuts or more. We can repeat this process as many times as we think necessary to achieve our desired form. Repeat this process in one to two years.

That's it. That's shrub pruning in a nutshell. When compared to using gas-powered hedge trimmers across a growing season, hand pruning is faster, easier, generates no harmful pollutants, creates no CO_2 emissions, and best of all, yields healthier plants. Have fun hand pruning and remember to take a moment to appreciate the plant's beauty!

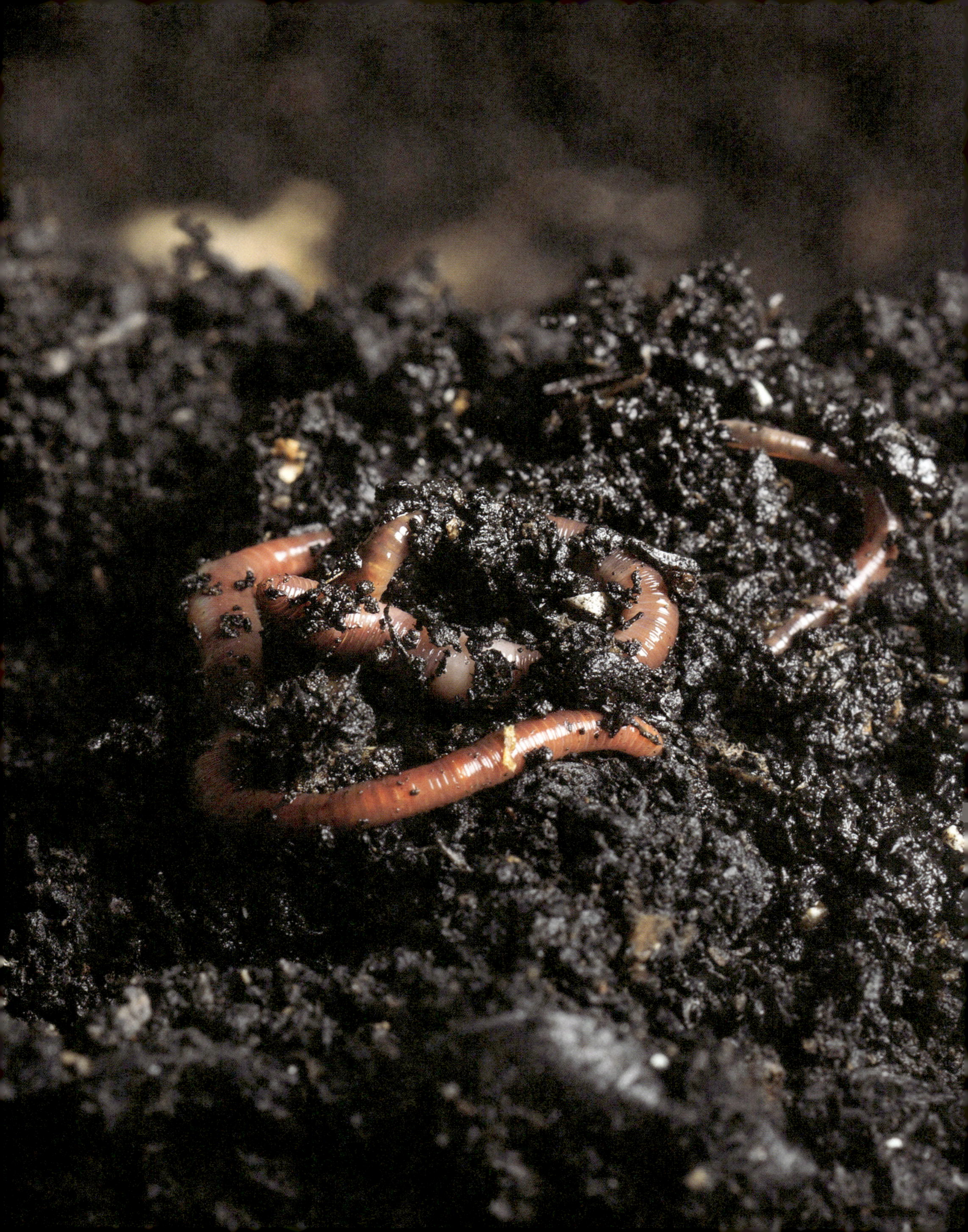

CHAPTER 14

promote soil bursting with life

Recall that to achieve maximum longevity for trees in the sub/urban landscape, **the two most important things we must do are maximize their strength and health.** Aside from avoiding harm, like construction in the CRZ, the best ways to do this are pruning to create ideal structure and improving the health of the soil in which they grow.

Unfortunately most of the sub/urban landscape consists of dirt, not soil. This is a result of hundreds of years of agricultural practices followed by recent land clearing to build neighborhoods, office parks, and shopping centers. Recall from Chapter 1 that dirt is sand, silt, and clay, while soil is dirt plus a living underground ecosystem. When trees are growing in dirt instead of soil, they are often sickly and die prematurely.

We can transform dirt back to soil with three basic approaches: First, plant many native trees, flowers, and grasses. Second, retain and add lots of organic matter. Third, avoid harmful products that kill life, such as pesticides and fertilizers. The second and third approaches are the focus of this chapter.

This video helps set the stage for what comes next:

Leave the Leaves

Imagine we are standing in the middle of an old forest. What do we feel under our feet? Leaves of course! The forest floor is covered in layers of decaying leaves that give way to dark, loamy soil. Rotting leaves form the very foundation of a healthy forest by providing organic matter for the living underground ecosystem. Recall that organic matter is the dead remains of anything that was once living. It is food for many species within the soil and helps enhance soil structure by acting as spacers between particles of dirt. The takeaway? **We should leave all leaves under our trees and shrubs to rot.**

Consider this: before leaves drop, around half of the nutrients within the leaves are sucked back into the trunk and roots for safekeeping during the dormant season. The rest of the nutrients remain in the leaf. In 10 pounds of leaves, we could expect to find roughly 5 pounds of carbon, 0.1 pounds of nitrogen, 0.01 pounds of phosphorus, 0.04 pounds of potassium, 0.17 pounds of calcium, 0.02 pounds of magnesium, 0.01 pounds of sulfur, and iron, zinc, and much more. That is a lot of nutrients! Leaves are literal fertilizers.

There is another layer worth considering. Leaf litter is a diverse ecosystem all its own, which further boosts the diversity on our property. Thousands of different species of insects rely on leaves for food, reproduction, cover to hide from predators, and warmth during the dormant season. These in turn provide food for birds, raccoons, and other larger species. Consider three examples:

- Luna moths, swallowtail butterflies, and many other species rely on leaf litter to camouflage and protect their cocoons.
- Bumblebee queens need leaf litter to protect their shallow burrows within the soil.
- Many species of beetles use fallen leaves to hide from hungry birds.

Some folks have concerns about leaving the leaves. Here are ones I hear most often (plus solutions):

"I want to keep the leaves, but not on my lawn."

Totally fine! Leaving the leaves does not mean we have to literally leave them where they land. Rather, it means we leave them on site and do not dispose of them nor burn them. In this scenario, we can move them into a natural area or beds under our trees and shrubs. If this is not possible, we can stage them in piles out of sight.

"I want the leaves, but they blow around and make a mess."

First, is it possible to rethink our definition of a mess? Perhaps it might be worth shifting to a new standard of beauty, one that helps other life? If not, then we could consider shredding the leaves with a lawnmower or leaf shredder. Shredded leaves generally blow around less. But it's very important to note that this shredding action will kill many of the insects in the leaf litter.

"I want to keep the leaves but I like the aesthetics of my designer mulch."

If aesthetics are a priority we can place the leaves under these top layers of mulch, or stage all the leaves somewhere else on our property or in the community. Then let them rot to create leaf mold and leaf compost (more on this soon).

"My HOA will not allow me to keep the leaves."

In this instance, we must educate the HOA and spread the word to others in the community. We can entice them with the idea of saving money and reducing effort while helping heal Earth.

"Snakes will hide in the leaves and bite me!"

Snakes are very rare within the sub/urban landscape. Most cause no harm. This deserves a deeper discussion—please see the sidebar for more information on this topic.

When we get rid of our leaves each year by burning them, bagging them, or blowing them offsite, we generate the following additional negative outcomes:

- Burning them releases CO_2 into the atmosphere.

- Bagging leaves and sending them to the landfill generates methane, which causes even more change in the atmosphere than CO_2 does.

- Gas-powered blowers generate toxic pollution, CO_2 emissions, and irritating noise for people nearby.

- If our municipality or a service provider removes the leaves for us, there are added CO_2 emissions and pollution from equipment being driven to and from our site.

Leaving the leaves saves us time, reduces harm, and is a powerful way to increase the outrageous diversity of the living underground ecosystem. Before we discuss arborist wood chips, here is a fun video summarizing much of what we have learned about leaving the leaves:

Create Beds of Arborist Wood Chips Around Trees & Shrubs

Arborist wood chips are one of my favorite products for increasing the health of soil. Let's imagine once more that we are standing in an old forest. What else is on the ground besides leaves? All sorts of twigs, branches, and fallen trees that provide even more organic matter for the living underground ecosystem. Arborist wood chips fill this role in the sub/urban landscape.

Arborist wood chips are generated when a tree service removes a tree or prunes limbs and shreds the material in a machine called a *wood chipper*. This results in nutrient-rich arborist wood chips. Most tree services give these away for free because the alternative is to pay to dump them at a landfill or wood waste processing center. The best wood chips are those that have more chipped branches than trunk wood, since roughly 75% of nutrients, aminos, and enzymes in a tree are contained within the leaves, needles, twigs, and small branches. But no need to be picky—all arborist wood chips are great!

Creating beds is easy. We can spread arborist wood chips around our trees to a depth of 3–6 inches. Ideally we extend the beds to the edge of the canopy. But the distance does not matter; something is better than nothing. We must avoid placing wood chips on the root collar

The Truth About Snakes

Snakes get a bad rap as being harmful and dangerous. The reality is that snakes are neither. They fear us and rarely bite, except when threatened or surprised. They help create healthy ecosystems. Some of a snake's favorite foods are mice and rats, animals that can harbor awful diseases like Lyme Disease, leptospirosis, Rocky Mountain Spotted Fever, lymphocytic choriomeningitis (LCMV), and *Salmonella*, among others. Mice and rats also cause property damage by chewing through electrical wiring.

Let's use the copperhead, the most common venomous snake in the Piedmont of North Carolina, to take a deeper dive into this topic. Copperheads are quite timid and would prefer to stay far away from people. This is true for most snakes. These shy reptiles tend to freeze when frightened. They prefer to leave the scene if possible, but will strike if they feel threatened. Copperheads can release toxic venom when they bite. However, roughly 40% of their bites are *dry* bites, meaning no venom is injected.

In the United States there have only been 101 fatal bites from 1989 to 2018 (this excludes accidents related to caring for exotic pet snakes). Let's put this in perspective:

- The CDC reports that in the United States over 300,000 people are sent to the emergency room by dog bites yearly; only about 7,000 are bitten by venomous snakes.
- In 2021, 42,939 people died in car accidents.
- Last but not least: in 2012 one person in the United States died from a snake bite. During that same year, 33,000 people died from the common cold and 791 were killed by toasters.

If we are going to manage risk in our lives, snakes are of no concern. The chances of being harmed by a snake are infinitesimally low. The truth is that our fear of snakes is driven by ancient evolutionary traits that mattered in our past but have virtually no modern day relevance. They are obsolete and irrational based on the data.

Still worried about snakes? There are ways we can further decrease the near-zero likelihood of being bitten.

- Wear gloves and shoes while working outside.
- If we see a snake, leave it alone. Most snake bites occur when people try to handle them.
- If we absolutely must relocate it, consider hiring a professional to do the job.

The truth is, we need snakes. Their populations are in decline throughout the world due to human-inflicted habitat destruction. So instead of removing leaves and underbrush to reduce snake populations, let's do the opposite. Let's learn to co-exist with our shy, slender neighbors and celebrate when we see them.

because doing so will harm the health of the trees and possibly kill it. When we pile arborist wood chips (or mulch or dirt of any kind) on the base of a tree, we form what is known as a *mulch volcano*. This is one of the worst landscape practices to emerge in recent decades, at least as far as trees are concerned. If you have any trees with mulch volcanoes, remove the mulch and uncover the root collar right away (or hire a professional to do so). Mulch volcanoes kill trees. Here is a detailed video to learn more:

When installing these beds, avoid using landscape cloth and landscape fabric for weed suppression. These products are usually made of plastic and limit both water and gas exchange within the soil. They typically cause tremendous harm to trees and to life in the soil ecosystem.

A better option for weed suppression is cardboard because it rots over time. We can lay down 1–2 layers of cardboard and place the arborist wood chips on top. If weeds become an issue again in the future, we can add new layers of cardboard and new layers of arborist wood chips. Another option for controlling weeds is to use other plants to outcompete them. We can preemptively fill any vacant growing spaces with plants that we find to be more desirable.

A Note About "Weeds" & "Pests"

"Weeds" are simply plants growing in a place that we do not want them to grow. They often appear because they are taking advantage of a vacant growing space. The term "weeds" is disparaging but there is nothing inherently wrong with them. They are plants like any other.

While we are on this topic, the term "pest" is also disparaging. We label some insects as "pests" and view them in a negative light because they interfere with one of our artificial landscape systems, such as growing lawns. There is nothing inherently wrong with them. Much like humans and the rest of life, they want food, shelter, and the ability to live a long and happy existence. They participate in larger ecosystems and serve necessary roles.

I'm using the terms "weeds" and "pests" for the sake of conventional communication.

Beds of arborist wood chips around our trees and shrubs have some other benefits as well:

- They make it easy to leave the leaves under our trees.

- They keep trees safe from string trimmers and lawnmowers by creating a gap between the trunk and the lawn. Repeated trunk damage harms and kills trees and shrubs.

- They help retain more moisture within the soil by keeping it from evaporating.

- They help regulate soil temperature. This is especially important in the growing season when wood chips can physically protect the soil from being damaged by the sun's rays.

One last tidbit on this topic of arborist wood chips, because it is a concern I hear frequently: arborist wood chips do **not** suck nitrogen from the soil or spread disease. Quite the opposite. They make more nitrogen available and reduce the spread of disease by bolstering plant health.

119

What About Using Other Mulches for Making Beds?

Double and triple shredded mulches tend to become waterproof after a few months. We can test this by lifting some mulch. Does it lift the way we would expect (crumbly and loose) or does it lift in layers and sections? If the latter, it is preventing water from reaching the soil and causing harm. In this instance, we must turn the mulch using a pitchfork or potato hoe. Typically, when using double- and triple-shredded mulches, we do this every three to six months. In contrast, arborist wood chips rarely if ever become waterproof. Instead, they develop porous fungal mats that keep the chips in place but still allow water to pass through.

With double- and triple-shredded mulches, there is also the fact that they are shredded in giant, gas-guzzling machines either twice (double-shredded mulch) or three times (triple-shredded mulch), resulting in a larger carbon footprint as compared to arborist wood chips.

Then there are dyed mulches. These have the issue of being soaked in chemicals, which is not healthy for the soil or plants. Even the "safe" and "organic" dyes aren't truly safe. In addition, production results in a larger carbon footprint as compared to arborist wood chips.

What about inorganic mulches, such as rocks and rubber? These options may seem promising, but they provide no value to life in the soil. Because our goal is to improve the health of the soil, these options are not viable.

Another popular alternative is pine straw. Some claim it changes the pH of the soil or that it does not provide organic matter. Neither of these is true. But unfortunately, pine straw does not provide the same quantity of organic matter as arborist wood chips. A good compromise between arborist wood chips and pine straw is to place the former on the bottom layer and the latter on top for the sake of aesthetics.

Skip Fertilizers Because They Kill Soil

For the sake of clarifying language, I'm going to call anything we purchase from a hardware store, gardening store, farm supply store, or lawn/tree service provider a fertilizer. The only exceptions to this are compost, compost tea, and a small handful of other products that specifically focus on feeding life within the soil without the use of any nitrogen, phosphorus, and potassium (these three are known as *NPK*).

Fertilizers in the sub/urban landscape are a destructive (and expensive) scam, plain and simple. Plants have been thriving for hundreds of millions of years, thanks to the living underground ecosystem we call soil. Soil is full of the nutrients that plants need. We don't have to introduce nitrogen, phosphorus, potassium, boron, or magnesium—these and other nutrients are often naturally available from sand, silt, and clay. All we need to do is to ensure that the soil in which our plants are growing has an outrageous diversity of life. They will provide our trees and shrubs with all the nutrients they need.

Fertilizers ignore these basic concepts and create harm in multiple ways. Here are some examples:

- Phosphorus and nitrogen are two of the most common ingredients in fertilizers. Adding them to the soil damages the essential relationship between a plant and its mycorrhizal fungi (see the sidebar for more information about these incredible fungi). Without that relationship, the plant is vulnerable to a decline in health and death during droughts and other hard times.

- Most nitrogen never makes it into plants and instead leaches into waterways and evaporates into the atmosphere. As we learned in Chapter 5, this destroys aquatic ecosystems, creates dead zones that kill aquatic life, damages the ozone layer, and generates smog.

- We use a tremendous amount of energy to produce fertilizers. Making nitrogen fertilizer requires approximately 2% of global energy and produces 5% of global annual greenhouse gas emissions.

- Creating phosphorus fertilizer generates radioactive waste called *phosphogypsum*. For every ton of phosphorus fertilizer we produce, we create 5.2 tons of radioactive waste.

I'm only scratching the surface on the many serious issues created by fertilizers. The good news is that we do not need them in the sub/urban landscape. We have amazing alternatives that are easy to make and cause none of these issues. These alternatives are compost and compost tea.

Fantastic Fungi

Mycorrhizal fungi are especially important. These fungi form a mutually symbiotic relationship with 85–90% of all terrestrial plants. In exchange for sugar, fungi provide plants with water by using their tiny hyphae to access places that are too small for plant roots. Through this relationship, mycorrhizal fungi can extend a plant's root system by 1,000-fold. This is a huge boost for plant health, especially during times of drought.

Mycorrhizal fungi also provide plants with essential nutrients by mining dirt (recall that dirt is sand, silt, and clay). They do this by secreting organic acids onto the dirt and then redigesting the resulting slurry. This enables them to access nitrogen, phosphorus, and a variety of other nutrients for the plants.

If this reminds you of lichen, you are correct. The modern plant-mycorrhizal partnership is a more advanced symbiotic relationship that evolved because of its lichen predecessor. Indeed, the fossil record suggests that mycorrhizal fungi predate plant roots and that plants may have actually developed roots for the sole purpose of interfacing with these fungi.

Mycorrhizal fungi provide plants with other benefits as well. They boost plants' immune systems, filter toxic compounds, and protect them from parasites. There is even emerging research to suggest that they provide an underground network through which plants can communicate to exchange nutrients, provide food for young saplings, and warn each other about pest attacks. This is all relatively new research. We are still learning a lot about the soil ecosystem.

Use Compost & Compost Tea

We know from Section 1 that when things rot they provide food (organic matter) for life in soil. Feeding life within the soil produces a healthier ecosystem that benefits all its members, including the plants growing there. We can tap into this natural cycle by using existing waste streams to produce incredible products that have many of the benefits that fertilizers promise (but do not deliver) with none of their negative outcomes. These products are compost and compost tea. *Compost* is basic: it's organic matter, i.e., the decayed remains of things that were once living, like leaves, grass, and food scraps. *Compost tea* is compost in water, which generates a liquid solution that is easier to apply.

We can buy compost or make it. If we choose to buy it, look for products with natural, recognizable ingredients. For example, earlier in my career I used a product called Black Kow made purely of cow manure. Other common compost ingredients include other types of manure, blood meal, mushrooms, worm castings, food scraps, grass clippings, seaweed, fish, leaves, and other things that rot. Bonus points if the compost is produced locally from an existing waste stream. Avoid anything with added nitrogen, lime, and other industrially-produced fertilizers. In addition, avoid nonrenewable resources and especially those for which extraction harms Earth. Peat moss is a great example. It comes from bogs, moors, and other wetland ecosystems that must be drained, smashed, and heavily degraded to harvest peat moss. These are fragile ecosystems that hold a tremendous amount of stable carbon—an estimated 30% of Earth's soil carbon! We should avoid using peat moss.

This said, I much prefer making my own compost because it is so simple. Here are easy ways to do so:

How to Make Leaf Mold & Leaf Compost

Rake leaves into a pile or ask a landscaping company to dump a load of leaves. Let them sit for six to 12 months. Congratulations! We now have leaf mold, which is partially rotted leaves.

Let the leaves sit for another one to two years. Congratulations! We now have leaf compost, which are fully rotted leaves. Leaf compost looks like black soil.

Yeah, it's that easy. Leaf mold and leaf compost are pure gold when it comes to increasing the diversity of the soil ecosystem. And why not? This is basically what happens on the forest floor.

At Leaf & Limb, we have examined these products under a microscope to verify that they are, in fact, teaming with beneficial life. The results are incredible and confirm that these are indeed remarkable products.

How to Make Compost from Food, Grass Clippings, and Leaves

I will begin with a video showing what this compost setup looks like:

Before we get started, here are the tools and supplies we will need:

- ❏ Two or four pallets. We can usually get these for free from a furniture store, big box hardware store, or any other place that generates a lot of pallets.

- ❏ Brackets with screws for attaching the pallets to one another. I recommend corner brackets or straight brackets, but the options for what we can choose are endless, so long as they can hold pallets together.

- ❏ Screwdriver or power drill with bits for screwing the brackets to the pallets.

Here is what we do next:

1. Determine where we want to set up our compost bin. I generally position these in a corner of the property. Especially when using two pallets, a corner is ideal.

2. Place the pallets on one of their outer edges and use them to form a box. The box will be as tall as the pallets are wide because each pallet is on its side.

3. Alternatively, use two pallets and form a corner (half of the box). I prefer this approach because it leaves the back of this configuration open, which allows me to stage other green waste like tree branches and chunks of wood behind it.

4. Use angle brackets, straight brackets, or some alternative fastening method to attach each pallet to each other.

5. That is it—the compost bin is complete.

Next, place all green waste from our property and kitchen into this enclosure. This includes grass clippings, leaves, weeds, and all food scraps—if it rots, put it in the compost bin. Some say to be discerning about what type of food we put in our compost, e.g., to avoid adding meat, citrus, or a variety of other specific items. Ignore this advice. If it rots, it makes compost.

We do not need to turn our compost or tend to it in any way. Let it sit and rot. Over time, we will begin to see what appears to be black soil accumulate at the bottom of the bin and pour out of the open slats on the sides. This is compost. Grab a handful and smell it. It should smell earthy and fresh, like the smell of rotting leaves on the forest floor. It should not smell rotten, dead, or gross in any way.

I hesitate to even mention this, since it is not the norm, but compost can attract rats. Hopefully we have snakes nearby to eat those rats. But in some sub/urban settings, this may not be the case. I had a rat infestation once and I used a trap called the Uhlik Repeater. It was effective at catching the rats quickly. I will include a link for this in the Appendix. Alternatively, hire a vendor who can solve this issue without poisoning the site.

When it comes to making compost, there are many options to choose from, in terms of both processes and products. There are countless resources and books available on this topic. I will list some in the Appendix. Here is another challenging option that I especially like.

Vermicomposting: A Challenging, Yet Amazing Compost

For those who are compost nerds like me, or want to become one, let me introduce another incredible composting method called vermicomposting. Essentially this process involves becoming a worm farmer and harvesting worm poop, which we call *worm castings*. This sounds positively delightful, right?

In fact, worm castings are light, airy, smell amazing, and are chock-full of life. Earthworms are prolific decomposers that can quickly turn a variety of organic materials into high-quality compost. By grinding and aerating organic matter, the worms create ideal conditions for soil microbes to thrive and multiply. In turn, the microbes secrete enzymes that unlock nutrients for plants to use. When it comes to creating high-quality compost in record time, the research proves that vermicomposting is hard to beat.

In short, the worms need a home that is relatively dark and full of oxygen, certain types and quantities of food, and adequate clean water (we will learn more about what constitutes clean water shortly). They must also be kept safe from harsh weather, such as freezing conditions and hot summer temperatures. There are many ways we can achieve these objectives. If we carefully maintain the appropriate conditions and keep the worms healthy, we will be rewarded with incredible worm castings, which we can harvest from their home. Here are resources for making vermicompost:

How to Use Our Compost

Once we have compost, whether we make it or buy it, we can scatter a very light layer around trees and other plants of our choosing. Either leave it where it falls or use a rake to further distribute the compost. We can use a little or a lot—a little always goes a long way and it's hard to use too much.

In addition, we can steep our compost in water to create a liquid solution that we call compost tea. We can pour or spray this compost tea on the ground around trees and shrubs and in our flower beds. We can even spray it directly on plants to bolster their health.

Before I dive into the written instructions for how to make compost tea, here is a how-to video:

To make compost tea we need the following tools and supplies:

- ❏ 2–4 cups of compost.
- ❏ A 5-gallon bucket or something similar for mixing.
- ❏ A mesh tea bag large enough to hold the compost. We can make these or buy them online.

When making compost tea, there are two vital concepts we must keep in mind:

First, the fungi, bacteria, and other life within the compost have a limited time in which they can survive in liquid. Do not leave them in liquid solution for longer than a day. After that, they could die and the compost tea may become harmful to soil and plants. It is worth noting that this compost tea is generally safe for more than eight hours, but without the ability to verify this using a microscope it's best to observe this time constraint.

Second, we must be careful about what water we use. If we use tap water that has been cleaned by our local municipality, it generally contains chlorine, which can kill the life in the compost tea. Here are alternatives and methods for cleaning chlorine from the tap water:

- Untreated water collected from the rain (e.g., water captured in rain barrels or via a cistern system).

- Untreated well water.

- Municipal water treated with ascorbic acid, which is Vitamin C. This is also used to treat fish aquariums. It is often labeled as "dechlorination tablets."

- On this same note, there are other products used to treat water in aquariums that are generally labeled as "water conditioners." So long as they keep fish safe, they will keep the life in compost safe.

- Finally, if none of these are options, leave the water sitting in the 5-gallon container with an open top for a minimum of 24 hours and most of the chlorine will evaporate.

Some municipal water systems use a product called chloramine to treat water, which is a combination of chlorine and ammonia. Unfortunately, the methods for removing chloramine are more limited. The easiest option is to buy three-in-one chlorine, chloramines, and ammonia treatment tap water conditioner.

Now it's time to make five gallons of compost tea. We can easily scale these ratios up and down to meet our needs.

1. Fill a 5-gallon bucket with clean water.

2. Scoop 2–4 cups of our favorite compost and place it inside of the mesh tea bag.

3. Seal the bag and drop it into the water. Let it soak for 5–10 minutes.

Biochar—Another Powerful Tool for Building Soil

Biochar is an ancient product that has been rediscovered in recent decades. It is created by burning organic matter with little or no oxygen. When it is added to soil, biochar sequesters carbon for thousands of years. It also attracts nutrients, provides a great boost to life in the soil, and helps retain more water. We can buy it or make our own. Then we can add it directly to the surface of the soil as-is, soak it in compost tea before applying it to the soil, or add it in conjunction with leaf mold, leaf compost, or some other compost of our choosing. Then we should add arborist wood chips on top.

4. Then massage the bag within the water for 5–10 minutes. More massaging time will help release more microbial life into the solution.

5. Remove the compost bag from the bucket.

Presto! We have living compost tea! We can pour it where we please or place it within a pump sprayer for easy application on soil, plants, beds, seeds, and most anywhere in the sub/urban landscape. Do note that if we have no intention of spraying the compost tea, we can dump the compost in the bucket of water without a mesh bag, let it soak for 20–30 minutes, then pour the mixed solution where we please.

Leaves, arborist wood chips, and compost form the easy trifecta for generating soil bursting with outrageous diversity. Trees and other plants flourish in healthy soil. More soil also boosts the land's ability to retain water, carbon, and support life.

To reiterate an earlier point, the two best ways to maximize tree longevity, aside from doing no harm, are through structural pruning (makes trees stronger) and promoting soil bursting with life (makes trees healthier).

Tests That Matter & Those That Do Not!

Notice that not once have I mentioned soil tests in this chapter. For reasons that are hopefully obvious by now, most soil tests are a waste of time. We do not need advice about how much nitrogen or phosphorus to add to the soil—we should add none. These tests were created to support the agriculture and sub/urban landscape practices that are harming Earth.

If we want to get a soil test—and this is still unnecessary—the best option is a microbiology test. This provides us with information about the abundance and diversity of life within that sample. That is a more useful set of information, especially in the context of compost. I will list my favorite microbiology testing companies in the Appendix.

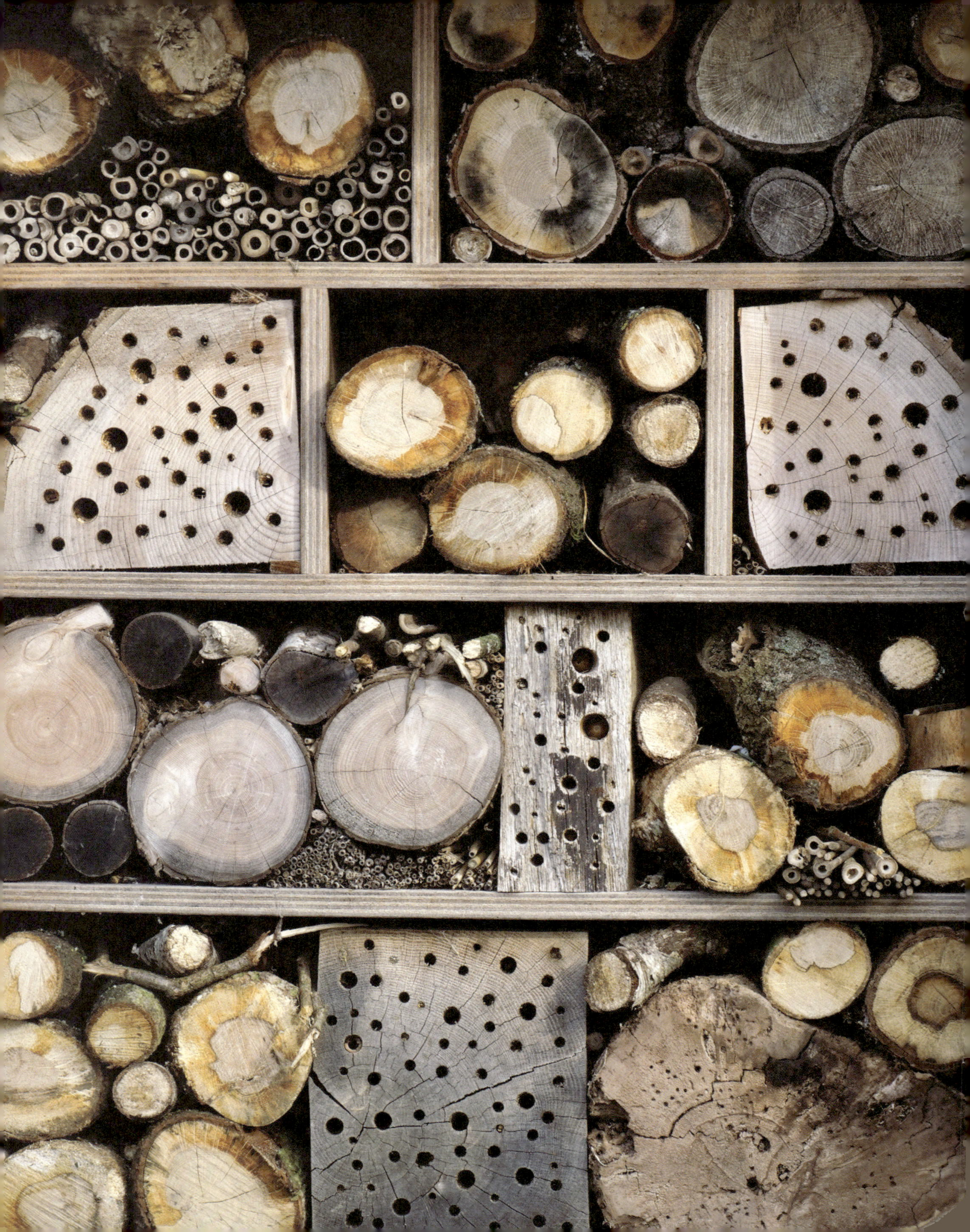

CHAPTER 15

more easy ways to promote outrageous diversity!

There are all sorts of fun and easy things we can do on our property to promote even more abundance and diversity of life! What's good for bats and beetles is also good for trees, soil, water availability, and carbon sequestration. Aside from improving the health of Earth, promoting more life means more twittering birds during the day and more glowing fireflies at night. Yes, please!

A quick note about the ideas that follow. I'm only featuring a handful of my favorites that also happen to be easy (with one exception at the end of this chapter that is difficult, but important). There are many other impactful things we can do that are not included here, such as reducing pollution in waterways, building rain gardens, and creating wildlife corridors.

Retain All Organic Matter

We can do more than retain grass clippings, leaves, and kitchen waste. We can retain **all** organic matter from our property. If it's organic, it rots and supports more diversity in the process. This includes all branches and logs.

We can use branches, stalks, and stems to form a brush pile behind or near the pallets that hold our compost. A brush pile provides food and shelter for birds, all sorts of insects, chipmunks, salamanders, turtles, and other life. It also supports possums, hawks, and raccoons that feed on the creatures that live in the brush pile. Worried what neighbors or clients think? Put up an educational sign. Or hide the pile out of sight.

Logs and chunks of wood create another thriving ecosystem for frogs, lizards, and fungi. In particular, logs are excellent for supporting beetles. Beetles help facilitate the breakdown of organic matter by eating pollen, leaves, fruit, dung, and rotting wood. They also prey on pests, pollinate plants by patrolling across flowers, and help control weeds by eating their seeds. We can stack logs and chunks of wood behind or near the compost pile. We can also use sections of logs to create beautiful borders around or between spaces. We can either lay them on their long sides or stack them vertically on their short ends depending on how much wood we have available. This accomplishes an aesthetic objective while also providing extra habitat for more ecology. Win-win!

This can be done on any property, whether at a home or commercial site. Our goal should be to prevent any organic matter from leaving the property. This boosts the abundance and diversity of life, sequesters more carbon, and reduces the CO_2 emissions associated with having those materials moved to the landfill or yard waste center.

Create Understory Layers

An understory layer is one or multiple layers of plants underneath larger plants. For example, planting flowers and a dogwood under an existing white oak creates two new understory layers. I often see trees in the landscape with nothing growing underneath. This is the perfect place to plant smaller trees, shrubs, and flowers. These new plant layers benefit insects (and all the life that rely on insects for food) because many insects need an understory layer to complete their life cycles. For example, many caterpillars feed on the canopy of a large tree and then drop to attach themselves to smaller plants below where they transform into butterflies and moths. If these layers do not exist, these caterpillars will die.

more easy ways to promote outrageous diversity!

Leave the Dead Stems

Traditional landscape paradigms recommend cutting dead flower stalks, removing seed heads, and generally cleaning dead material from the landscape every year. But these dead plants are so important for housing insects and their young through the dormant season. All the life we see during the growing season still exists within the landscape during the dormant season, but it is quietly hidden away in its dead cracks and crevices—the very material that traditional landscaping practices would have us cut and remove.

We can either leave them in place permanently (they will eventually rot), or remove them when the growing season begins, which gives the insect a chance to emerge. If these options are not possible, then stage the plant material in a pile somewhere on the property since some of the insects and their young will survive.

Here is additional information for those who want to learn more:

Help for the Jewels of the Night

Do you remember growing up and seeing the magic of fireflies (often called *lightning bugs*) in Summer? I sure do. I would sit outside to watch them slowly emerge from the landscape as the sunlight receded. The darker it became, the higher they flew. I loved gently catching these flying jewels on the back of my hand.

Sadly, much like most other life on this planet, populations of fireflies are in decline. A recent study found that of the 62 firefly species in North America for which sufficient data could be found, 18 species—or about 29%—are threatened with extinction. The primary issues are habitat degradation, chemicals, and light pollution. The good news is that the practices outlined in this chapter—and the book as a whole—are the very actions necessary to help promote a thriving population of fireflies. Here is a great resource for those interested in learning more:

Install Houses and Hotels

We can buy or build all sorts of specialized houses to help bats, birds, owls, and various pollinators. I especially love hotels for native bees. They come in all shapes and varieties. They usually include wood, bricks, tubes, straw, pinecones, and other nooks and crannies for native bees and other pollinators to call home. They are not suitable replacements for natural, high-quality habitat, but they certainly help.

Xerces Society offers several free plans and specifications online. We can find countless other resources on YouTube and the internet in general. Here is a link to a great resource on this topic:

Turn Off Exterior Lights at Night

Light pollution is devastating insects, birds, bats, amphibians, and all sorts of other life. It can affect reproduction, nourishment, sleeping, predation, and more. Here are some examples from the world of insects:

- Many moths and other nighttime insects are drawn to lights, thinking they are the moon. They swirl around the light all night, flying to exhaustion. Up to one-third of these insects will be dead by morning, either from exhaustion or being picked off by predators.

- Lights interfere with insects that rely on bioluminescence to attract mates, such as fireflies.

- Insects often confuse light reflections on streets and sidewalks with bodies of water, causing them to lay eggs on hardscapes instead of in streams.

- Insects are attracted to headlights—for example, 100 billion insects die on German highways each year due to headlights.

There are many other types of life that are affected, including birds, bats, frogs, and turtles. Lights alter the path of migrating birds, confuse sea turtles laying eggs, and deprive daytime-loving species of sleep. As we increasingly light up the night sky—and nearly 20% of the planet's land surface is now affected by light pollution—we throw more natural ecosystems into chaos.

There are easy ways we can help. We can get rid of any outdoor lighting that is not necessary for safety or accessibility. For any remaining lights, we can make sure they are on timers, or better yet, motion activated. We can trade traditional bulbs for red bulbs, which are less damaging.

more easy ways to promote outrageous diversity!

Bats Are Amazing—and They Need Our Help!

Bats often get a bad rap—undeservedly so. Bats are entangled in mystery, mythology, cultural norms, and fear. They are commonly associated with vampires, evil, and things that go "bump" in the night.

The truth is that bats are fuzzy, cute little flying mammals who play an essential role in creating a healthy ecology. They eat insects and pollinate plants. According to the US Fish & Wildlife Service, bats eat enough pests to save more than $1 billion per year in crop damage and pesticide costs in the United States corn industry alone. Across all agricultural production, bats save us more than $3 billion per year.

Unfortunately, populations of bats are declining. Part of this is due to the usual causes, like habitat destruction. In addition, many folks actively kill bats or usher them out of their roosts, often due to unfounded fears. Many do this because they fear getting rabies. But getting rabies from bats is very rare. There are typically only one to three reported cases of rabies from bats each year. A person living in the United States is more likely to catch leprosy or the plague than to contract rabies from a bat.

If bats are living inside of a building, we can install a bat home outside or on the exterior of the building to help them relocate. We should avoid this process during the mating season because young bats are flightless and will starve to death if they are separated from their mothers. We should also avoid trapping bats within buildings since they will starve to death.

Here is my last plug for bats for those still not convinced: they happily gobble up mosquitoes! Think about bats as free mosquito control. Estimates vary widely about how much they eat. I have seen estimates ranging from hundreds to thousands per night, with variations based on the species and the study. Regardless of the number, any mosquito control is helpful.

We can petition our city to transition to motion-activated streetlights and to require all businesses and buildings to turn off lights at night.

If we could accomplish this goal, we could also gaze up at space each night and stare in awe at a galaxy full of stars. To those of you who already have access to these views, I'm jealous. I am not able to see more than a handful of stars here in Raleigh due to light pollution.

Stop Using Harmful Chemicals

In some cases, the best actions are inactions. This is certainly the case with most every chemical that is traditionally used as part of lawn and tree care maintenance plans. Here are some of the common ones we usually see in these programs: herbicides, pesticides, fungicides, and miticides. (NOTE: "-cide" literally means "denoting an act of killing"—think homicide and suicide). They pollute water, kill soil, and devastate populations of birds and insects.

Insect populations are declining at the skyrocket rate of 2% per year, due in large part to pesticide use. As insects decline, so too do the species that rely on them—like birds. Here in North America, most birds rely on live insects to feed their young. Research shows that over the past 50 years the population of birds in the United States and Canada has decreased by roughly 2.9 billion, which is a 29% decrease. Scientists theorize this is tied to having fewer insects in the world. It is also tied to cats, which we will discuss next.

These "-cides" also harm us humans. Mosquito sprays are nerve agents (more on this later in this chapter). Exposure to neonicotinoids, which are common in many pesticides, has been linked to heart and brain disorders. Acephate—another common chemical in the landscape—damages the nervous system. Fungicides can be carcinogenic. The list goes on and on.

To be fair, there may be specific times and places that we need help from some of these chemicals. For example, herbicides can help with ecological restoration and sometimes toxic chemicals should be used to address a specific pest for which there is no other solution (this is common with invasive pests such as the emerald ash borer). But none of these should be used as part of ongoing landscape maintenance.

If we need help reducing weeds or pests, there are alternatives available that cause less harm, no harm, and in some cases are even beneficial to life.

- **Cold-pressed pure neem oil:** Neem oil is extracted from seeds from the neem tree. It has been used for hundreds of years to help control various pests. It can help boost plant health by stimulating an immune response that helps ward off fungal pathogens and by feeding bacteria and fungi within the plant's roots and canopy.

- **Horticultural oil:** Horticultural oils are either petroleum- or vegetable-based oils. They help control insects and mites by smothering them. Horticultural oils are not as beneficial as neem. But they evaporate rapidly and leave no toxic residue, which makes them a great alternative to many other pesticides.

- *Bacillus thuringiensis*: This is a species of bacteria that lives in the soil and only harms certain insects, particularly those that feed on leaves. This can help with situations where a leaf-eating insect is defoliating a tree to the point where it is threatening the survival of the tree.

- **Compost tea:** In the last chapter we learned how compost can boost a thriving soil ecosystem. It can also be used as a foliar spray that helps build a healthy community of fungi and bacteria in the canopy, which boosts the plant's health and ability to defend itself from pest attacks.

- **Beneficial insects:** We can buy beneficial insects and release them onto our property to eat pests. Two especially beneficial insects that eat a wide range of pests are ladybugs and green lacewings. We can also procure parasitic wasps to help control various scale insects in large canopy trees. There are more examples. But before we buy a beneficial insect, we must make sure it is native or near native to where we plan on releasing it. We do not want to release an invasive insect.

- **Herbicide alternatives:** There are a number of herbicides made from edible oils and food grade ingredients. They kill weeds by preventing photosynthesis and cause no harm to the soil ecosystem. The downside is that they are generally expensive and less effective than traditional herbicides.

- **Meadows, pocket forests, and thickets:** These are the ultimate in terms of pest control. They attract a wide variety of insects, butterflies, bees, pollinators, and birds. These insects and birds feed on the pests that attack our trees and shrubs. Ditto for gardens, orchards, and crops in general. Not only that, but we can use these ecosystems to outcompete weeds, thus replacing the need for an herbicide. We will go into great detail on these topics in Section 4 of this book.

There are other examples of products that cause less harm, no harm, or are beneficial to life. I recommend books and articles from Xerces Society. Here is a helpful list of organic pesticides:

I also recommend products that have been certified by the Organic Materials Review

more easy ways to promote outrageous diversity!

Institute (OMRI). These are generally safer than most. Here is a link to a list of OMRI-certified products:

Keep All Cats Inside

As we learned earlier, bird populations in North America have declined by 29% in the past 50 years. Outdoor cats have played a role in this decline. There are tens of millions of free-range cats in the United States that kill millions of birds each year.

We can help by keeping our kitties inside. Always. When we see cats outside, check to see if they have a tag. If not, call animal control. If yes, call the owner and ask them to please pick up the cat. If they refuse, call animal control. Some folks recommend using bells and bright collars to deter cats from killing birds. These are helpful, but do not solve the issue.

Stop Using Mosquito Spray Services

Traditional mosquito control is devastating to all life, including humans. Most of these sprays contain pyrethrin or pyrethroids (the synthetic version of pyrethrin). Both are nerve agents that disrupt our nervous system and brain function. Ditto for all life affected by the spray. Some mosquito spray companies advertise their products as being all-natural. Indeed, pyrethrin is all-natural. But so is asbestos. Being "all natural" does not necessarily make a product safe.

As if all this was not enough, mosquito sprays are downright ineffective. Think about it—the mosquitoes can still fly in from neighboring properties. We would have to spray all the neighboring properties, and perhaps the entire city, to keep them out of our property. Even then, this assumes the spray actually kills all of the mosquitoes on site. It will kill many, but some will survive. Those that survive have fewer predators to eat them, since many of these predators were killed or harmed by the spray. With fewer predators, the mosquito population rebounds more quickly.

Because mosquitoes reproduce so quickly, they can develop resistance to chemicals. As we speak this is happening—mosquitoes are becoming resistant to many of the usual chemical approaches, such as pyrethrin.

What are our alternative options for controlling mosquitoes? We can do the following:

- Create habitat so predators like bats and lizards take up residence in our landscape. They love eating mosquitoes.

- Mosquitoes breed in water and puddles. We should reduce standing water by ensuring none collects in buckets, gutters, downspouts, pots, hollows, etc.

- For standing water we can't dump or drain, buy BTI mosquito dunks. These contain a substrain of the *Bacillus thuringiensis* bacteria we learned about earlier that eat baby mosquitoes.

- Remove English ivy because it holds water and creates the perfect breeding ground for Asian tiger mosquitoes. It is also invasive in the United States.

- Garlic spray can serve as an alternative to traditional mosquito sprays. It is approximately as effective as traditional sprays (i.e., not very effective), but without the damaging consequences.

- Use fans. Mosquitoes are bad at flying. Strong fans blowing across a patio or porch will rid it of these blood sucking fiends.

- **My preferred approach:** We can apply nontoxic balms and sprays on our bodies or wear long sleeves, tuck our pants into our socks, and wear a head net. By protecting ourselves at the point of contact, we can generate the most effective defense against mosquitoes.

Here is additional help on this topic for those who want more:

Because we are now deep in this topic, let me touch on one other ineffective approach: bug zappers. These devices use ultraviolet (UV) light to draw in mosquitoes where they then contact an electrical grid that kills them. Unfortunately mosquitoes are not attracted to UV light. They are attracted to CO_2 that we and other life exhale. The insects that do get zapped include beneficial solitary wasps as well as moths, whose caterpillars support our bird populations. Skip the bug zappers.

Before I leave this topic, I want to note that all life has value, even mosquitoes. At a minimum, they provide a huge amount of food for other insects, birds, and bats.

Remove Invasive Plants

Removing invasive plants is challenging. I almost excluded it from this chapter because it requires being able to identify invasive plants, understand their growth and reproductive strategies, tailor a removal plan based on those findings, and then execute that plan. This is not easy, but it is so important. We know that invasive plants cause great harm.

My best and easiest recommendation for this task? Hire a qualified professional to remove invasive plants.

For those who have the time and desire to learn how to do this work, here is a basic overview for how we can proceed:

- **Learn to identify invasive plants:** We can start by searching "invasive plants (insert location)" online to find many resources. Typical culprits here in North Carolina are Bradford pear, English ivy, ligustrum, mimosa, Tree of Heaven, and a number of others.

- **Learn about the plant:** To control a plant, we need to understand its life cycle and how it likes to grow, spread, and reproduce. This is going to influence our strategy. For example, if a plant spreads by seed, then our goal should be to prevent it from ever seeding.

- **Evaluate resources:** What resources do we have available for this project? What is our funding or labor availability? What is the setting? What tools will we need and what do we have?

- **Establish goals and parameters:** Is our goal to get rid of all non-native plants? Or only invasive plants? By when do we want to have this work completed? What products and tools are we willing to use and not willing to use? The list of options is long.

- **Craft and execute our strategy:** With sufficient knowledge we can now create a plan and implement it.

There are many reputable organizations offering in-depth information and resources regarding this topic. Here is one that I find helpful:

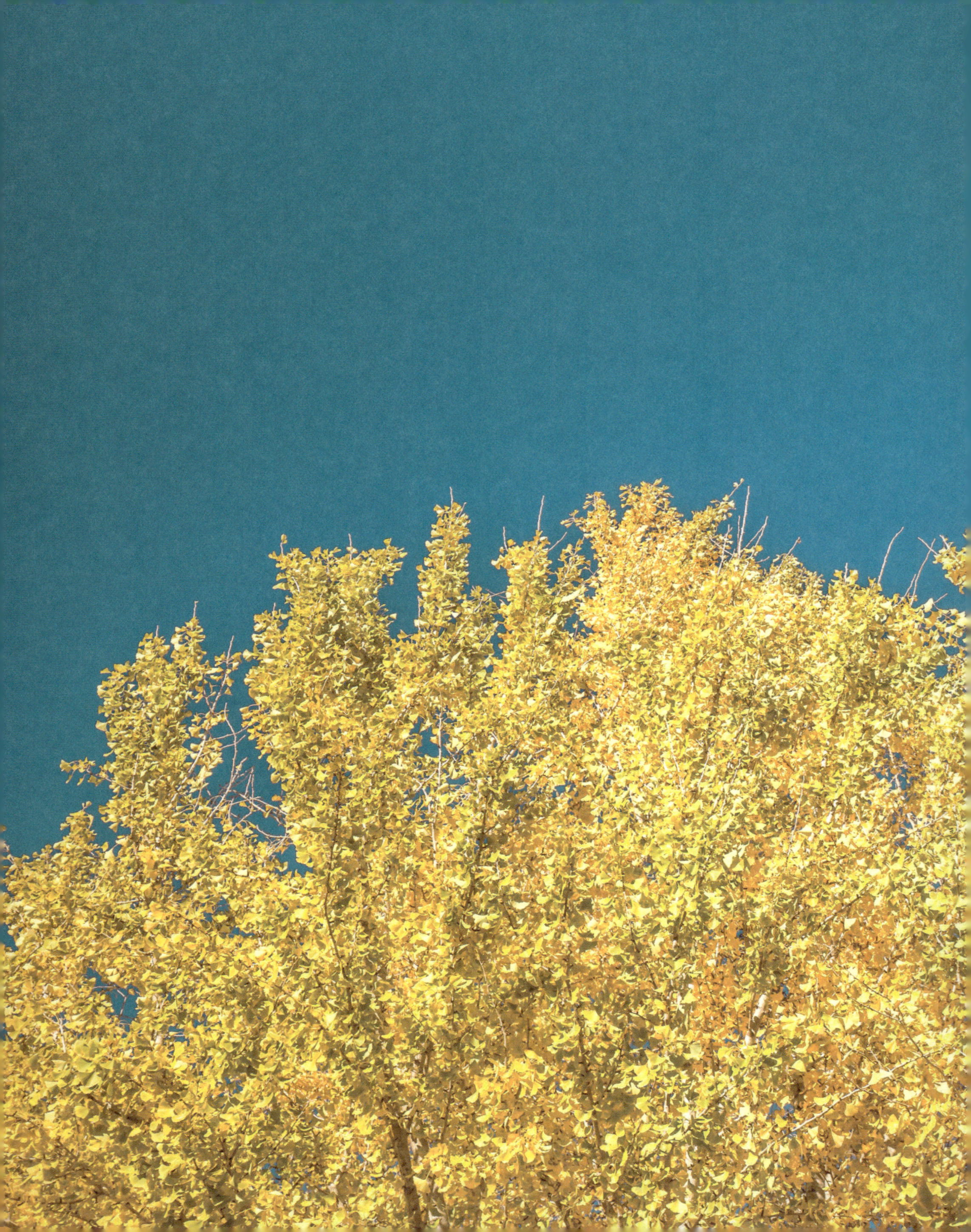

SECTION 4

more powerful ways to help heal earth

Our strategy remains the same: increase photosynthesis and build soil. Plant native trees, flowers, and grasses. Help them attain a long, healthy life. Preserve existing and mature trees. Get rid of lawns. Stop using fertilizers and harmful chemicals. **Do everything we can to increase outrageous diversity.**

In Section 3 we learned how to plant native saplings, preserve existing trees, and help them achieve long, healthy lives through ideal structure and soil. We learned a handful of ideas that help boost life both below ground and above ground. These actions (and in some cases, inactions) increase photosynthesis, soil, water availability, sequestered carbon, and the abundance and diversity of life. In short, they help heal Earth while also saving us time and money.

In this section, let's build on what we have learned and increase our ability to achieve our strategy by orders of magnitude. **Enter meadows and pocket forests!**

Meadows and pocket forests enable us to fill entire communities—neighborhoods, shopping centers, and business parks—with a diversity of native plants. Both are radical departures from traditional landscape paradigms. Though they are more challenging than anything we have learned thus far, these systems are still easier and a heck of a lot more fun than the status quo.

We use meadows full of native flowers and grasses to replace lawns, which are ecological wastelands, as we will learn in Chapter 16. We plant these meadows from seeds, not from individual plants grown in trays (called *plugs*), which has been the norm for most sub/urban meadows. With pocket forests, we plant saplings in dense groups consisting of many different native species. These take the place of what has typically been one stand-alone tree surrounded by a bed of mulch.

In both cases, by working with communities of plants instead of individual plants, we reduce maintenance requirements considerably. Both systems are cheaper, more resilient, more stable, and more beautiful than the status quo. They also virtually eliminate the need for all the harmful "-cides" we learned about in Section 3.

Best of all, meadows and pocket forests do even more to boost photosynthesis, soil, water, and stored carbon compared to what we have learned thus far. Then, of course, there is the incredible life that both systems help generate and support. To illustrate this, I want to share a personal story:

It was a hot, sweaty June afternoon. I simply could not—or rather, would not—mow my front yard any longer. Growing up, my siblings and I used a small push mower to cut the giant field that surrounded our house. Because of this, I really hated mowing.

On that summer day I decided to plant some trees and shrubs in my front lawn to get rid of the grass. But they were not enough; I needed some smaller plants to fill the gaps. I turned to flowers and ground covers to fill the many open spaces.

Though I knew a good amount about trees and shrubs through my work at Leaf & Limb, back then I knew absolutely nothing about flowers. I was starting from scratch. After some research and a handful of visits to local nurseries, I got to work planting all sorts of new flowers in my front yard.

I quickly discovered that I *loved* flowers! They bring beauty and a burst of life. I was fascinated by the slow growth and evolution of every plant. They each behave, react, and age differently across seasons. It turns out the Butterfly Bush was not much of a butterfly magnet at all. It's non-native and provides little food for those who need it. I learned that the **real** butterfly magnets were native species like Joe Pye weed, coneflowers, and mountain mint. Speaking of butterflies, I'll never forget the first time a monarch butterfly gently glided into my garden one warm October afternoon to feed on the butterfly milkweed. Its name suits it well; I felt as if royalty had indeed arrived.

As it often happens, my life got busier, especially after I became a father. I was not able to dedicate as much time to my garden. In particular, I could not spend hours every weekend pulling weeds. I began questioning the practice of pulling weeds—why do I have to weed? There is nobody pulling weeds out in the fields and forests. Yet breathtaking ecosystems exist. Perhaps I could recreate this in my yard? So I set out once again to reimagine what my yard could be.

Monarchs Are Nearing Extinction

Sadly, as I write this, monarch butterflies are close to extinction. The use of pesticides has played a big role in their decline, as has development in general. But another one of the big reasons for their decline is that they simply do not have enough food. Imagine that—an entire species dying for lack of food. Yet their food is butterfly milkweed, a beautiful orange flower that we can all plant in our yards, city parks, and along roadsides. It's easy to grow from seed and is quite tolerant of hot, dry conditions. It does well here in the Piedmont. We can have something of beauty and help save a species. It's a win-win!

With time, I discovered meadows. Because meadows create a tight-knit community of plants that grow *with* one another, they are largely able to avoid being invaded and overrun by weeds. I spent a lot of time learning about these ecosystems through research, visiting Piedmont Prairies across North Carolina, and experimentation. I planted two meadows: one in my backyard and one in the front yard. Next I converted my neighbor's front yard from lawn into meadow, after he graciously allowed me to experiment with his space.

I found that a meadow requires patience; nothing about it is fast or provides any sort of instant gratification. But once it gets going, a meadow is incredible. It requires little maintenance—essentially only one cut per year—and no watering, fertilization, pesticides, or treatments of any kind. These plant communities form deep and dense roots that build rich soil to great depths. I learned first-hand that they suck down an incredible amount of water. Before meadows, I used to have streams of water flow through my yard during rain events. I had a small rain garden that would quickly fill to the brim before overflowing. Once the meadows were established, those streams disappeared and the rain garden rarely filled.

But the best part was that my meadows were **wild** with life. I had no idea that we have so many different types of bees in North Carolina! Some drone about like fluffy blimps while others zip from flower to flower like hyperactive hummingbirds. Some shine green, some cut leaves, and some dig holes. I saw an assassin bug for the first time and watched transfixed as it stalked after its prey through the dense goldenrod. After a few seasons, male anoles appeared. During hot summer afternoons I would spot them signaling potential mates with their red throats.

Apparently, the red throats worked because I noticed a cohort of smaller anoles some months later. I watched as butterflies soared in for landings like planes at a busy airport. Five bats began showing up each evening to swoop around for food. I remember walking outside one morning before sunrise and hearing two great horned owls for the first time. My skin prickled and I stood silently, soaking in their haunting calls for as long as they would linger. I had never seen bats or owls in downtown Raleigh, but I knew why they showed up—mine was the yard with an abundance of life.

I felt deeply connected to this little vibrant ecosystem. I still do. This connection grows with time. I love this place, and all the life in it—I never could have anticipated how much it would change my life for the better.

This brings me to my final highlight for meadows and pocket forests: **they are a place where life thrives, my own included.**

Before we dive into the details, I want to share a video to provide inspiration. Keep in mind that I am not a landscape designer of any kind. All I did was measure the space, assess basic site conditions (sun and water), decide approximately where to put each system, and then install the plants using the methods outlined in the next two chapters. There is nothing fancy; I'm simply putting together the basic parts from this book. The outcome is incredible.

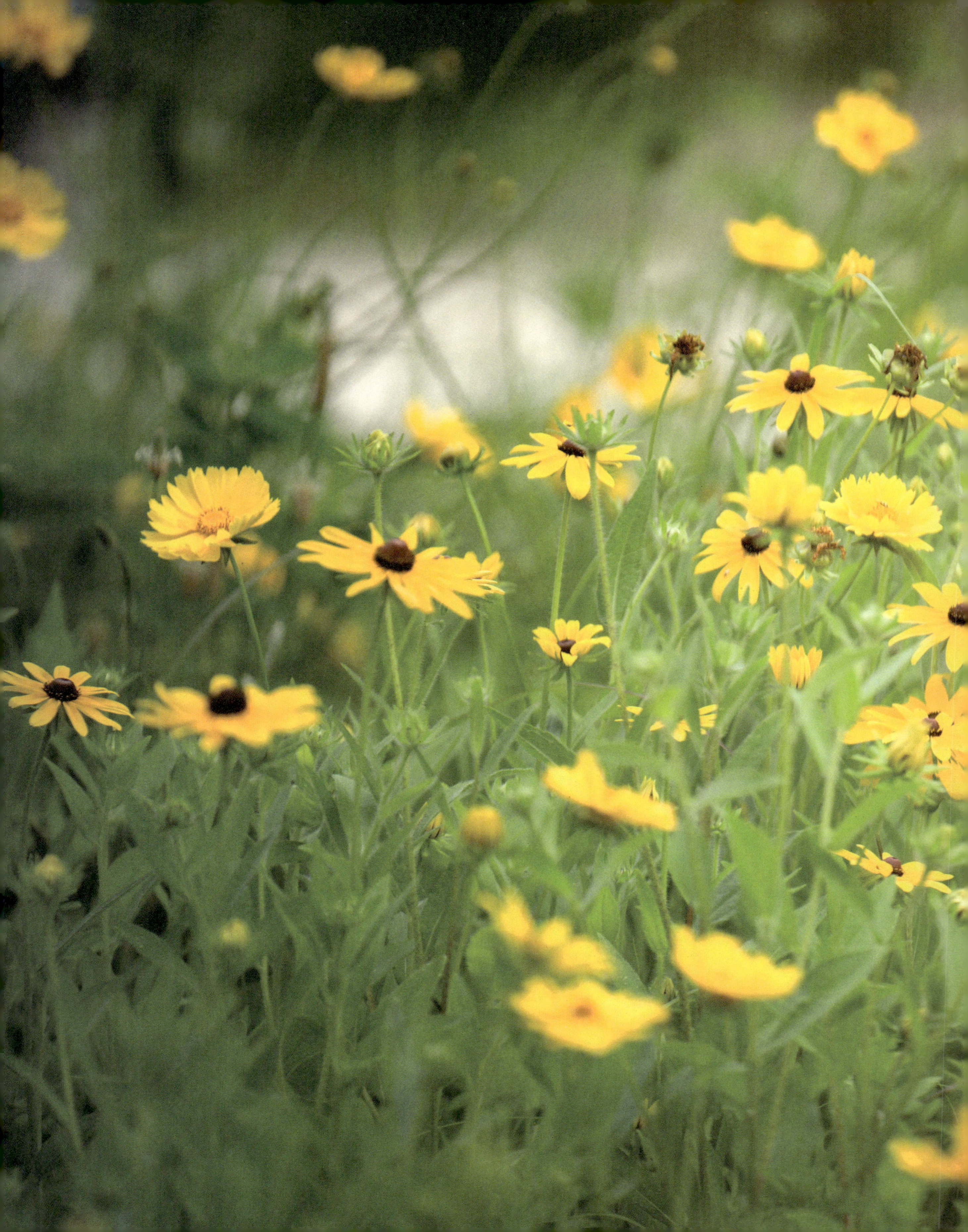

CHAPTER 16

lawns are ecological disasters—replace them with meadows from seed

To begin, let's consider the following:

- Lawns in the US form a whopping 63,000 square miles, an area close to the size of Georgia.

- Lawns are the #1 largest crop grown in the United States, surpassing even corn. Yet they produce no food.

- One-third of all annual water use in the sub/urban landscape in the United States is used to water our lawns.

- Lawn care is resource intensive. We use an estimated 1.2 billion gallons of gas, over 850 million pounds of fertilizer, and 59 million pounds of pesticides every year to tend to the sub/urban landscape.

- Over 10 million tons of grass clippings and other yard waste are sent to landfills each year. This results in a tremendous amount of methane being released into the atmosphere.

- Lawnmowers burn fuel inefficiently, emitting roughly four times more smog-forming pollution per hour than cars.

- Lawns have shallow roots, which means they build little soil (a plant can only generate soil to the depth to which its roots grow) and hold little water. In fact, lawns are only slightly better at soaking up water than sidewalks!

In short, lawns are ecological wastelands that do not support life and cause massive harm to our planet. All this for a space that very few people even enjoy—research shows that we spend less than 10% of our time outside!

Let's pause as we collect our jaws from the floor.

Luckily, we have an amazing alternative: meadows. The premise of a meadow (also called a prairie, or Piedmont Prairie here in the Southeast) is that we plant a variety of native flowers and grasses to replace a lawn. By doing so, we reverse every one of the issues listed at the start of this chapter. Meadows have deep roots that build rich soil, which sequesters loads of carbon and holds a great deal of water. Meadows have far more resilience in the face of drought and damaging pests. They do not need to be irrigated, fertilized, aerated, or sprayed with any chemicals of any kind. Once established, they need only be cut once per year, which means less work and less emissions from lawnmowers, blowers, trucks, and other equipment. Best of all, native meadows promote a fantastic abundance and diversity of life.

Meadows can be planted from plugs (individual plants grown in trays and small containers) or from seeds. When using plugs, we must individually install each plant then pull or cut weeds from around the individual plants for several growing seasons. Both are excruciatingly laborious tasks. Planting meadows from seed is much easier than installing individual plants. Then as the seeds begin growing, we mow the entire area repeatedly for one to three growing seasons using a lawnmower or string trimmer—no pulling weeds necessary. Once the native flowers and grasses establish, we only need to cut them once per year and perform a handful of basic maintenance tasks throughout the growing season. For these reasons, we will be learning how to plant a native meadow from seed, not plugs. This is not to say that planting meadows from plugs has no value. Plugs are excellent for certain scenarios, such as small sites and sites where we must achieve a very specific aesthetic outcome.

A Bit of Grasslands History

There were grasslands in the Midwest and other parts of the United States that predate the arrival of humans. They were maintained by fire from lightning, periodic drought, and herbivores ranging from mammoths to the giant bison. Later many grasslands—especially the Piedmont Prairies that covered parts of the US Southeast—were also cultivated and maintained by indigenous people. By using fire and other cultivation techniques to attract huge herds of bison, elk, and other herbivores, they were able to promote a wide array of life while satisfying their needs for food and materials.

Unfortunately, as we learned in Chapter 5, these native grasslands are nearly extinct. We need native grasslands as much as we need native forests. Ditto for all the other various ecosystems that are under threat, including wetlands, mangrove swamps, estuaries, and many others.

How to Grow a Meadow from Seed

Like every other topic in this book, meadows can get really complicated. For example, if we choose to sow seeds early in the growing season instead of the dormant season, this will require a different process and additional tools. We are going to skip a lot of complexity and focus on the easiest way to plant meadows that works for most sub/urban properties (recall the 80/20 Rule from Chapter 9). There are other ways to install native meadows from seed that work well, and there are also some sites for which the approach outlined in this chapter may not work.

Here are the six steps for growing meadows from seed:

1. Evaluate basic site conditions.
2. Kill existing vegetation during the growing season.
3. Plant seeds in the dormant season.
4. Perform maintenance during the first growing season.
5. Perform maintenance during the second growing season.
6. Perform maintenance during the third growing season and beyond.

Before we begin, here is the list of tools and supplies we will need:

- Cell phone or tablet with a sun tracker app
- Glyphosate herbicide without any added surfactant
- Sprayer to apply herbicide
- Wheelbarrow
- 5-gallon bucket
- Jute fabric and jute pins to cover the site after sowing seeds
- Heavy-duty, sharp scissors for cutting jute fabric
- Hammer to secure jute pins into the ground
- Kitty litter (a basic clay litter with no additives is best)
- A native seed blend
- Bags for measured portions of seeds

It is worth noting that this process takes time and requires patience. From start to finish, three years is normal. Sometimes it may only take two years for the meadow to establish, but it could also take four years or more. **There is no instant gratification when it comes to meadows.** The good news is that once they establish, meadows are resilient and remain for many years, assuming proper maintenance.

Here is a video showing the full installation process:

Step 1: Evaluate Basic Site Conditions

Meadows need lots of direct sun, typically at least five hours per day. This is a loose guideline; some can survive with as little as four hours, especially where there is additional dappled sun.

There is generally no upward limit to how much sun a meadow can tolerate. Make observations or use a sun tracker app to ensure the site of the intended meadow receives adequate sunlight during the growing season. The amount of sun exposure during the dormant season does not matter.

Here is another option: evaluate what is in the space now. Presumably it is a lawn, which is generally an excellent site for a meadow. Or perhaps it is a space filled with weeds and other herbaceous plants? *Herbaceous* plants are those that have no persistent woody stems above ground, i.e., not trees, shrubs, or vines.

A Native Flower Case Study

So that we have some sense for how much outrageous diversity native flowers and grasses support, here is an excerpt from *Nature's Best Hope: A New Approach to Conservation That Starts in Your Yard* by Doug Tallamy. He writes:

Goldenrod leaves support 110 species of caterpillars in Southeast Pennsylvania and many species of leaf beetles and June beetles. In our area, its flowers provide pollen and nectar for 35 bee species, 15 of which use only goldenrod pollen; myriad wasps; as well as long-horned, scarab, blister, phalacrid, ripiphorid, and ladybird beetles. And don't forget that goldenrod nectar is an important source of energy for migrating monarchs. Goldenrod flowers are favorite hunting sites for crab spiders and praying mantids, and its seeds feed a number of wintering sparrows, juncos, and finches—and birds use them to line their nests in the spring. Its stems provide housing for native bees throughout the year and support four species of gallers [insects that create galls] as well as several stem-boring caterpillars, and they are feeding sites for many plant and leafhoppers. Who knows how many species goldenrod roots support.

Once we determine sun exposure, next we look at soil moisture. All we need to determine is whether the area is very dry, normal, or very wet. We use this to help choose the right seed species. We can look at more variables that may enhance outcomes somewhat, but it is not necessary to do so at this basic level.

Step 2: Kill Existing Vegetation During the Growing Season

Our next objective is to get rid of the lawn (or weeds) that currently exist on the site. **This is one of the most crucial steps in this process.** The degree to which we reduce competing vegetation correlates with how successful the meadow is likely to be.

For this, I recommend using an herbicide called glyphosate. Of the many herbicides available on the market, glyphosate currently has the best balance of maximum killing power and minimum negative consequences. We should choose one that has no added surfactants. While herbicides are typically harmful and we should generally avoid using them, they can be helpful tools in the context of ecological restoration. Turning a lawn into a native meadow is a form of this work.

Some who read this may be surprised and even upset by my decision to recommend an herbicide. I get it; I used to be strictly against the use of herbicides, with no exceptions. But experience and research have required that I take a more nuanced

This too should be a good place for a meadow. What if the area is covered by leaves, moss, or rocks and little vegetation is growing? This will not suffice for a meadow. The land often shows us what we need to know based on what is growing there now.

Please note that if the space is filled with mature trees, shrubs, and vines, this will not suffice. We should not remove them to plant a meadow, unless they are invasive. If they are invasive, we must first eliminate them from the site using targeted strategies for each different species before proceeding.

approach. For those who want to learn more about my position on this topic, here is additional information:

Before proceeding, mow the vegetation to a height of 3 to 6 inches. We want to avoid having tall, dead plants later in the process. Once it has been mowed, begin spraying. Follow all safety requirements, including the following: We must strictly follow the label and always wear the necessary protective gear. People and pets should not enter the sprayed area until four hours after the application. We should avoid spraying if there is a possibility of rain within the next six hours. Most crucially, we must not spray creeks, ponds, and other bodies of water.

A 5% solution is generally an adequate strength, though we should consult the label for exact instructions. We should include an herbicide dye so we can visually confirm that all vegetation has been sprayed. Perform the first spray during the middle of the growing season. Then we should monitor how fast new vegetation grows. Once it reaches 6 inches, spray again. Repeat until the end of the growing season. For most sites, we only need a total of two sprays—one in the middle of the growing season and one near the end.

If after the first application nothing happens, we may need to consider using a stronger dosage (consult the label) or another herbicide. There are some lawns, such as Bermuda grass, that can be quite difficult to kill.

For those who simply refuse to use glyphosate, here are two alternatives that can be somewhat effective in the right setting.

Occultation: Using opaque tarps, silage tarps, old vinyl billboards, or anything that blocks the light from reaching vegetation below is called *occultation*. Lay the tarps down early in the growing season, after everything has come to life. Do not lay them earlier because we want vegetation to begin growing. Place sandbags, chunks of wood, or anything heavy that can hold the tarps in place, especially during gusty thunderstorms. After 1 month, lift the tarps to allow sunlight to reach the plants. This causes them to resprout. Keep them lifted for two to three days and then cover the area again. Repeat this every month. We may need to repeat this process for multiple growing seasons.

Glyphosate Alternatives: For some sites, it may be possible to use glyphosate alternatives. This approach will be similar to using glyphosate, with one modification: we should spray every time the vegetation reaches 4 inches. We will likely need to spray many times throughout the growing season and may need to repeat this process for multiple growing seasons. Use the maximum recommended dosage for each spray.

A Word Regarding European Honeybees

Meadows support an incredible number of native bees, many of which are in decline thanks to pesticides and habitat destruction. Another threat to native bees is competition from non-native European honeybees.

Unfortunately, European honeybees are the face of many "save the bees" campaigns. These are also the species that many beekeepers care for, which is unfortunate, because this puts even more pressure on our native bee populations. I'm all for saving the bees—but the native ones, not European honeybees.

Yet I always hesitate to criticize the European honeybee, especially around new gardeners. It is often the very thing that gets folks interested in flowers and the outdoors. It has been powerful in helping change the tide of public perception regarding important topics like the overuse of chemicals and lawns. From this standpoint, the European honeybee is an ally to the efforts described in this book.

My thoughts on related topics, like No Mow May, are very similar. In a strict ecological sense, they are not helpful and even harmful at times. But from a social standpoint, they are powerful agents for change that could make a positive difference. These are complicated issues. I like to remind myself that there was a time when all of this was new to me as well (and I still have a lot to learn). We are all in various stages of our journey.

Step 3: Plant Seeds in the Dormant Season

The next step is to buy a blend of native flower and grass seeds from a reputable vendor. We should choose a blend that is suitable given what we found during the basic site assessment. It should also contain a diversity of native species, preferably at least 20. So long as we meet these requirements, we can pick any other traits that we prefer, such as short or tall, more flowers or more grasses, and so forth.

NOTE: it is possible to create our own custom blend of native seeds. But this process is challenging. For those who want to learn more, there are additional resources available in the Appendix.

Buy two times more than the vendor recommends—this will leave plenty of seeds after birds and erosion have taken their cut. If the vendor has a lower and upper limit to how much seed we should use, double the upper limit, not the lower limit.

Example: For a high-quality seed blend from Roundstone, they recommend 7–11 pounds per acre. Buy 22 pounds per acre (2 times the upper range). An acre is 43,560-ft^2. If the site is 4,000-ft^2, then we will need (4,000/43,560) × 22 pounds = 2.02 pounds. Round to two pounds.

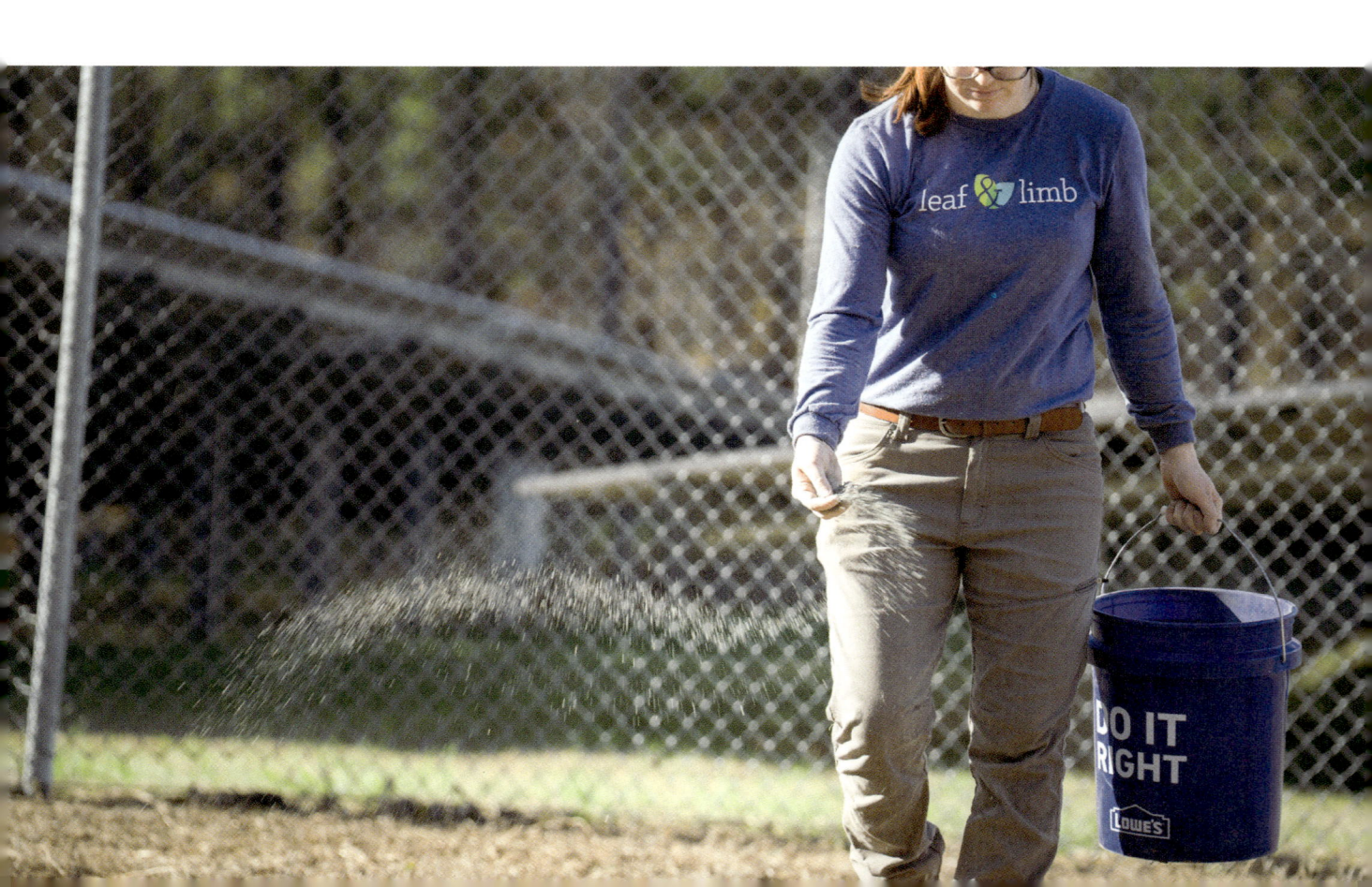

After we receive our seed blend, the next task is to portion it into 1,000-ft^2 sections. Let's stick with the prior example where we have a 4,000-ft^2 site. 4,000 divided

lawns are ecological disasters

by 1,000 is 4, so divide the seed into four portions that are approximately 0.5 pounds each. Once we portion out the seeds, store them in bags that can be closed so the seeds do not spill.

Next we begin the process of installing the meadow. Meadows can be installed in every season, and each has its advantages, disadvantages, and unique procedural nuances. In my experience, the best time to perform installation is during the dormant season, preferably near the middle. For those who experience heavy snowfall during the dormant season, I recommend installing the meadow before the snow arrives.

Do not rake, till, or otherwise disturb the soil. Doing so can activate dormant weed seeds and give rise to challenging issues. If there is dead vegetation on site, leave it in place. The dead roots help prevent our seeds from washing away. If leaves are covering the site, blow them out of the way. Otherwise, the leaves will prevent our seeds from reaching the soil.

When we are ready to sow the seeds, we need to mix them with a filler for better distribution. If we spread the seed blend without a filler, we will overseed and quickly run out before covering the entire site. My favorite filler is kitty litter. It's light and readily available at many pet stores. We will need 50 pounds per 1,000-ft^2 of area to be seeded.

For the 4,000-ft² example we have been using throughout this chapter, we will need four bags of kitty litter in total.

Begin by pouring 50 pounds of kitty litter into a wheelbarrow. Add a bag of seeds, which is enough seed for 1,000-ft². Mix them thoroughly.

If there are many 1,000-ft² sections, it may help to mark each one. Pour half of this seed/filler mix into a 5-gallon bucket. Begin spreading the mix in the first 1,000-ft² section. For each 1,000-ft² section we make two passes: using the first half of the mix (25 pounds), we should walk in east–west directions. Scatter it in a consistent fashion. I like to turn my right palm up and flick it to my left, like I'm casting a fishing line sideways. But there is no right or wrong way to do this, so long as we thoroughly spread the mix across the intended area. The goals are to be consistent with our hand motion, take slow steps, and implement a method that creates a methodical spray pattern.

We do not want clumps; we want even and thorough distribution of the mix.

Make sure we spread conservatively so that we have enough mix to cover the entire area in our east–west pattern. Once we are done with the first bucket, refill the bucket with the remaining half of our mix. With this second bucket, walk in a north–south direction. This allows us to create a crosshatch pattern over the 1,000-ft² section, which ensures better coverage. Please note that we do not actually have to walk east–west and north–south; I only chose these to illustrate the need to create a crosshatch pattern. Repeat this process for all 1,000-ft² sections until the entire area has been seeded.

Finally, we must install a biodegradable fabric to help reduce erosion and seed loss. Some experts argue that this is unnecessary, but I find that it can make a big, positive difference in the outcome of the meadow. One good option is jute fabric, which is made of plant fibers that rot over time. To install the jute fabric, roll it out across the entirety of the meadow. Use a hammer and jute pins to fasten the fabric to the ground. There are many techniques, tools, and supplies we can use. Whatever we choose, the goal is to cover the entire area in a biodegradable fabric that remains securely attached to the land and holds seeds in place during rain events.

Step 4: Perform Maintenance During the First Growing Season

We must closely follow what I consider to be one of the most crucial rules for success: **no matter how well a meadow performs in its first growing season, and no matter how amazing we might find it to be, we must cut it every two to three weeks.** We will be tempted to ignore this rule—especially when the flowers are dazzling—but we must not.

We have two primary goals during the first growing season:

1. Keep weeds from producing mature seed.

2. Make sure the small native grass and flower sprouts receive plenty of sunlight.

We can achieve these goals by mowing every two to three weeks. Cut all plants to a height of 5–6 inches with a string trimmer or lawnmower (assuming it can be positioned to the appropriate height). We should avoid using a lawnmower on days when the ground is wet, since this can damage the sprouts. If we use a lawnmower, attach a bag to the side to catch debris if possible. This will help reduce something called *thatch*. Thatch is what occurs when we leave layers of cut vegetation in place. If thatch builds up, it will shade out the young native sprouts and prevent them from receiving adequate sunlight. Luckily even if bagging the thatch is not an option, cutting every two to three weeks minimizes this issue.

If for some reason we cut less frequently than every two to three weeks—and we should not—we will need to remove the resulting thatch. Place the thatch in a compost pile.

We do this for the entire growing season. Our meadow will look like a semi-mowed patch of weeds. This is ok. It paves the way for something beautiful later.

At the end of the growing season, let the plants grow a bit taller than usual. We want them to have extra mass to weather cold temperatures during the dormant season. Ideally, the meadow plants should be 10–12 inches tall during the dormant season.

If leaves or pine straw fall onto the meadow from nearby trees, rake or blow them off the meadow sometime before the end of the dormant season. They will obstruct the growth of the flowers and grasses during the second growing season. From the meadow's perspective, we can think of leaves as a type of thatch.

If budget allows, we should spread seeds again during the dormant season (this is called *overseeding*). This should be done after removing leaves. We use the same seed blend and the same processes outlined in Step 3 of this chapter, but without installing more jute fabric. Overseeding is not necessary but will help bolster the meadow.

Step 5: Perform Maintenance During the Second Growing Season

Here is a video providing some thoughts, tips, and so forth to help with maintenance in the second growing season and beyond, since this can be more tricky than the first growing season.

During the second growing season, our goals are the same as the first growing season. The difference now is that we have more flexibility to make decisions about what to do next. Some may decide that there are minimal weeds, plenty of robust native plants, and it's time to let the meadow grow freely. Determining whether this is true requires the ability to distinguish weeds from desirable flowers and grasses, which is not easy to do.

If in doubt about what to do, or if you want to maximize the probability of long-term success, keep up the work from last growing season, with one modification: cut to a height of 10–12 inches instead of 5–6 inches. Given the height change, this will require the use of a string trimmer instead of a lawnmower. We will still need to cut regularly every two to three weeks to avoid creating a lot of thick thatch.

Once the dormant season arrives, we need to perform our first annual cut. We perform the annual cut to reduce thatch and to prevent tree and shrub species from turning the meadow into a forest. Ideally, we would burn the meadow instead of cutting it, but that is not an option for most sites in the sub/urban landscape.

When performing the annual cut, we begin by cutting the entire meadow close to ground level. We should aim to cut all debris to a height of 2 inches or less, but we must not cut so low that we scalp the soil. There are many tools we can use, including a lawn mower, string trimmer, hedge trimmer with an articulating cutting head, or scythe. Once the cutting is done, we gather all the large stalks and place them in a brush or compost pile.

What About Leaving Dead Stems?

In Chapter 15 we discussed the importance of leaving dead stems for pollinators. My instructions to perform the annual cut during the dormant season are at odds with that recommendation. This is due to an underlying tension: on the one side of this tension is something known as *ecological succession*, which is the idea that ecosystems evolve and change over time. Meadows often turn into forests. On the other side is the need to leave dead stems for the insects that need them.

My recommendation is to default towards preventing ecological successions during the meadow's early years since we want it to establish. Make a thorough annual cut, even at the expense of destroying habitat for pollinators. As a compromise, we can stage the debris in a brush pile somewhere on site. Some insects will survive and return to the meadow next growing season.

As the meadow matures, we can favor pollinator habitat more heavily. Perhaps we cut half of the meadow one year and the other half the next year? Or do this in thirds across a three-year rotation? We could try cutting different sections at different heights. Or vary the timing of the annual cut, e.g., late growing season, early dormant season, and late growing season. Or skip a year altogether. There are many possibilities. Whatever we choose, we must monitor pressure from young trees, saplings, and invasive plants, since these are what will transform our meadow into a forest.

Ultimately how we manage this meadow depends on our goals and preferences. We should be experimental, make decisions, and observe what happens. We can use first-hand experiences and observations to guide the way.

Step 6: Perform Maintenance During the Third Growing Season and Beyond

By the third growing season, most meadows will be established. Now it is time to enjoy the incredible beauty and buzzing life that calls this space home.

There will be exceptions, of course. Some sites may take longer, especially those with heavily compacted dirt. For these sites, repeat Step 5 (maintenance for the second growing season) for one or two more growing seasons. Eventually the meadow will flourish. Every meadow evolves in its own unique way based on site conditions, weather, and other factors outside of our control. Each season will bring unexpected surprises and changes. **This is part of what makes meadows so exciting!**

From here on out, all we need to do is the following:

- Perform an annual cut.

- Spend some time each growing season monitoring for unwelcome plants taking root in the meadow. A pass every month is sufficient. I recommend snipping intruders with scissors or clippers. Keep a close eye on the edges of the meadow where wind and water often move weed seeds in from surrounding areas. Make methodical passes through the interior as well.

A Patch of Livable Grass

If we want a patch of livable grass in or near our meadows, we can use the same method outlined in this chapter to grow native or near-native turf. One great species to consider is buffalograss. There are other native/near-native grass options to choose from, pending our location and site conditions, such as Halls' bentgrass, seashore bentgrass, blue grama, sideoats grama, seashore saltgrass, red fescue, St. Augustinegrass, and Texas bluegrass. There are others.

Another class of plants to consider are native sedges. They are low maintenance, drought tolerant, and highly adaptable. The only downside to sedges is that we cannot easily grow them from seed; these will have to be planted from plugs. Here is more information on this topic:

- If we observe that an invasive species of some kind is taking over the meadow at a pace that cannot be controlled with cuts and other non-chemical solutions, we may need to use targeted herbicide applications to eradicate it. Otherwise, the invasive species could destroy the meadow. For this, I recommend using a glove or brush to apply a glyphosate herbicide that has no added surfactants directly on the invasive plant. Spraying herbicide will create too much damage to nearby plants.

There is another important consideration we should bear in mind: by keeping the edges of our meadows mowed or trimmed we can create pleasing visual frames and the appearance of order. It indicates to passersby that this space is cared for—it is not neglected. This may matter for some properties where aesthetics are a concern and for meadows bordering sidewalks, paths, and streets. For this I recommend using a string trimmer to cut the edge of the meadow down to half its height or to create a rounded contour (in other words, sculpt the edge of the meadow so the plants do not drape over the walkway or street). We can also use a lawnmower to create a low, mowed strip along the relevant edges.

Finally, above all else we should remember to perform what is by far the most important task: enjoy the meadow! Soak in its magnificent beauty, watch the wonder of life humming about, and experience moments of peace.

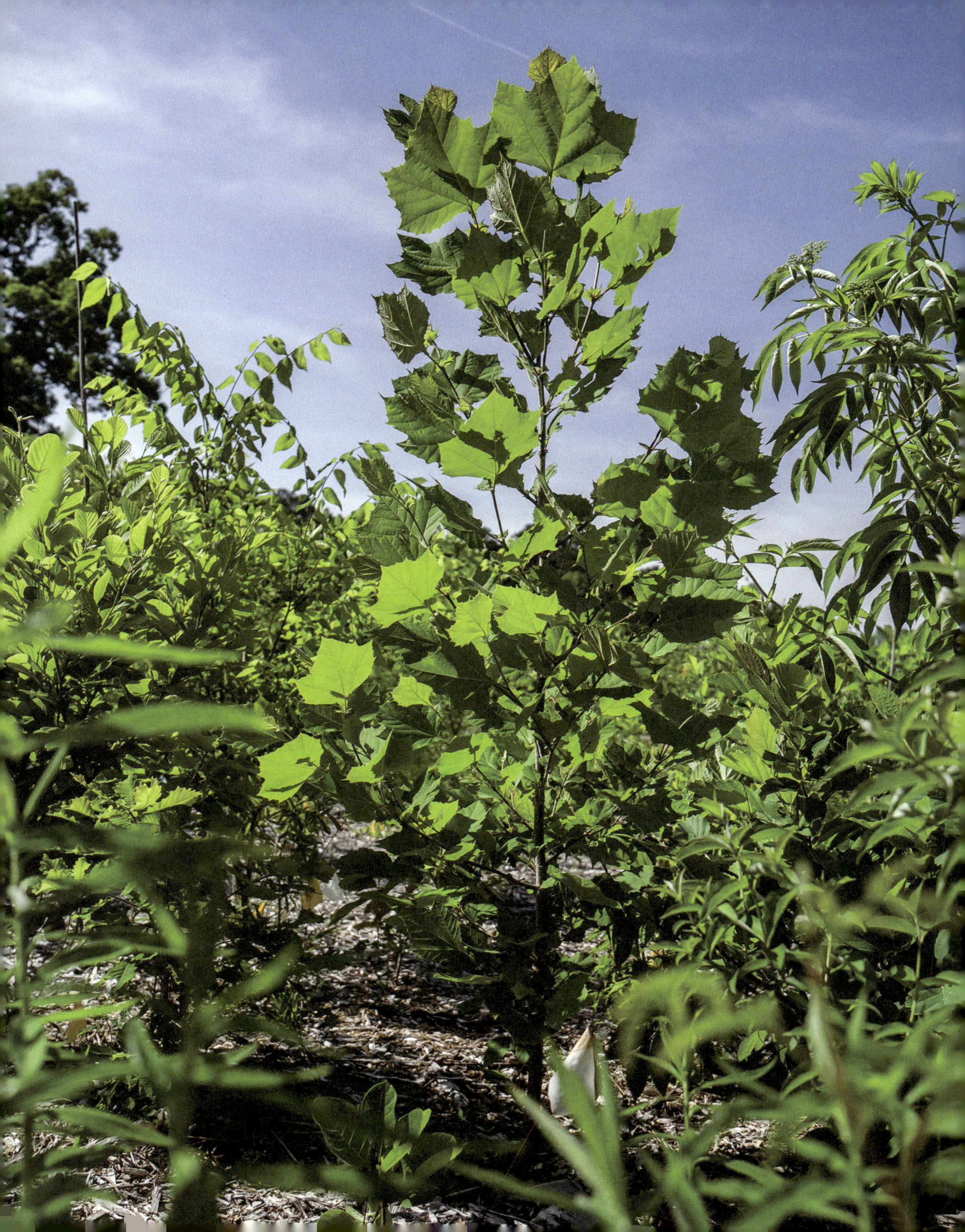

CHAPTER 17

pocket forests— a better way to plant trees

Most trees in the sub/urban landscape are planted individually within a bed of mulch. The bed surrounding the tree must be cared for—this is called *bed maintenance* in the landscaping industry. Bed maintenance is a major expense and frustration for many homeowners, HOAs, and commercial sites. We spend a great deal of time and money on weed control, replenishing mulch, edging, removing leaves, and a variety of other tasks associated with bed maintenance.

Bed maintenance is also a hub for toxic chemicals since many homeowners and service providers continuously apply herbicides to control weeds in these spaces. Unlike with ecological restoration, this is an application that must be repeated in perpetuity and harms life without providing any benefits. Most who want to transition away from herbicides are unable to do so because of the effort required to pull weeds by hand.

This set of issues and frustrations surrounding bed maintenance is where my work with pocket forests began. By then I understood the benefits of working with communities of flowers and grasses to create meadows. I surmised that this approach could work with trees and shrubs too. Perhaps we could eliminate bed maintenance altogether by planting trees and shrubs together in communities instead of as individuals? Better yet, this would increase photosynthesis, soil formation, sequestered carbon, water availability, and outrageous diversity.

I returned to one of our guiding frameworks: **when in doubt, look to ecosystems for guidance.** Trees and shrubs naturally grow very close to each other in forests. When young trees take over old fields, they are often growing within a foot of each other. Even after three or four decades they are still within 3–6 feet of each other. Over time, the spacing between the largest trees increases—but that creates new gaps for all sorts of other species to enter and occupy middle and lower layers within the forest ecosystem. I observed the same thing within the Amazon. Plants want to fill every available open space; they naturally grow very close to one another and fill many vertical layers.

The Benefits of Pocket Forests

We know from Chapter 10 that saplings are cheap and easy to plant. We can comfortably plant 20 saplings per hour, and more if we hustle. With approximately the same time and costs necessary to plant one traditional nursery tree in a 10-ft × 10-ft bed, we can fill this entire space with a variety of native trees and shrubs. The saplings do not need to be watered because even in dismal conditions we typically see no more than 30% mortality (this is based on Leaf & Limb experiments in Raleigh, NC). That leaves plenty of trees to continue.

The only maintenance required during the first several growing seasons is to remove other trees and shrubs that take root. For easy reference, a 10-ft × 10-ft area requires around 20 minutes of maintenance each growing season. That is it. Over time, the pocket forest will naturally shade out competing plants and sustain itself.

Compare this to the typical model of planting one traditional nursery tree in the same 10-ft × 10-ft space. We need to water it for several years. Since it is our only tree in that space, we do not want to lose it. Then we need to perform annual bed maintenance practices in perpetuity.

Over the ensuing years, a pocket forest has greater resilience and stability than a single tree. If one tree dies, or if one species is killed by an invasive pest, there are many others still present. From

The only time I observed open forests with lots of spacing between trees and a lack of middle and lower layers were those under intensive management and with too many deer. Unfortunately, with wolves being extirpated from most of the US, deer are a major threat to the well-being of many American forest ecosystems, especially east of the Mississippi River. With no predators to hold them in balance, deer feed on the young trees and shrubs, thereby eliminating future generations of growth.

I began experimenting with planting many young saplings close to one another, to fill areas that would normally only be occupied by one or several trees. I found that it eliminates many maintenance tasks without an increase in installation costs and provides all of the outcomes we hope to achieve in this book. Here are some of the specific benefits of this approach.

a safety standpoint it is always better to plant more trees versus fewer. Trees that grow together have interwoven root systems, which makes them all collectively more stable in the face of storms and hurricanes. Trees in groups are less likely to fall as compared to individual trees.

As pocket forests grow, some trees will survive and others will pass on, but the community as a whole will grow healthier because of the high density of roots below ground and layers of leaves above ground. More roots, more leaves, and more species of plants result in more photosynthesis, turn more dirt into soil, sequester more carbon, soak up more water when it rains, and produce more outrageous diversity as compared to single traditional nursery trees in managed beds.

How to Plant & Maintain a Pocket Forest

Pocket forests can be planted almost anywhere in the sub/urban space. Most any size will do, though I typically recommend an area that is at least as large as a parking space for a vehicle. We plant pocket forests using saplings for all the reasons we learned in Chapter 10. What comes next builds on that chapter, so please reread it if necessary.

Like many things in this book, what follows are not strict rules. There is plenty of room to experiment and build on these ideas. Here is the process in a nutshell:

1. Prepare the site.
2. Buy native trees and shrub saplings.
3. Plant the saplings.
4. Perform maintenance.

Before I begin, I want to make note that I'm attempting to teach the easiest way to plant a pocket forest. For a more challenging approach we can grow our own saplings using the Project Pando model outlined in Section 5 of this book. We can also create our own "recipe" of specific species to plant. This is beyond the scope of this book, but here is an example of a pocket forest recipe for those interested:

Before we begin, here are the tools and supplies we need:

- ❑ Some way to measure the planting area (measuring tape, measuring wheel, etc.).
- ❑ Enough cardboard to cover the planting area, preferably reused from packages. Avoid cardboard treated with wax or other preservatives—we want the cardboard to rot.
- ❑ Optional: enough leaf mold to cover the area in a 2-inch layer.
- ❑ Enough arborist wood chips to cover the area in an 8-inch layer (if no leaf mold) or a 6-inch layer (if using in conjunction with leaf mold).
- ❑ A sapling planting tool.
- ❑ A sufficient number of durable markers to indicate the location of each plant. I recommend driveway markers. Landscape flags are also an option, but not as good since the plastic flags tend to fall off during the first or second growing season.
- ❑ A variety of native tree and shrub saplings.

Miyawaki Method

Our pocket forest process shares some commonalities with the Miyawaki Method developed by Dr. Akira Miyawaki. He was a professor at Yokohama National University and director of the Japanese Center for International Studies in Ecology. Our approach requires less resources for soil preparation, fewer plants, and less maintenance after planting. This yields less sapling survivability as compared to the Miyawaki Method—though still more than sufficient. I believe our approach is more practical for projects where time and budgets are limited, which is often the case in the sub/urban landscape. For those wanting to learn more about the Miyawaki Method, I recommend the book *Mini-Forest Revolution: Using the Miyawaki Method to Rapidly Rewild the World* by Hannah Lewis

Here is a video showing the installation process:

Step 1: Prepare the Site

To begin, we measure the available planting space. Once we have the total space, divide by 4. This tells us how many saplings we will need to buy to plant them approximately 2 feet from each other, which is our ideal target.

Example: We have a 4,000-ft^2 area where we want to plant a pocket forest. 4,000 divided by 4 is 1,000 total plants.

This spacing is not strict. We can increase the distance to 3 feet, or even to 4 feet if we must. However, spacing modifications will change the math. If we use a 3-foot spacing, divide the total area by 9. This results in a total of 445 plants in the previous example. If we use a 4-foot spacing, divide by 16. This results in a total of 250 plants. Or we could change our approach and use 20 plants per 100 square feet, which is a tad more than a 2-foot spacing, but not quite 3 feet. Using the prior example, this would require 800 trees instead of 1,000.

Please keep in mind that changes in spacing affect the time necessary for maintenance, both in terms of duration for each maintenance session and the number of seasons for which maintenance will be necessary. More open space means there will be more competing plants to remove, and it will take more time for the pocket forest to shade the gaps. Using the previous example, a change from 1,000 to 800 plants would result in a minor increase in maintenance. But a change to 250 plants would result in a substantial increase in maintenance.

Next, we need to kill competing herbaceous plants. This work should begin during the middle of the growing season and is very important—inadequate control over existing weeds can stunt a pocket forest and add substantial maintenance time. Please note that the instructions outlined next will not suffice for sites where there are invasive trees, shrubs, and vines. If they exist, eliminate them using targeted strategies before proceeding.

Invasives aside, start by laying down 1–2 layers of cardboard across the entire area, then add 2 inches of leaf mold followed by 4–6 inches of arborist wood chips on top. The leaf mold is not critical; it simply enhances the health of the planting bed. We can substitute the leaf mold with an additional 2 inches of arborist wood chips instead, for a total of 6–8 inches of arborist wood chips. Do not exceed 8 inches of depth, since doing so can make planting more challenging. These layers will rot, control competing herbaceous weeds, and create the perfect environment in which to plant our saplings during the dormant season.

If in doubt about whether these measures will suffice, particularly on sites with aggressive weeds such as abandoned farmland, make one herbicide application per the instructions in the previous chapter about meadows before laying the cardboard.

Step 2: Buy Native Tree & Shrub Saplings

We need a variety of species, including large shade trees (e.g., oaks), small- to medium-sized trees, and shrubs. We want a range of sizes at maturity so that the end result has many vertical layers of leaves from near the ground to high above. I recommend using at least 25 different native species, but more is better. In some pocket forests I have used close to 90, which is excessive (but fun!). Using around 50 species should be more than sufficient. We can contact our local native nursery, an online native nursery, and/or the state forest service to ask them for a list of what they have available. Ask them for their favorite recommendations, pick 25–50 species at random, or make informed decisions based on research. So long as these species are native to our area and generally appropriate for the site (revisit Chapter 10 for guidance), it is hard to make a bad decision.

Buy enough saplings to fill the area based on the math in Step 1.

Step 3: Plant the Saplings

We start by subdividing the area into 1,000-ft² sections. If the area is less than 1,000-ft², we can skip this step. Next, we divide each species by the number of 1,000-ft² sections. We should create a collection of all the saplings we will plant in each 1,000-ft² section.

Example: We have a 4,000-ft² area. This yields four 1,000-ft² sections. We already know we need 1,000 total plants. Assume we are using 50 different species. 1,000 total plants divided by 50 species = 20 of each species. 20 plants of each species divided by four 1,000-ft² sections = 5 of each species per 1,000-ft² section. The end result should be 4 collections of 200 saplings, each containing 5 saplings of each of the 50 species.

Once we have our collection of saplings for each 1,000-ft² section, we plant the saplings in that space. When planting, we should follow three broad guidelines:

- We should generally attempt to be random. **We must not create a planting plan or neat rows**—this defeats the purpose. Natural ecosystems are not planned and they do not occur in neat rows.

- Attempt to meet the targeted space between plants. But do not be exact—approximations are encouraged.

- This last one is optional: avoid planting species of the same type near each other. Spread them out across the space.

If there are structures and sidewalks nearby, we can plant as close or far away as we please. I have pocket forests planted right next to the sides of buildings and others where I left 6 feet of space so I can maintain a gap through pruning. Some only have shrubs near the sidewalks. Others have oaks near the sidewalks. There is no right or wrong decision.

It is crucial that we add a marker next to each plant. This will make maintenance very easy later since we will know which saplings we planted and which we did not—this can become confusing as the plants age. Four-foot driveway markers are ideal but there are many options we can choose from, including landscape flags. Final options to consider—but do note that none are necessary.

- If we have access to compost or compost tea, per Chapter 14, we can spread it around these saplings or spray it directly onto the plants.

- If deer or rabbits are abundant in our area, we may need protection. See the sidebar for more information.

- Add a sign with a QR code to engage and educate passersby.

- Add labels on or near plants indicating their species names.

Now comes the best part: watching these plants grow over the coming years!

Step 4: Perform Maintenance

Our primary maintenance objective is to keep other trees and shrubs from taking over our pocket forest. Seeds will enter our pocket forest via bird poop, wind, and squirrels. It does not matter whether these saplings are native, non-native, or invasive—we want none of them. Sometimes we may have to keep aggressive vines out as well, such as English ivy. We can ignore herbaceous plants, since the trees will eventually outcompete these plants. But for the perfectionists among us (myself included) it does not hurt to remove these if we desire to do so. It simply requires a little extra time.

We should allocate three to five maintenance sessions per growing season spaced one to two months apart. Time for each maintenance session varies, but is typically in the range of 5 minutes per 100-ft^2.

Example: The 4,000-ft^2 area from the prior example would require around 3 ⅓ hours per session × 4 sessions per growing season = 13 hours per growing season for three growing seasons. This assumes that we (A) controlled competing vegetation in advance, (B) clearly marked each tree, and (C) planted saplings approximately 2 feet apart. Without these, maintenance time can easily balloon well beyond this figure.

Continue this practice for two to four growing seasons, to the point at which the pocket forest has fully shaded the ground below and other plants are not able to easily gain a foothold in this ecosystem. More time may be necessary, especially if we planted trees further than 2 feet apart.

Here is a video providing some additional thoughts, tips, and insights regarding maintenance.

Watering is unnecessary. Yes, some plants will die. That is ok. We should expect to see death in the range of 5–30% in the early years. Sites with ideal conditions often have mortality around 5%. Sites with especially harsh conditions might be closer to 30% mortality. This assumes adequate control over weeds and other competing vegetation. Without this control, we could see mortality approach 80%, especially on sites with very aggressive weeds (e.g., old farmland). If a sapling dies, leave it—they often make a comeback the next growing season. Saplings are impressively tough.

The best part? No bed maintenance required! We do not need to add any arborist wood chips, compost tea, or treatments of any kind. We certainly can—compost tea especially can be a helpful addition. But none of this is necessary. We also no longer need to worry about pest control services since this is a

Deer & Rabbit Protection

Here is a recommendation for protecting pocket forests from deer (I offer additional resources in the Appendix): stretch clear, deep sea fishing line between 4-foot poles positioned around the perimeter. Attach the line to each pole. We only need one line set 3 feet above ground. Though this will not physically keep deer out, the line will spook them when they touch it. This system is effective, cheap, and easy to build, which is why I love it. Here is a video showing how to make this fence:

For rabbits, the solution is a bit easier: we can set up chicken wire fence around the perimeter. It should be at least 2 feet tall, but 3 feet is better. We must anchor the fence down with sod staples (or some other method) to ensure they do not squeeze underneath.

Even if deer or rabbits eat our saplings, they often grow back. Saplings are highly resilient.

healthy ecosystem. There are exceptions, of course, especially in regard to invasive pests. For example, we may need to protect ash trees against the emerald ash borer.

As the installation matures, we should perform structural pruning on all the trees growing at the edges of the pocket forest since these tend to grow lopsided as they reach for available sunlight. We may also need to prune branches away from houses, buildings, and other structures using proper pruning cuts. This is ongoing for many years but is not unique to pocket forests. All trees in the sub/urban landscape need ongoing structural pruning.

Pending specific site conditions, we may also need to prevent aggressive vines and invasive plants from entering into the outer edges of our pocket forests.

Other Applications of This Process

We can use this pocket forest process for other applications. Here are some of my favorites:

Thickets

Native thickets are collections of shrubs and small tree species growing close to one another. They form an important ecosystem and often serve as transition zones between grasslands and forests and provide food and shelter for all sorts of insects and birds. Thickets were once far more abundant than they are now. But

173

due to hundreds of years of agriculture and development in general, these ecosystems have declined.

We can use the process for pocket forests to plant thickets. They are perfect for establishing borders and privacy screens between properties. Even with most of these plants being deciduous, they still provide privacy during the dormant season due to being planted so closely together; the plants become closely entwined. They work well under powerlines where height is a concern. We can also use thickets to provide fast and effective erosion control on hills and buffers along streets and streams.

The process is the exact same as for a pocket forest, with one modification: we only use shrubs and small tree species. Do not choose anything that grows taller than around 20 feet. I recommend that the thicket have a minimum width of 10 feet to create sufficient density.

For fun, we can also include edible species. I like to include native blueberries, native plums (Chickasaw plum is my favorite!), and sumac that I use to make sumac lemonade, a delicious and refreshing summer treat. We can invite neighbors to enjoy this food and create a social gathering place.

Filling in Shady & Wooded Areas

Many wooded areas in the sub/urban landscape have little to no understory plants as a result of over-management and predation from deer. To increase life while simultaneously decreasing the need to maintain these spaces, we can plant an understory of shade-loving shrubs and

Pests Diminish in Pocket Forests & Meadows

With a few exceptions like invasive pests, most pest issues are a symptom of a sub/urban wasteland, like plants growing in dirt instead of soil, lack of species diversity, and chemical overuse. These ecosystems contain stressed plants that emit various signals that attract pests from miles away and lack predatory insects to prey on the pests.

The key is to focus on fostering a healthy ecosystem humming with outrageous diversity both above and below ground. Within these spaces, plants tend to be healthier, which means they do not invite attacks and can defend themselves when attacks happen. There are also many predatory insects that eat pests. For example, spiders, beetles, centipedes, and mites eat young ticks. Opossums also eat ticks! In a healthy ecosystem, the idea of a "pest" nearly ceases to make sense—these are now insects participating in natural ecosystems.

small trees that thrive in these conditions. One of my favorites is the native paw-paw! Its fruit tastes like mango mixed with marshmallows and orange creamsicles.

When we dig, we need to minimize harm to existing trees, particularly their large roots. Luckily installing saplings requires minimal digging, so this is an easy issue to avoid.

Reforestation Efforts

The future of reforestation is still being written. Many methods are currently being used and tested—we have drones that drop seeds, robotic machines that plant saplings, humans planting thousands of saplings per day by hand, and many more.

The pocket forest process can also play a role. The idea is to plant islands of native pocket forests and thickets, then let those islands naturally spread out. The fancy name for this approach is *applied nucleation*. The new installations may require some form of deer protection in many areas of the United States. But once established and of a certain height, the fence can be removed and reused. The advantage of applied nucleation is that it is roughly as effective as a traditional tree-planting approach, but it requires fewer resources.

Replacing Invasive Trees & Shrubs

It is important to remove and eradicate invasive trees, shrubs, and vines for all the reasons we know. But we cannot leave that space vacant. Something will grow—presumably more invasive plants. We can use the planting methodology from this chapter to load that space with native saplings of our choosing. By densely filling this space with these plants, we reduce the likelihood that the invasive plants will return.

Combine Pocket Forest & Meadows to Create an Entire Landscape

All the methods from this chapter and the previous one combine beautifully. These systems form the colors on our canvas—we can blend them together in many ways to overhaul and blanket entire properties. For example, on one property we can:

- Plant pocket forests in the back.
- Install thickets for screening along the sides.
- Fill the understory of existing stands of trees with native saplings.
- Plant meadows from seed in the front.

Once in place, the maintenance requirements are as described in this and the previous chapter, with one minor addition: we must perform a bit of extra maintenance in the borders between the systems. For example, we may need to keep the pocket forests from advancing into the meadows and vice versa. The borders of these systems tend to be the most vulnerable to intrusion, especially when it comes to invasive species.

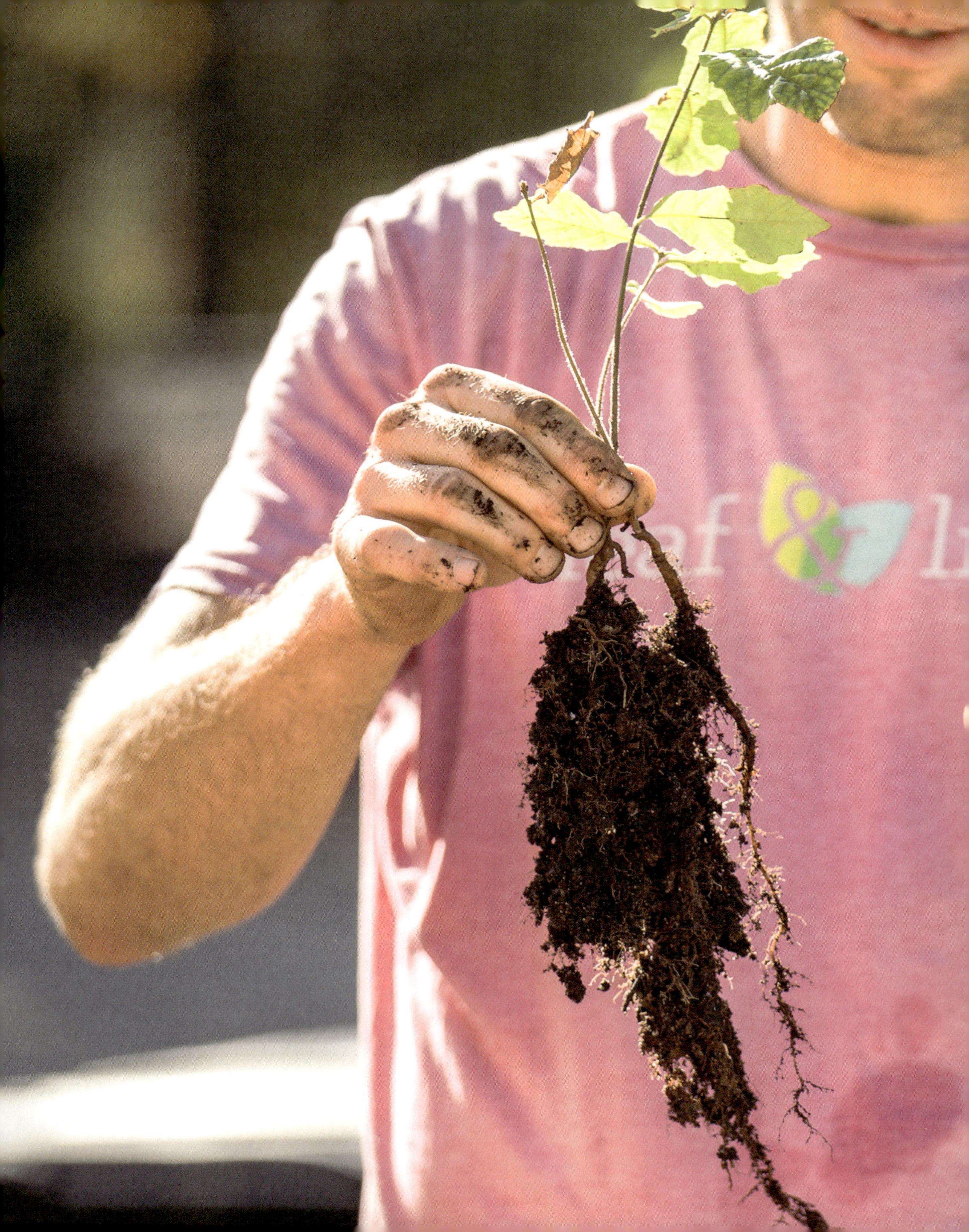

SECTION 5

lead & inspire communities to help heal earth

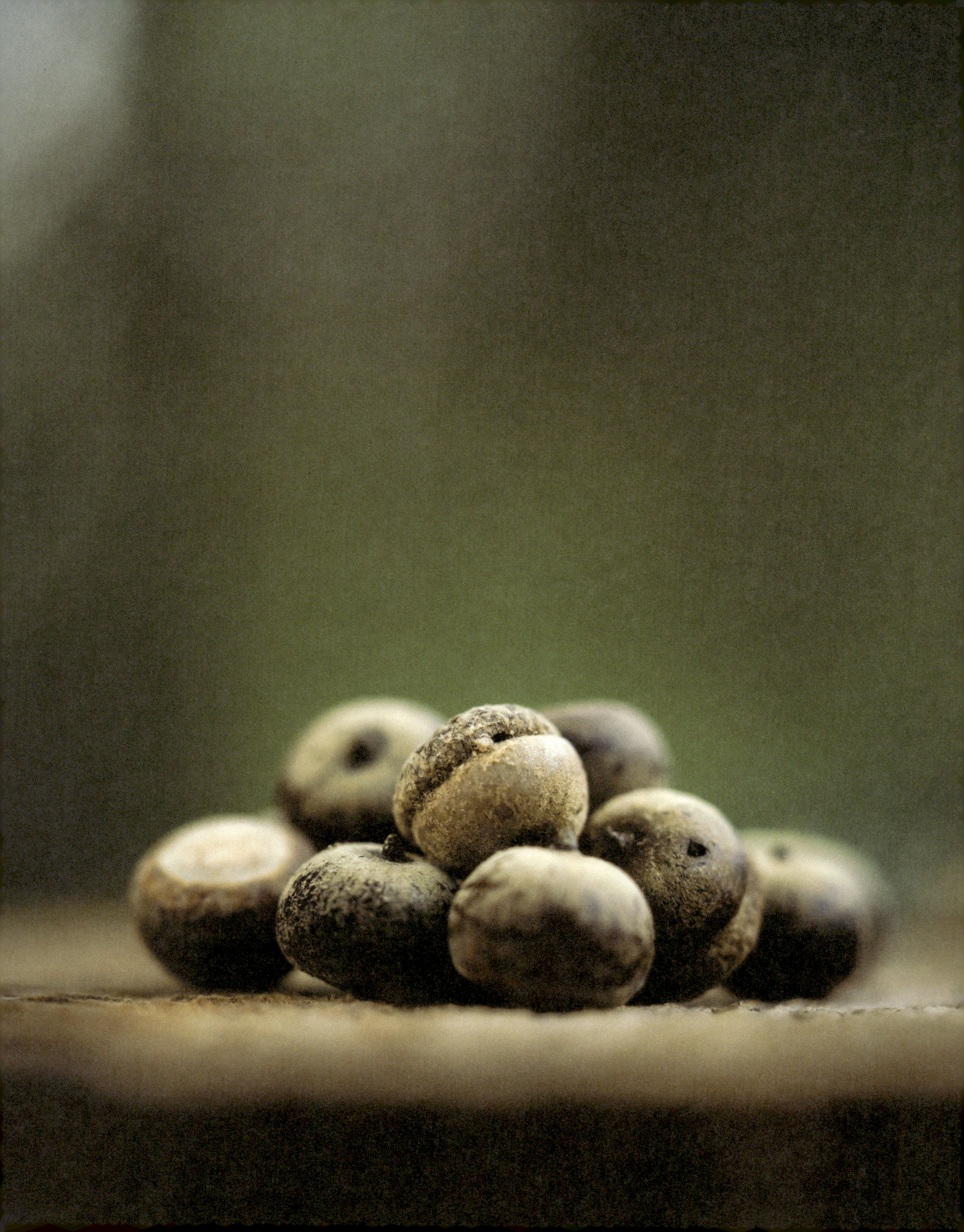

At this point, we know enough to understand and appreciate why these three points are true:

1. The way we currently manage the sub/urban landscape is creating a wasteland and harming the well-being of Earth.

2. The landscape paradigms and practices outlined in this book do the opposite—they help heal Earth.

3. When we work to help heal Earth, we save time and money because we are working with natural systems instead of against them.

If we make these changes where we live, work, and play we are actively helping change landscape paradigms from those that create an ecological wasteland to those that help heal Earth and create wonder. We are leading by example. According to Donella Meadows in her book *Thinking in Systems*, shifting paradigms is one of the most powerful ways that we can generate change.

For those who want to help shift paradigms even more, let me introduce Project Pando, which aims to do exactly this. At Project Pando we work with volunteers to collect seeds from native trees and shrubs, raise them into saplings, and give them away for free. This idea can also be applied to native flowers and grasses. This has all sorts of wonderful outcomes, like expanding the supply and variety of native species while bringing people together through a shared sense of purpose and community. But there is a deeper, more potent magic at work: collecting seeds and raising trees changes how we view them, which shifts our thinking and behaviors.

What follows next is the culmination of what we have learned thus far. There will be many future versions. We will continue to iterate and innovate because this project is constantly evolving as we learn more.

An Overview of The Project Pando Model

During my career I have donated time and expertise to helping various non-profit tree-planting organizations here in Raleigh and the surrounding cities. I have learned firsthand of their many challenges. Their primary ones are:

1. Tree planting efforts are often limited by small budgets and traditional nursery trees are expensive.

2. Volunteer planting efforts are limited by the technical expertise required to plant traditional nursery trees, which we learned about in Chapter 10. The trees often die due to lack of proper planting.

3. The ones that survive often die from lack of water since it is challenging to organize volunteer tree watering efforts.

One day it occurred to me: why not grow trees for these planting organizations for free, thus bypassing their budget limitations? While we are at it, why not attempt to shift away from traditional nursery trees toward saplings to eliminate the majority of the technical planting requirements and watering needs? Saplings would also result in healthier mature trees. Better yet, we could do this work together as a community! With funding from Leaf & Limb and space from Triangle Land Conservancy, a group of amazing volunteers, colleagues, and I banded together to turn this idea into reality.

We work with our community to collect seeds from native trees that grow in this area. Then we plant all the seeds in leaf mold in what are known as *air-pruning boxes* (we will learn more about these later in this section). Using this approach, we can grow many trees in a very small area.

A 4-ft × 2-ft box can easily yield 200 saplings, and far more for some species. Better yet, it produces saplings with well-formed root systems that are healthy, hardy, and ready for a future in the sub/urban landscape, where there is often more dirt than soil. After growing for one to two years, we extract the saplings from the air-pruning boxes and give them away.

This model has many benefits. The most impressive thus far has been the collective power that comes from working as a community to collect native seeds. By teaching folks how to identify native trees and shrubs, and by providing them with the information and systems necessary to support their efforts, we have been able to tap into the collective power that comes from many people working together. Essentially this is the idea that "many hands make light work." This has encouraging implications for other organizations and projects aimed at helping plant trees,

More Information About Project Pando

By now, you know a bit about Project Pando. Let me tell you more. Some of our specific goals are to:

- Create a robust supply of free native trees, shrubs, and other plants.

- Offer free education about why native trees, flowers, and soil matter, and how to care for them.

- Increase the genetic diversity of trees being planted in sub/urban spaces.

- Bring people together to strengthen ties in our community.

- Provide a fun way for folks to develop a closer relationship with trees, flowers, soil, and other life.

It has also been our goal to develop a set of helpful plans and guidelines that other organizations and communities can use to mimic what we are doing at Project Pando. I am happy to report that this section of the book contains these plans! My hope is that you and others will use this information to grow native trees and shrubs with your friends and community. If you want to learn more—or would like to get involved with Project Pando—please scan this QR code:

grasslands, and perform other forms of ecological restoration.

Another benefit is that we can grow many different native species of trees and shrubs that are from this immediate area, or an adjacent area. We can think of these as being hyper-native. A given species adapts to its local growing conditions. For example, a white oak has a native range across much of the eastern United States. But a seed from a white oak in North Carolina and one from New York are not the same—they have local adaptations and genetic variations. The seed from New York is better suited to grow there, and the seed from North Carolina is better suited to grow in NC. Species continuously evolve to match their specific growing conditions. Any seeds collected from native trees that grow in a certain area, and that are then planted in the same area, will have the best chance of long-term survival.

It also infuses more genetic variation back into the sub/urban landscape. Many traditional nursery trees are clones of one another, which means they are genetically identical. Sometimes this is due to propagation techniques and other times it is due to the plant being trademarked. This leaves these cloned trees vulnerable to a pest that could wipe out the entire population, which makes our sub/urban canopy less resilient and stable. Planting saplings grown with the Project Pando model does the opposite—it increases the resilience and stability of our canopy in the face of an uncertain future.

The Need for Native Seed Collectors

Collecting native seeds is a rare skill that is becoming increasingly important. A study published in the journal *Bioscience* outlined a troubling bottleneck: nurseries in the US do not grow nearly enough native trees to support the many ambitious tree-planting laws, acts, and initiatives aimed at collectively planting billions of trees. The issue is that we need more native trees and shrubs to reforest areas that have been ecologically destroyed but we do not have enough seeds to grow them. Worse yet, obtaining native seeds is not as easy as picking up a catalog and ordering them. Many are commercially unavailable. Those that are available are typically offered in small numbers. Why? The demand for native trees and shrubs has historically been somewhere between low and non-existent **Long story short: we need more native seeds.** The Project Pando model can help with this. Here is more information on this topic:

lead & inspire communities to help heal earth

Most important of all, this work supports all the goals outlined in this book while strengthening the bonds within our community and between all life—trees, humans, and insects alike. We experience joy and learn new things. Slowly, our hearts, minds, and paradigms begin to shift.

Here is an overview of the steps necessary to use this model. Please note that I have attempted to focus on the easiest and most essential components of this model to make it as fun and enjoyable as possible to get started. There are many opportunities to add complexity, some of which I will link to via QR codes.

1. Learn to identify native plants.
2. Build air-pruning boxes and fill them.
3. Find space to grow saplings.
4. Collect native seeds.
5. Plant seeds.
6. Nurture the saplings—then give them away!

The Joy of Project Pando

Project Pando has been one of the most fun and rewarding endeavors in which I have had the privilege of participating. When I stop for a moment to reflect, so many wonderful memories flood my mind. I think about all the joyous times I have spent working alongside volunteers from the community, chatting away under sunny, blue skies. I think of the thrill of overcoming challenges, the excitement of finding rare seeds, and the joy that comes with handing somebody a young tree that I tended to from infancy. In my mind I can envision seeds slowly transforming to eager saplings, I can hear the cheerful noises of my kids playing in the background, and I can feel my heart swelling so full of happiness I thought it might burst. Pando volunteer days—especially with my colleagues at Leaf & Limb—are some of my absolute favorites.

I also cannot help but to think of my Grandmama, who passed some years ago. She had a majestic white oak in her front yard that predated the Revolutionary War. When she was alive and I was young, we spent a lot of time under that tree. So much of my love for trees and my Grandmama was inextricably tied to that dear old oak. After she passed, her land was sold and developed. That lovely oak was destroyed. But before that occurred, my dad and I collected thousands of acorns that we raised and gave away through Project Pando. To this day, I still receive notes and updates from folks who received one of those trees (we called them Beryl's Beauties in homage to Grandmama). I also planted many at my home and in various locations around town. I keep a close eye on all those baby white oaks. Hearing the stories and seeing the saplings grow has helped me process the grief of my Grandmama's passing.

Perhaps this is the core of why I love growing trees—they embody new life, joy, and hope for the future.

Step 1: Learn to Identify Native Plants

To begin, please revisit Chapter 10, where I outline some strategies for learning what species are native to a given area. The next step is learning to identify those species. The best place to learn this skill is from a tree ID book. They provide processes and resources that work well. I have included some of my favorite tree ID books in the Appendix.

The good news is that learning tree ID is a skill that builds on itself. The first 10 species are the hardest. The more we learn, the faster we learn because patterns and similarities emerge. Here are some tips and ideas for how to proceed with developing this new skill.

- Commit to learning one new species each day, week, or month. Regularity helps.

- Have fun! Integrate this learning process into afternoon walks with loved ones or pets. Or turn it into a scavenger hunt or a game of bingo.

- Follow the processes outlined in the plant ID books—they work.

- Visit local arboretums and botanical gardens. Many of the species are labeled, which makes learning all that much easier.

- Join some local groups of plant enthusiasts. Look online at Reddit, Meetup, and in various social media groups.

- Check with local parks and preserves. Many of these groups even host tree ID walks.

- We all regularly get stumped at times—even the experts. Avoid becoming frustrated and move on. The key is to have fun and keep learning.

- Use apps to help, such as iNaturalist.

For those already familiar with tree and shrub ID, consider hosting educational tree ID walks. We began hosting these as part of Project Pando and they quickly became popular. They are a great place to meet like-minded people who want to learn more about trees. We also collect seeds along the way when they are available.

Once we know what plants are native and how to identify them, we can decide what we want to grow. One approach is to simply start collecting the native seeds we encounter during our daily routines. For example, what do we find when walking around our neighborhood, outside at work, or at the local park?

Or we may want to grow trees for a specific purpose or goal (e.g., to fill a wetland area). If yes, we will need to do further research about the various species that meet our goals. There are many plant databases and resources that can help with this task, per earlier recommendations in Chapter 10.

Step 2: Build Air-Pruning Boxes and Fill Them

As mentioned earlier in this section, our preferred method for growing trees and shrubs is using air-pruning boxes. This is an open frame built with wood on the sides and a wire mesh on the bottom. It is able to hold a large quantity of leaf mold for growing seeds. **The essential feature of an air-pruning box is the bottom: it's a wire mesh.** When roots grow through the mesh, they encounter air, and the root tips dry out, i.e., they are "pruned" by the air. This causes the plant to produce new branching roots, leading to a young sapling with extensive root development and excellent root structure. In addition, they are cheap, easy to build, grow lots of trees in a small space, and provide flexibility about where trees can be grown.

There are many ways to make air-pruning boxes. This means we have flexibility in terms of the size of box we build and the process we use, so long as the end result can hold a growing substrate and has a wire mesh at the bottom. Here's how we build our air-pruning boxes at Project Pando. Per usual, here is a video first, followed by written instructions.

Here are the tools and supplies we need for one air-pruning box:

- 12 feet of 2" × 8" treated lumber (There is some concern about whether the treated lumber might affect the saplings, but we have never had any issues. We can choose other lumber, but it must be rot-resistant.)
- 12 feet of 2" × 6" treated lumber
- 4 feet of 2" × 2" treated lumber
- Eight 3" angle brackets
- Four 3" T brackets
- Approximately fifty 1-¼" deck screws
- 4 feet of 2-ft tall ½" × ½" hardware cloth
- Hammer
- Fence staples or industrial staple gun with matching staples
- Power drill with screwdriver bits (or screwdriver if a drill is not an option)
- Eight bricks or four cinder blocks
- Miter saw, circular saw, or hand saw for cutting lumber
- Offset snips for cutting wire
- OPTIONAL: #8 2-inch wood deck screws for additional support

Before we begin, here is an overview: our box frames are 4-ft long by 2-ft wide, using 2" × 8" treated lumber. In addition, we place a second frame (we will call this a *riser*) on top of the box frame. This riser can be removed, which makes it easier to extract the saplings when they are ready. It is made from 2" × 6" lumber and helps increase the rooting area and water retention within the box. The frames are connected using brackets and screws. We attach 2" × 2" crossbars at the base of the box to help hold the growing substrate.

Now it's time to build the box. Here are details:

1. Let's begin by cutting our pieces:
   - Two 4-foot sections of 2" × 8"
   - Two 4-foot sections of 2" × 6"
   - Two 21-inch sections of 2" × 8"
   - Two 21-inch sections of 2" × 6"
   - Two 21-inch sections of 2" × 2"
   - PRO TIP: Sometimes stores that sell lumber will cut it to specified lengths for free.

2. Attach the 2" × 8" boards to form a rectangle frame with the shorter lengths on the inside of the longer lengths so that the entire box is 2-ft by 4-ft. In other words, the 21" sections are attached inside of the 4-ft sections. Use 3" angle brackets with 1-¼" deck screws on the inside the frames.

3. Repeat this process for the 2" × 6" boards. We now have two frames.

4. It's ok if the frames are a little wobbly. But if we prefer less wobble and want the added support, we can drill the #8 2-inch wood deck screws into the outside corners of the box. Drive them through the outside of the 4-foot section into the end of the 21" section. Use two screws per corner per frame.

5. We add two 21-inch 2" × 2" crossbars to the 2" × 8 main box frame to provide additional support for the hardware cloth. Space each approximately one-third of the distance across the box so they are evenly distributed. We use 3" T-brackets with 1-¼" deck screws to attach these crossbars to the inside of the bottom of the frame.

6. Once this is done, we should have a reasonably sturdy frame. It is ok to have some wiggle. But we do not want too much; the frame needs to be strong enough to hold 100+ pounds of leaf mold and trees.

7. The final step is to attach the screen to the bottom of the 2" × 8" frame (NOTE: the bottom is the side with the 2" × 2" crossbars). We use a product called hardware cloth. The hardware cloth we use is ½" × ½". We can firmly attach it to the bottom of the box using fence staples placed along the outside of the frame and along the crossbars. We typically use at least 20 of these staples per 4-ft × 2-ft box. If in doubt, use more because the substrate is heavy. We don't want our screens to fall off during the growing season.

8. If we are building a lot of boxes, we may want to consider using an industrial staple gun powered by compressed air to save time and effort.

9. We do not add center beams or hardware cloth to the 2" × 6" frame. This is the riser and does not need additional construction.

10. Now set the riser on top of the box—we are done!

lead & inspire communities to help heal earth

Before we fill our box with leaf mold, place it on bricks, cinder blocks, or some alternative option. The bottom of the box should be at least 5" above ground, though more is fine. The blocks should be located at each corner of the box and must not cover up the hardware cloth on the bottom. Remember, the defining trait of the air-pruning box is the gap of air underneath that will air prune roots and generate extensive root development with excellent structure.

Next, we fill the box with leaf mold and gently compress it to minimize future settling. We prefer leaf mold because it mimics the leaf litter in a forest, which is where many seeds grow naturally. We also prefer leaf mold because we have access to a large supply of it from our local municipality. But there are other substrates we can use, such as compost and soil.

If we have a lot of squirrels, mice, deer or other animals that love to eat seeds and saplings, we need to make a cage to protect them. Here are instructions for how to make a protective cage.

For the protective cage we need the following items:

- Four 45.5"-length sections of ¾" PVC pipe
- Eight 21.5"-length sections of ¾" PVC pipe
- NOTE: When we add PVC pipe connectors to both sides of the PVC pipe, we add an extra 2.5 inches of pipe, which is why we are cutting these shorter than 4 feet and 2 feet.
- Eight ¾" × ¾" 90° side outlet elbow connectors
- Chicken wire that is 2 feet wide
- Offset snips
- Zip ties
- Something to cut PVC, e.g., hand saw, power saw, PVC cutters

We begin by cutting the PVC into appropriate lengths. Then we connect the sections with the elbow connectors to create the box shape. First, we make two square frames using the 21.5" sections. Then we connect them with the four 45.5" sections. We don't use any glue with these connections. They are sturdy enough without it. Once we have our rectangular PVC box frame, we add the chicken wire as follows:

1. Roll out the chicken wire on the ground. Use bricks or something sturdy to keep it from rolling back on itself.

2. Lay the PVC box frame on its side on top of the chicken wire. The 2-foot height of the frame should match the 2-foot width of the chicken wire.

3. Connect one edge of the chicken wire to one of the 2-foot PVC sections with zip ties.

4. Roll the outside of the PVC box frame along the chicken wire and bend the wire around each edge of the frame. This lightly holds the chicken wire in place around the outer 2-foot edges of the frame.

5. Secure the chicken wire to the PVC box frame with zip ties. Make sure to use lots of zip ties because squirrels will climb through small gaps. The sides of the frame have now been covered. Cut off excess chicken wire using the offset snips.

6. Now we need to cover one remaining panel of the PVC box frame, which will be the top of the protective cage. Cut out a section of chicken wire for the top and secure it in place with zip ties.

There we have it! The protective cage is complete. Set it on top of the air-pruning box to keep the seeds safe from predation.

lead & inspire communities to help heal earth

Step 3: Find Space to Grow Saplings

There is plenty of room to grow saplings all over the sub/urban landscape. This is part of the beauty of air-pruning boxes—they allow us to grow in small areas, such as a common area in an HOA, our home, on an outdoor patio at a local restaurant, outside an office building, or in a community garden. At Project Pando we have set up air-pruning boxes on many different sites. We have partnered with Triangle Land Conservancy to grow many boxes full of trees on land they hold in conservation. We grow trees behind Leaf & Limb's office on a concrete pad and in the woods behind the pad. We grow trees in air-pruning boxes on volunteers' driveways and patios. We also grow trees at local schools with the help of students. The possibilities are endless. The main considerations for any site are:

Water: We do not need to water our trees very often, if at all. But we may need to water them at some point, especially in the event of an extended heat wave or drought. Therefore, it is best to choose a site where we have access to water if necessary.

Enjoyment: People love following the progress of growing saplings! Set up chairs, benches, or stump rounds nearby to encourage folks to engage. Include an educational sign if it makes sense. The air-pruning boxes at Leaf & Limb have become a central point of interest, observation, and conversation for all of us. It's so fun and interesting to follow along for a growing season. We even attracted a growing family of anoles who now call this space home!

Sun/Shade: While many tree saplings can be grown in full sun, they often benefit from some shade. Shade is especially good if we are not able to water our saplings very often because it helps reduce water loss during the growing season. Therefore, I recommend placing the air-pruning boxes under the dappled shade of large trees if possible. Plus, this is how they often grow in the wild. This can certainly vary by species, though—some species will do well in full sun and even prefer it.

If natural shade is not an option, we can make our own with shade cloth. This can be attached on top of the protective cage using zip ties or we can build a simple structure to hold the shade cloth. Here is an easy way to build a shade structure:

We need the following supplies. How much of each will depend on the size of the shade structure we choose to build.

- ❏ Bungee cords
- ❏ Shade cloth
- ❏ 5-gallon buckets
- ❏ Instant concrete or gravel
- ❏ 2" × 4" treated lumber in 8-ft sections
- ❏ Hooks/loops that can be attached to the lumber to hold the shade cloth

Here are the steps:

1. Attach the hook or loop to one end of the 2" × 4" treated lumber.
2. Position this 8-ft section of 2" × 4" treated lumber upright in the center of a 5-gallon bucket. Make sure the hook/loop is on the side opposite the bucket.
3. Pour concrete or pack in gravel around the lumber to hold it firmly in place within the bucket.
4. You have now created a support beam. Repeat this process for as many support beams as necessary.
5. Position the support beams around and between the air-pruning boxes and drape the cloth across the 2" × 4" ends. Use bungees to secure the shade cloth to the hooks/loops.

After we build this structure and set it up, see how it reacts to the wind. Depending on the site conditions, it may need additional weight or support. For example, we may need to anchor each support beam to the ground with lines attached to tent stakes. We can also add weight to the support beams in the form of sandbags or cinder blocks. If digging is an option, we even partially bury each bucket for an extra-firm hold.

On a related note, we subjected some of our saplings to extreme growing conditions to test their ability to withstand heat, sun, and drought. We set them up on a south-facing patio with a white wall in the background, which is as hot a setting as we can create here in Raleigh. We provided them with no supplemental watering outside of normal rainfall, and we did not provide them with any shade. The results were impressive. This goes to show that even without any care, many saplings still grow. Here is a video featuring this experiment:

Step 4: Collect Native Seeds

Seed formation follows flowering. Seeds mature through most of the growing season, though many are not ready until early in the dormant season. They usually start out with a green color, which means they are not ripe and thus not ready for collection. When they are ripe, they often change to a red, orange, yellow, or brown color. There are exceptions to this, of course. Typically, we know seeds are ripe when they begin falling to the ground.

Our first step is to determine when various species are ready for collection. The precise timing for when seeds become available only matters if there are specific species we want to collect. In this case, we must research when each of our target species produces ripe seeds. Research can include reading books, consulting resources, and searching for answers online. It can also include visiting a tree or shrub multiple times to make observations. If we are collecting seeds at random, we can skip the research and collect whatever we happen to find.

Here is a calendar we use at Project Pando to help guide collection times. This can vary based on many factors, such as rain.

An Annual Seed Drive

To help promote a boost of seed collection at a time when many seeds are available, we hold an annual native seed drive at the start of the dormant season. This means we spend extra time spreading the word that we are collecting seeds. We send out newsletters, make announcements on social media, ask like-minded organizations to share the details with their members, hold events, reach out to news organizations, and more. We provide volunteers with easy access to helpful information, such as the seed identification database and other resources listed and linked in this section of the book. We also set up a network of seed drop-off sites throughout our collection area, generally at volunteers' homes and businesses. For each site we install a sign indicating this is a drop-off location and place a large plastic bin in an obvious spot near the sign. People drop their bags of seeds in the bin and fill out a small form that we store within the bin. On this form, we ask for contact information, the species if known, when the seeds were collected, and where they were found.

Once we know when the seeds are available, the next task is to find trees bearing those seeds. Again, this assumes there are specific species we hope to collect. Here are some general tips for finding these trees and shrubs:

- Explore nearby local, state, and national parks. Land conservancies are another great option. Since part of the objective is to increase genetic diversity, looking for species that are growing in the wild is optimal.

- Older trees are generally better than younger ones. It is very exciting when we can collect from old species that predate the clear-cutting that took place across much of the United States during the 1700s and 1800s. Many states and cities will call these "Champion Trees" or "Heritage Trees" or "Historic Trees." There are often databases available that list where these trees are located. These are often great places to collect seeds (with permission, of course).

- The sub/urban landscape can also be a good place to find species, especially at college campuses, churchyards, old cemeteries, public green spaces, and along roads with uncleared forest.

- Check with local arboretums, botanical gardens, native nurseries, and science museums. These organizations may allow us to collect seeds from their specimens—and some may even have labels to make ID easy!

- We can use apps to help with seed collection. For example, we can use the search function on iNaturalist to find specific species.

- Some organizations—especially museums, municipalities, and universities—may already have tree maps for their own in-house purposes. There are several such organizations here in North Carolina that allow us to use their maps to collect seeds from specific trees.

- Look for like-minded groups on the internet, social media, Meetup, Reddit, etc., that are into trees and plants in general. They can often help.

As we find specific species, we should document where we found them if we want to collect from them again in the future. We can do this in many ways. At Project Pando we create digital maps using Google Earth or ArcGIS that show the location of various species of native trees and shrubs. This makes it very easy for folks to help collect seeds from specific plants.

When the time is right and we know where the trees and shrubs are located, it's time to collect the seeds—*woo hoo!* Here are some helpful tips and considerations:

- If we are collecting seeds directly from the plant (versus those that have fallen to the ground), an easy way to determine if the seed is ripe is to feel how easily it releases from the plant. If it detaches easily with little effort, it is likely ripe. If we must pull and tug with any sort of force, the seed is not likely to be ripe.

- Collecting a seed slightly before it is fully ripe is not necessarily a bad thing. Especially for seeds that birds love, this may be the only way we can collect that species. It may decrease how many grow into saplings, but we are still likely to have some good results from these slightly unripe seeds.

- For acorns, pecans, walnuts, and other nuts, we can buy tools that allow us to collect them without bending over. If we are collecting a lot of these types of seeds, these devices will save future back pain and speed up the process.

- If we are collecting seeds that require us to be on our hands and knees, I recommend getting knee protection. There are all sorts of knee pads and cushioned devices made for gardeners and carpenters that we can find online.

- Windborne seeds are often easy to collect from hard surfaces. Examples include along street curbs, sidewalks, and on decks where the wind blows them in corners.

- Many trees and shrubs go through a process called *masting*, where they produce an abundance of seeds in some years, and very few in other years.

- We can lay tarps, nets, baskets, cages, and so forth to help catch seeds. This is especially useful in a forest setting, where it can be very hard to distinguish seeds from the leaves.

- When we are collecting seeds, be careful to minimize damage to nearby plants, fungi, and other life. We should aim to collect seeds responsibly with little to no impact!

- Remember to leave some seeds in place—many birds, raccoons, and other creatures rely on them for survival.

After collecting seeds, we may need to temporarily store them. For this, we can place them in a sealed bag and store them in a refrigerator. For bigger seeds like acorns or black walnuts, we can store them in buckets or other large containers in a cool, dark place. Basements or crawl spaces work well. The key to these storage options is the word "temporarily," which generally means weeks but not

lead & inspire communities to help heal earth

months or years. For long-term storage we may need to use different methods.

Step 5: Plant Seeds

At this point, we should plant the seeds. The easiest method, which generally follows the natural life cycle of many seeds, is to simply plant them as soon as possible after collection. Before we begin planting, there are some simple things we can do to filter out dead seeds and increase how many trees we grow. Here they are:

- Inspect the seeds. Do they look plump and have a solid color? Or are they black and shriveled? The former are likely good candidates to be planted and the latter are not.

- Pick a few samples from the seeds and break them open or cut them in half. Is the inside light green or white? Or is it black, shriveled, empty, or hollow? The former are likely good candidates to be planted and the latter are not.

- Perform something called the *float test*, which is when we put our seeds in a container of water. Do they sink or float? The former are likely good candidates to be planted and the latter are not. This test is especially important for nuts and acorns. Note that the float test does not always work for some species. If in doubt, open them up for closer inspection.

LIVE SEED ON LEFT, DEAD SEED ON RIGHT

When planting, we place the seeds directly onto the top of the leaf mold in our air-pruning boxes. There is a lot of flexibility on how we space seeds, but in general it is best to sow lots of seeds. Spread them out so they create a roughly even layer. Put a thin layer of leaf mold over them—we want this layer of leaf mold to be about as deep as the seeds are large. We can also add an optional thin layer of arborist wood chips. Once this is done, we should place cages on top of the air-pruning boxes if we are worried about predation.

When we have plenty of seeds, we should only grow one species per air-pruning box. However, if we have limited quantities of seeds, we can sow two or more species per box by leaving a little bit of unplanted space between the different types of seeds. In all cases, we should attach weatherproof labels to each box that contain the name and planting date for the species within that box (or use another record-keeping method of our choosing).

Finally, our seeds can become exposed over time, especially after the first several rain events. If this happens, cover them again with more leaf mold.

Step 6: Nurture the Saplings—Then Give Them Away!

The next step is to decide how much we are able or willing to care for the growing saplings. They don't need much, but some attention will deliver higher yields and larger saplings. The main objective is to provide some water whenever conditions become too dry. To determine if the saplings need water, grab a pinch of leaf mold from below the surface and evaluate the moisture. Is there any discernible moisture?

Processing Seeds to Increase Yields of Saplings

There are many things we can do between collecting seeds and planting them if we want to increase the number of saplings that we can grow. We call these acts *seed processing*. Many of the seed processing options mimic the natural life cycle of each species. Be warned, though, that seed processing can generate dizzying complexity. But for some goals and organizations, the additional effort is worth it. For those who want to learn more about seed processing, here is additional information:

Or is it dry and flaky? If it is dry, water the saplings thoroughly, until we see water dripping from the bottom of the box. If in doubt, err on the side of too much water since all the excess will drain out of the bottom. We should only water on an as-needed basis.

Other care options include removing unwanted trees and weeds when they appear. Seeds from nearby trees often take root in the boxes. We can also douse the saplings in compost tea one or multiple times during the growing season if we have some available. This is not necessary but will boost their health.

We leave the saplings in air-pruning boxes for at least one growing season. If they are small after one year, we can leave them in for another growing season. The term "small" is subjective but we usually draw the line at less than three inches. Generally, we do not leave saplings in a box longer than two growing seasons, though there are some slow-growing species that may need a third growing season.

Now comes the fun part—unboxing the saplings! Since the dormant season is the best time to plant, we typically unbox them for projects and giveaways during this season. It is best to do this as close to these events as possible to minimize the amount of time we need to store the saplings outside of the air-pruning box. **Our goal should be to move the saplings from the air-pruning box to their permanent destination within the ground as quickly as possible.**

Here is a video showing how to remove the saplings:

Begin by removing the riser from off the top of the box. This exposes the upper portion of the sapling roots. We can slowly wiggle our hands along the inside edge of the box until we can gently lift what will likely be a chunk of intertwined saplings. Once we have a chunk of intertwined saplings out of the box, carefully and gently tease the saplings apart from one another. The key is to move slowly, but firmly. They will untangle from one another. The goal is to minimize tearing and breaking the roots. We should only remove the trees that we need and leave the rest in the air-pruning box. If saplings remain in the air-pruning box, we should cover their exposed roots with extra leaf mold.

With all these saplings we have lots of options for what we can do with them next. We can plant them, offer them to friends, family, volunteers, and organizations that need them, and we can host tree giveaway events. Whatever we choose, the key is to ensure the saplings are planted as soon as possible. We should avoid placing them in pots for more than several weeks. Otherwise, the roots will become malformed within the pot.

If the saplings are headed to a giveaway or tree-planting event we may need to store them temporarily. We can gather them in bundles and cover their roots with soil, leaf mold, compost, or the leftover substrate from the boxes. This is called *heeling* the plants. Heel them in bundles in the ground, bags, or pots to help retain vital moisture. The goal is to keep the roots damp and cool—but not too cold. We must prevent the roots from freezing for multiple days. For the sake of logistical ease, we will often store set amounts of a given species (e.g., 50 saplings) in larger pots filled with substrate from the boxes and additional leaf mold. We always label the pots with a Listo grease pencil (they write on most anything). If the saplings are being planted, we can extract them from the bucket and plant them directly in the ground. If they are being given away, we can place a sapling (or 20) in a used plastic grocery bag and then secure the bag in place by fastening a used grocery twist tie around the base of the sapling, above the roots. This method helps maintain moisture in the roots, makes transport easy with little mess, and makes use of an existing waste stream.

One final pro tip: the substrate that remains after extracting the saplings is pure gold! We have found through tests and observations made through a microscope that this substrate has an incredibly rich soil ecosystem. It is an ideal compost that can also be turned into a compost tea solution for future saplings.

What Next?

It is important to remember that the core of this work is meant to be fun: this is a group of people collecting native seeds, raising trees, enjoying each other's company, and in the process, helping heal Earth. Fun can be simple: collect some seeds with friends and put them in old pots full of leaves. Plant whatever grows or share the saplings with friends and family. Or throw some native seeds on the ground to see what springs to life.

Fun can also be more involved and complex: work to maximize yields by focusing on seed processing and tinkering with every element of the growth process. Keep meticulous records and observations then use those to further improve future yields. Invest in equipment and increase the number of trees growing. Generate enough saplings for many pocket forests and thickets throughout the community. Apply for grants and funding. Use this same model to collect, grow, and distribute seeds for native meadows. Develop partnerships with like-minded organizations and municipalities. Host volunteer events and tree ID walks. Provide educational events regarding

lead & inspire communities to help heal earth

all the topics in this book. Host tree-giveaways and tree-planting events for the surrounding community. Find ways to engage groups and stakeholders that may not otherwise be interested in trees. Use this model to increase food resilience. The possibilities are endless!

Both journeys—and all the many other possibilities—are steps in the right direction. Whether they result in one more native tree being planted or changing the paradigms of an entire community, they help heal Earth. That is the beauty of Project Pando; amid all the fun, we find ourselves connecting more deeply with trees, soil, and other life. As we learn and develop new relationships, our paradigms slowly change. It has been truly inspirational to watch as people from all walks of life find joy and "ah-ha!" moments through their work with Project Pando. Folks go from knowing absolutely nothing about trees to being catalysts of change in their neighborhoods, schools, and workplaces.

My hope is that this is the beginning of a collective effort that connects many communities in different areas. Should you choose to use this model, I hope that you consider helping expand this work by adding contributions relevant to your area. With enough participation and input, we can create resources applicable to many regions and growing zones.

A Growing Database of Helpful Information for Project Pando Volunteers

We are creating a database of information to help with seed identification, research for various species, and more. We share these with volunteers and use them during events. This is a growing body of work and we hope that in the future it will contain information for native plants in many different regions (please let us know if you would like to help build this database for your region). Scan this QR code to access this information:

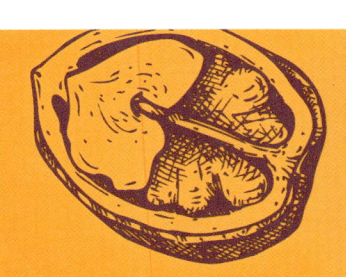

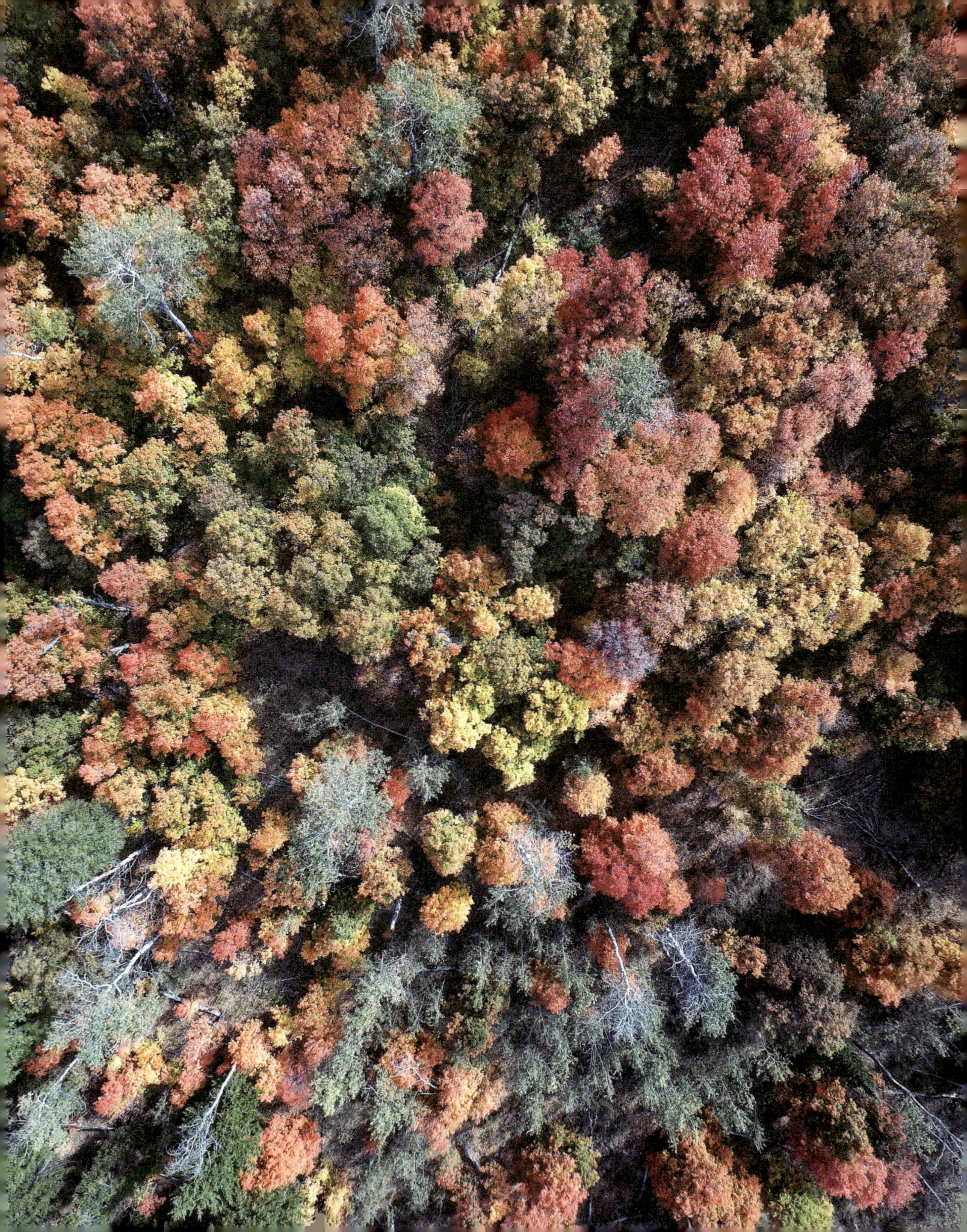

in closing

Before I go, I want to share an excerpt from Thích Nhất Hạnh's book *Love Letter to the Earth*:

> At this very moment, the Earth is above you, below you, all around you, and even inside you. The Earth is everywhere. You may be used to thinking of the Earth as only the ground beneath your feet. But the water, the sea, the sky, and everything around us comes from the Earth. Everything outside us and everything inside us comes from the Earth. We often forget that the planet we are living on has given us all the elements that make up our bodies. The water in our flesh, our bones, and all the microscopic cells inside our bodies all come from the Earth and are part of the Earth. The Earth is not the environment we live in. We are the Earth and we are always carrying her within us.
>
> Realizing this, we can see that the Earth is truly alive. We are a living, breathing manifestation of this beautiful and generous planet. Knowing this, we can begin to transform our relationship to the Earth. We can begin to walk differently and to care for her differently. We will fall completely in love with the Earth. When we are in love with someone or something, there is no separation between ourselves and the person or thing we love. We do whatever we can for them and this brings us great joy and nourishment. That is the relationship each of us can have with the Earth. That is the relationship each of us must have with the Earth if the Earth is to survive, and if we are to survive as well.

Wherever we go next, let's take time to enjoy the beauty and wonder of life all around. It is marvelous. Let's sit under a tree for a while, watch a butterfly feed on a flower, and enjoy the antics of a bat at sunset. Let's pause, take a deep breath, and feel the Sun's warmth on our face. To be born on Earth—the only planet we know of with life—and to be able to participate in this crazy thing we call consciousness is one of the most improbable events of all time. **We won the galactic lottery, my friend.**

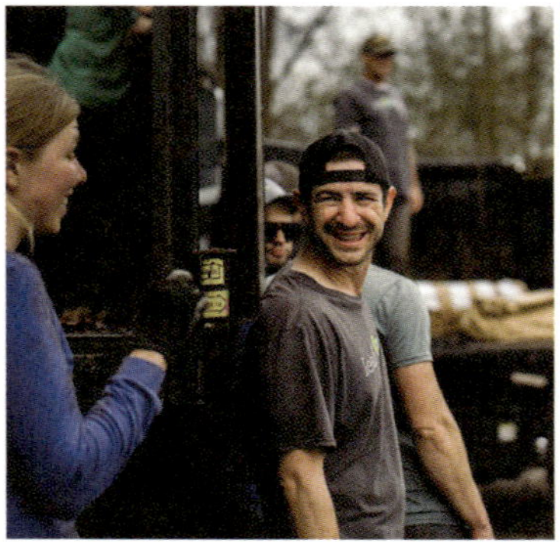
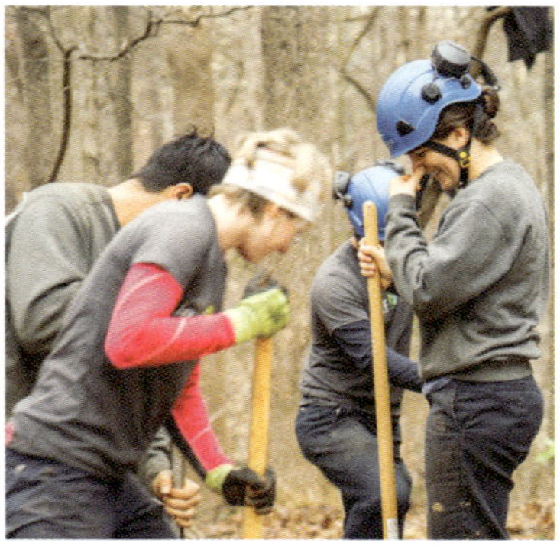
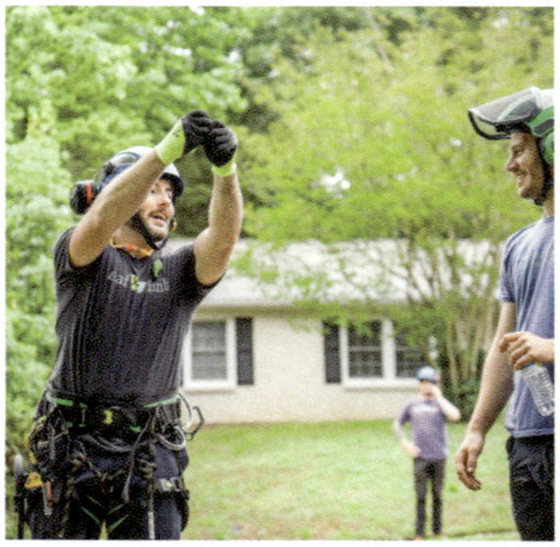
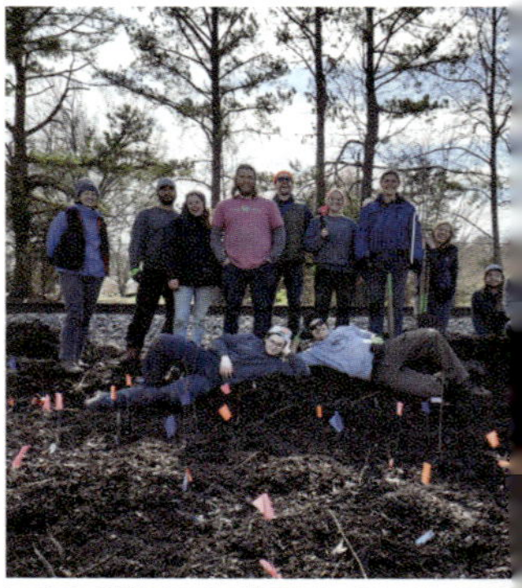
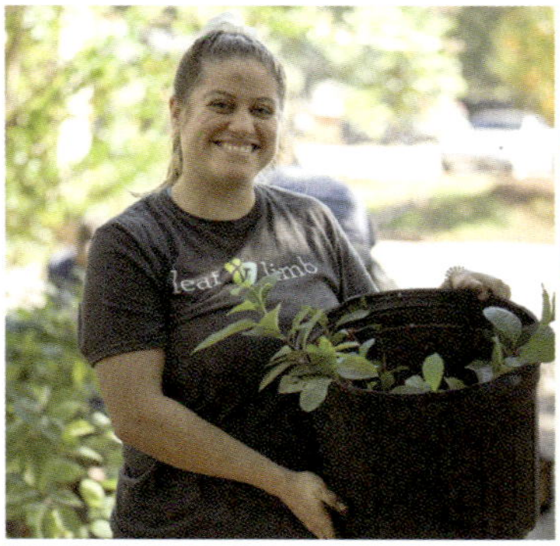
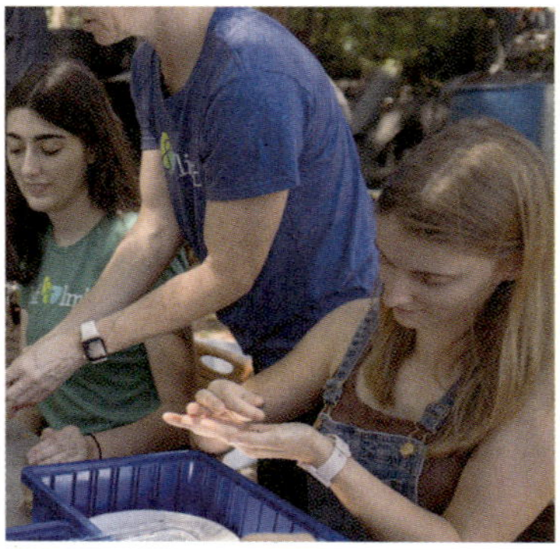
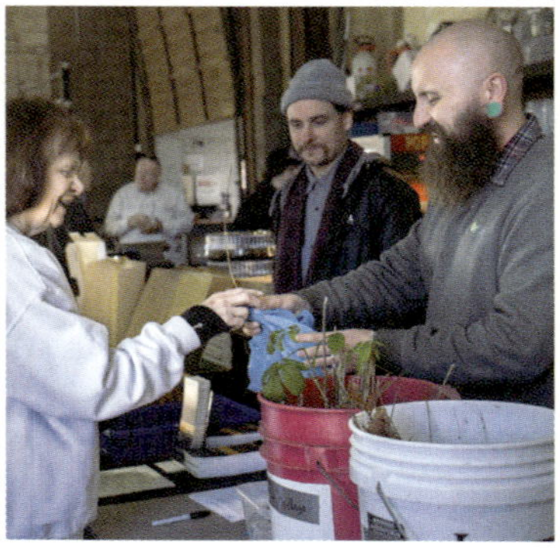
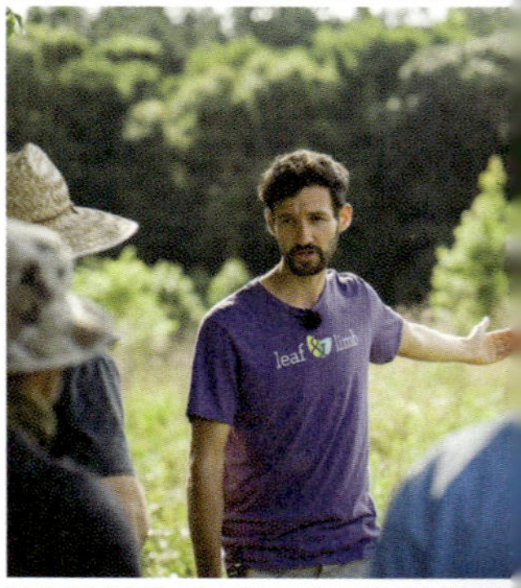
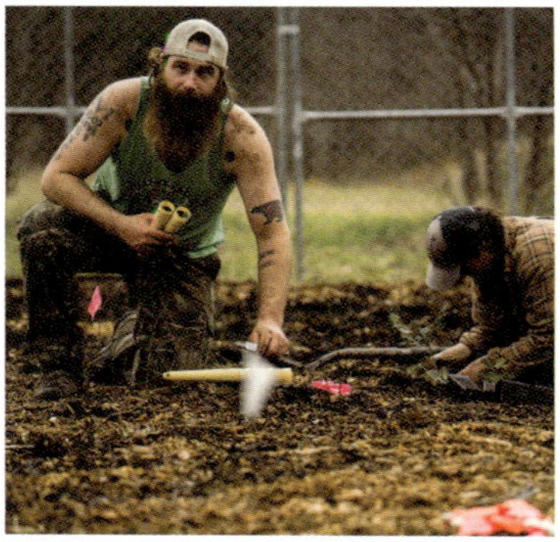
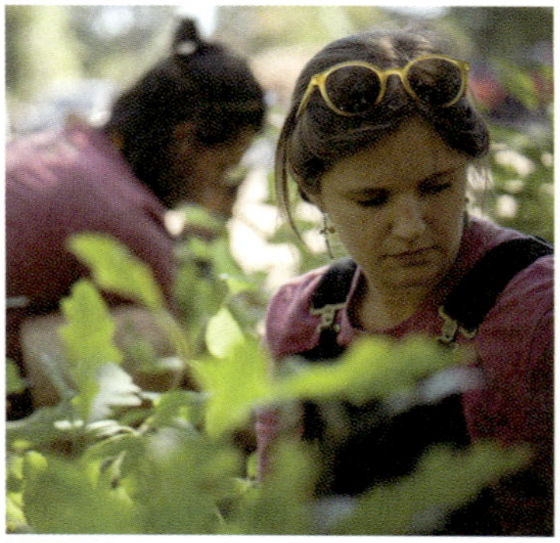
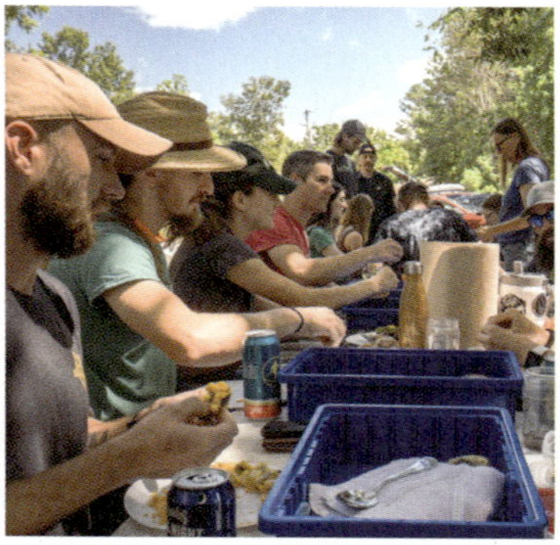
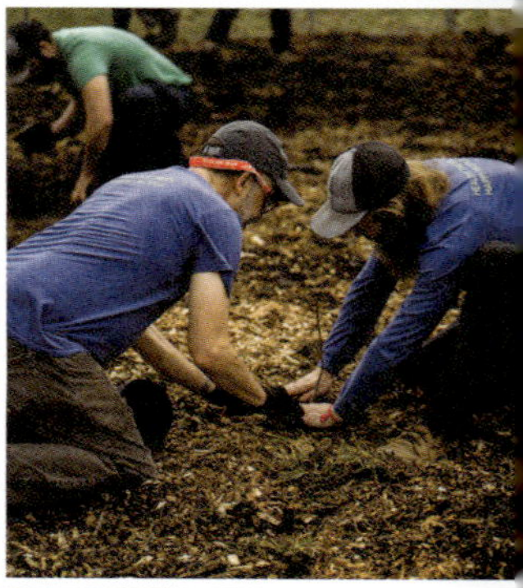
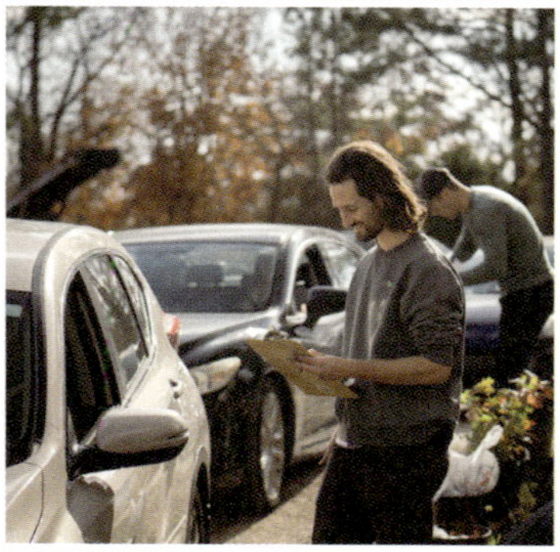
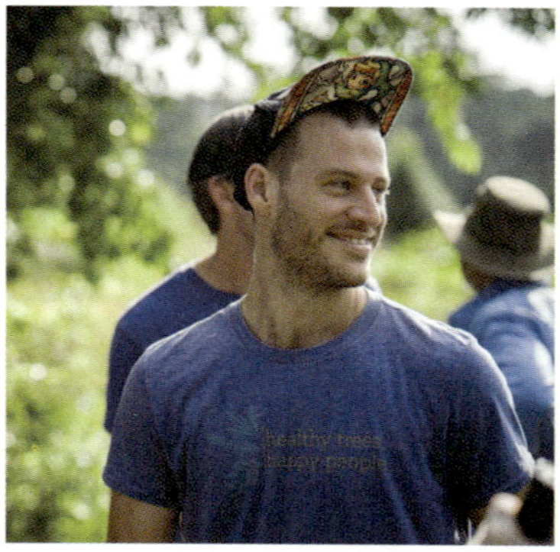
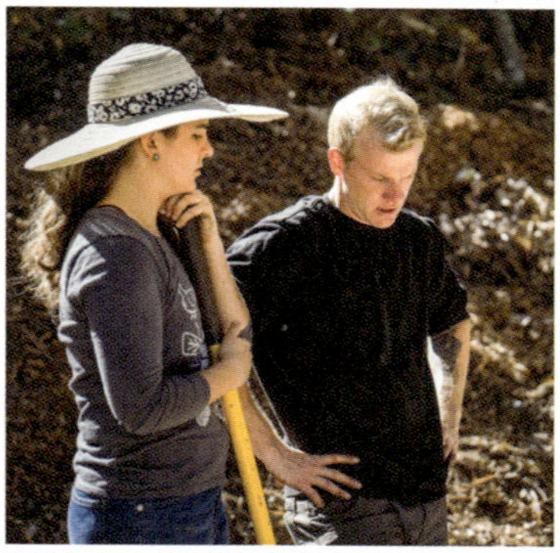
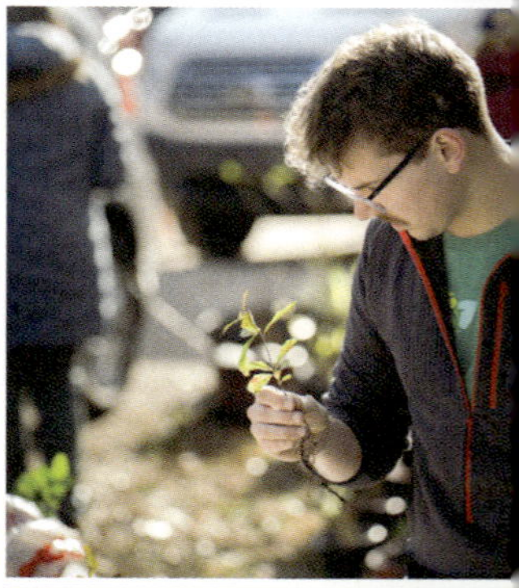
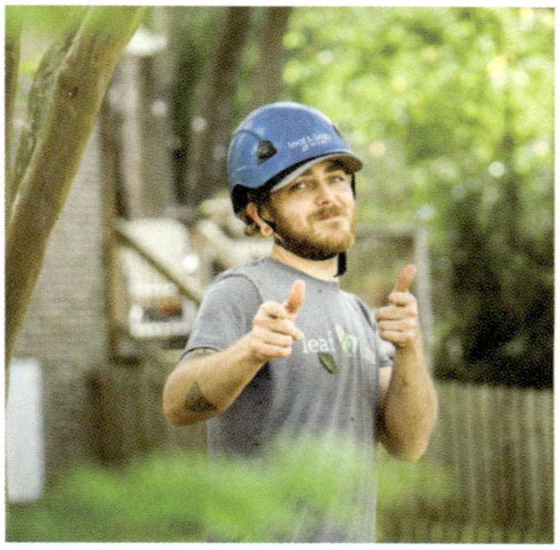
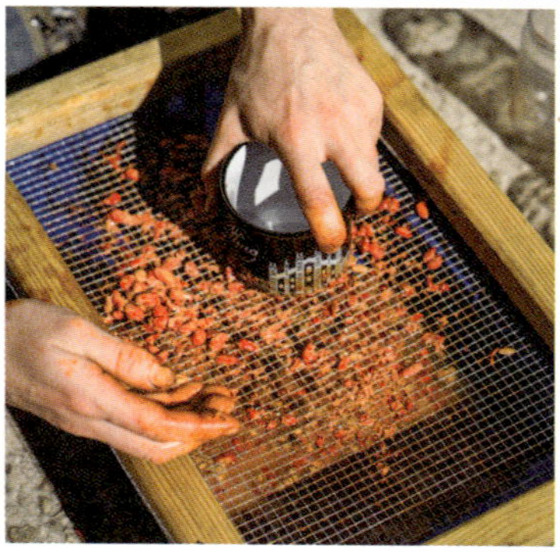
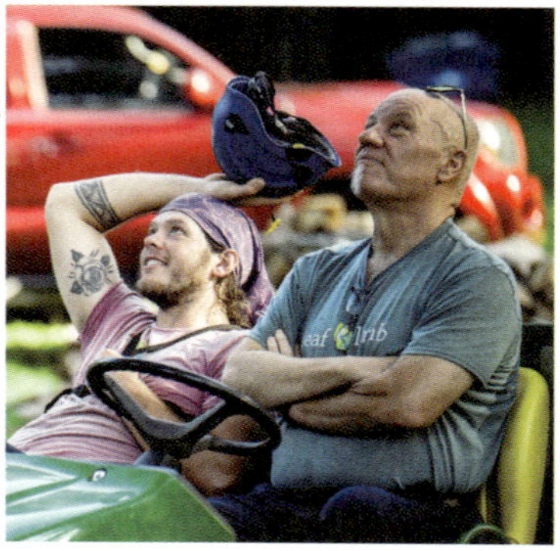
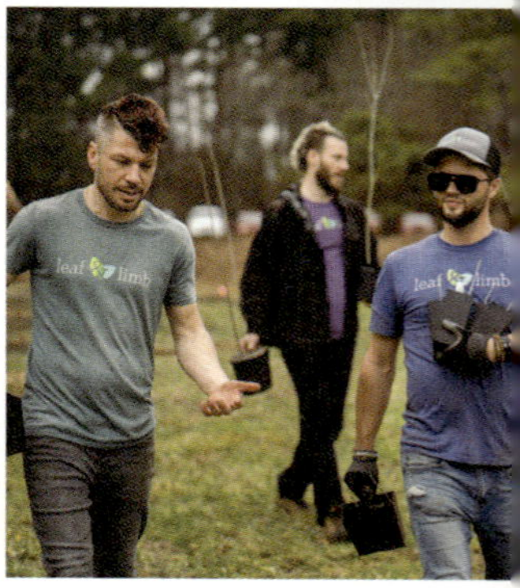

please donate to project pando & help heal earth

Now that you know what we do at Project Pando, will you consider donating? Everything we do is aimed at helping heal Earth.

Should you decide to give—and thank you in advance for even considering—I promise that every penny you donate will directly support Project Pando. I do mean literally *every* penny.

We will use this money to do the following and more:

- Fund additional seed collection efforts, air-pruning boxes, saplings, giveaway events, tree ID walks, and educational programming in Raleigh, NC and surrounding cities.

- Help communities around the country begin their own Project Pando models, using the instructions in Section 5 of this book.

- Finance further research and experiments about other ways we can use the sub/urban landscape to help heal Earth. For example, we have begun working on how we can use trees to create food resilience in our towns, cities, and neighborhoods. Our list of possible research and experimentation projects is long.

How to Donate to Project Pando

You can donate by using this QR code, texting **"PANDO" to 53555**, visiting **www.leaflimb.com/pando-donations**, or contacting us directly at **wonder@leaflimb.com**.

For those who prefer more traditional methods, you can also send a check to Project Pando, 511 Nowell Road in Raleigh, North Carolina, 27607. Please make payments out to "Project Pando."

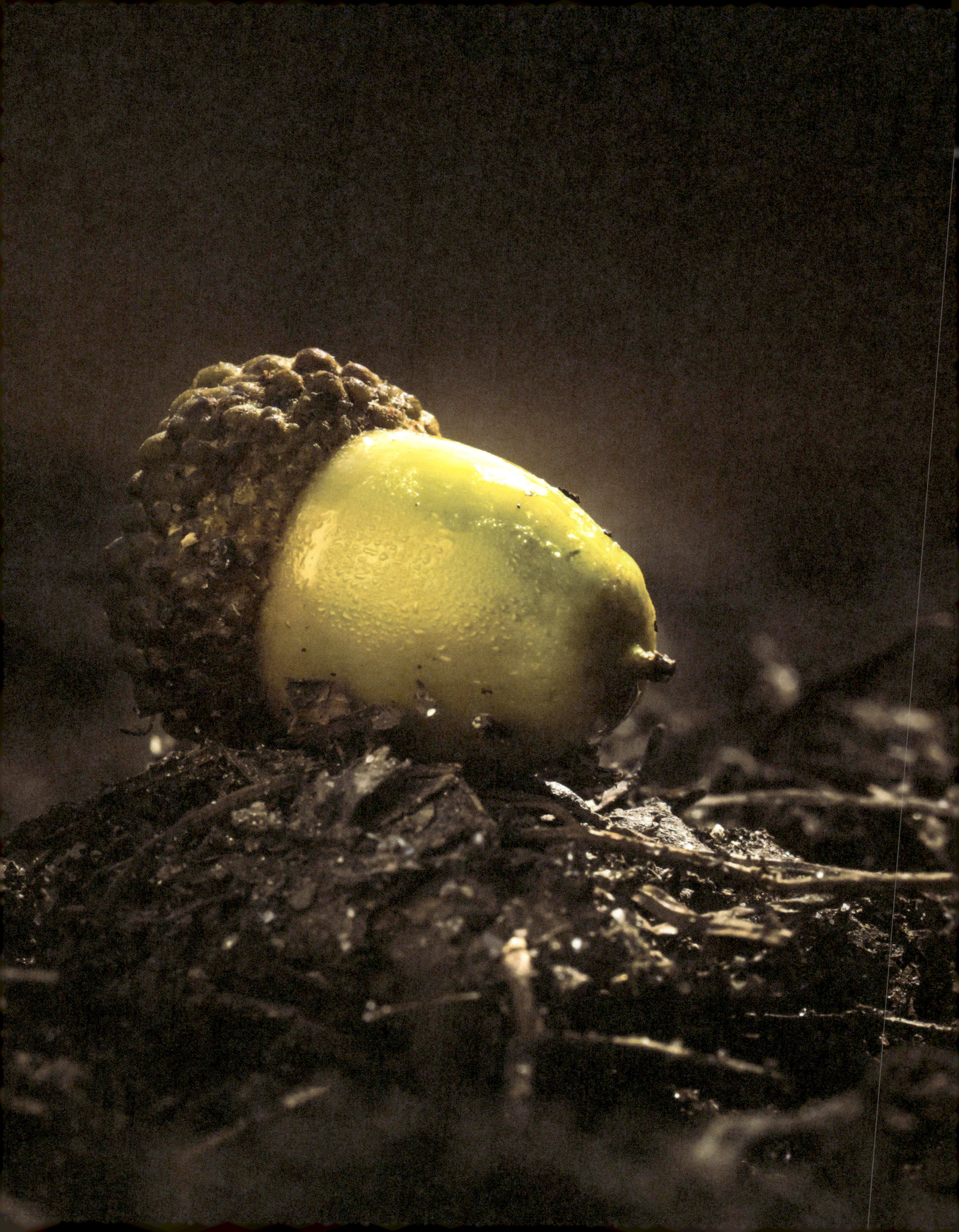

a note of gratitude

First, a note of gratitude to you: from the bottom of my heart, thank you for reading this book!

Second, I want to thank my colleagues and friends at Leaf & Limb and Project Pando. Some of you are still with us and some have moved on to new endeavors. This book is a culmination of the many incredible things we have learned and accomplished together. Especially with Project Pando, none of this would exist without the time, thought, and labor that so many of you freely gave.

This book began as a simple presentation in 2020 called "How Trees Can Save the World & What We Can Do to Help." I was shocked by the number of people who experienced an "ah-ha!" moment during that presentation and then doubly surprised by the number of speaker requests I received. But I was (and still am) limited on time. It was then that I decided to write this book so that everybody can freely access what I know.

I could never have completed this monumental task without help from my family, friends, and colleagues. First, I want to give a special thanks to those who read drafts of this book, gave me feedback, and helped me refine it. In no particular order, a big thanks to: Andrea Genna, Joe Sullivan, Cedric Camu, Chris Palmeri, John Brier, Robin Camu, EB Brown, Matt Fraley, Lila Camu, Nora Bryan, Zeb Baukhagen, Colin Camu, Matt Archibald, Katie Rose Levin, Nick Wrenn, Caroline Richardson, Morgan Camu, Anne Tyson, Thomas Kevin, Kyle Camu, and Patrick Kelly—without your help, suggestions, and feedback this book would only be a shadow of what it is now. Thank you!

Thanks to Jack Nestor, Letitia Glozer, and their colleagues at Technica Editorial Services for providing me with support through the publishing process—thank you Jack and Letitia!

Thanks to Elizabeth Newton for giving this book the perfect amount of professional copyediting during its final iteration. Thank you, Elizabeth!

Thank you to Josh Smith at Quartz Studio for all his help in creating and setting up webpages, Shopify, donation options, and various other technical wizardry necessary to host and distribute this book. Thank you, Josh!

Thanks to Tessa Williams for all of her beautiful videos and photography that are featured throughout this book. I am grateful for the many ways that Tessa brings beauty into Leaf & Limb, Project Pando, and my life in general. Thank you, Tessa!

Thanks to Joe Sullivan for not only helping read and edit, but for also checking sources, strengthening citations, and ensuring this book is backed by peer-reviewed science. This was a challenging and tedious task. Thank you, Joe!

Thanks to Emmanuel Brown for all his help with Project Pando. He first lived what is now Section 5 of this book as we worked to build Project Pando across many years. Then he helped write and edit (and edit, and edit, and edit) that same section. Thank you, EB!

Thanks to Kristi Stout for providing me with excellent editing help. Her suggestions and input helped transform this from a 400-page, 150,000 word muddy manuscript to what you hold now. Thank you so much, Kristi! I'm so glad we had the opportunity to work together.

Thank you to Rebekah Miel and her team at Miel Creative Studio for the incredible work they did in designing this book. It is an artistic masterpiece! I have worked with Rebekah and her team for many years, and I'm always impressed by them. They are pros at marketing, design, and communications. If you need a creative studio that is not only excellent at what they do but also cares about the health of Earth and other issues that matter, I cannot recommend Miel Creative Studio highly enough. Thank you, Rebekah!

A special thanks to Doug Tallamy and Johnny Randall for reading a draft of this book and providing feedback as well as words of encouragement. Both Doug and Johnny have spent their lives helping heal Earth. I greatly admire them both. Thank you, Doug and Johnny!

Finally, I want to give a particularly emphatic note of gratitude to the three people who have played the biggest role in my life:

I'm especially grateful for my dad, Colin Camu. He helped with this book by writing, editing, making videos, and brainstorming new ideas. But more importantly, he has been an amazing business partner. Without him none of this would have happened. He gave me the confidence I needed to become an entrepreneur when we began our first company together (Lark Tours). Looking back, dozens of happy memories spring to mind, like the shindig we threw after we bought our office, Friday nights at Mission Valley Cinema, holiday parties at Leaf & Limb, and the first time we made enough money to treat our family—all the Camus—to a fancy dinner. Of course, there were also the terrible days when everything went wrong, chaos ensued, and we faced utter ruin.

a note of gratitude

There are no words to describe the lows and the highs of this entrepreneurial road unless you have walked it. I love you Dad and I'm so grateful we were able to walk this road together!

I'm hugely grateful for my mom, Robin Camu. She is amazing! She fostered my deep love of learning and reading by homeschooling me and my siblings all the way to high school. She taught me the importance of integrity and grit not through words, but through living them in every aspect of her life. Few people are as tough and ethical as my mom. But it did not stop there. She was a force for positive change during my adult years. She introduced me to meditation back in my 20s, which played a critical role in me becoming a better version of myself. Then she introduced me to the Enneagram and coached me for many years. Understanding more about myself and others around me was another powerful force for change. Without my mom and her bountiful wisdom over the course of my life, I would not be here writing this now. I love you Mom and I'm hugely grateful for you!

Then there is Morgan, the best thing that ever happened in my life. We were both college freshmen looking for new friends on our first day of school. We hit it off famously and became chums right away. Now our roots are inextricably bound. She is whip smart, understands all the intricacies of Leaf & Limb, and is a crucial advisor on growth strategies and the stuff that really matters, like whether we should do something as crazy as quit offering tree-removal services (which was 40% of our revenue at the time). She helps pick up the pieces of my soul when the dark days of the entrepreneurial journey tear me apart. She cheers passionately during every celebration and happy milestone that matters most to me. And she does all this in her spare time—she has a far more distinguished career than I do. Best of all, we made two incredible little humans, Hugo and Jasper, whom I love so deeply. I love you so much Morgan and I'm eternally grateful for you! And thank you for all the time you invested in this book—discussions, brainstorming, and edits ad nauseam. I will do my absolute best to never write another book.

I'm so grateful for the amazing community that has helped me along my life journey. I have benefited from so many favorable circumstances and so many generous and incredible people. They are too many to list.

Last and most certainly not least, I am grateful beyond measure for the blink of an eye we call being alive. That fact that I see, breathe, smell, touch, experience, and love is mind-melting. I know it will be gone sooner than I would like. But I'm going to soak it up while I can by doing my best to practice mindfulness and to care for this marvelous, pale blue dot we call home.

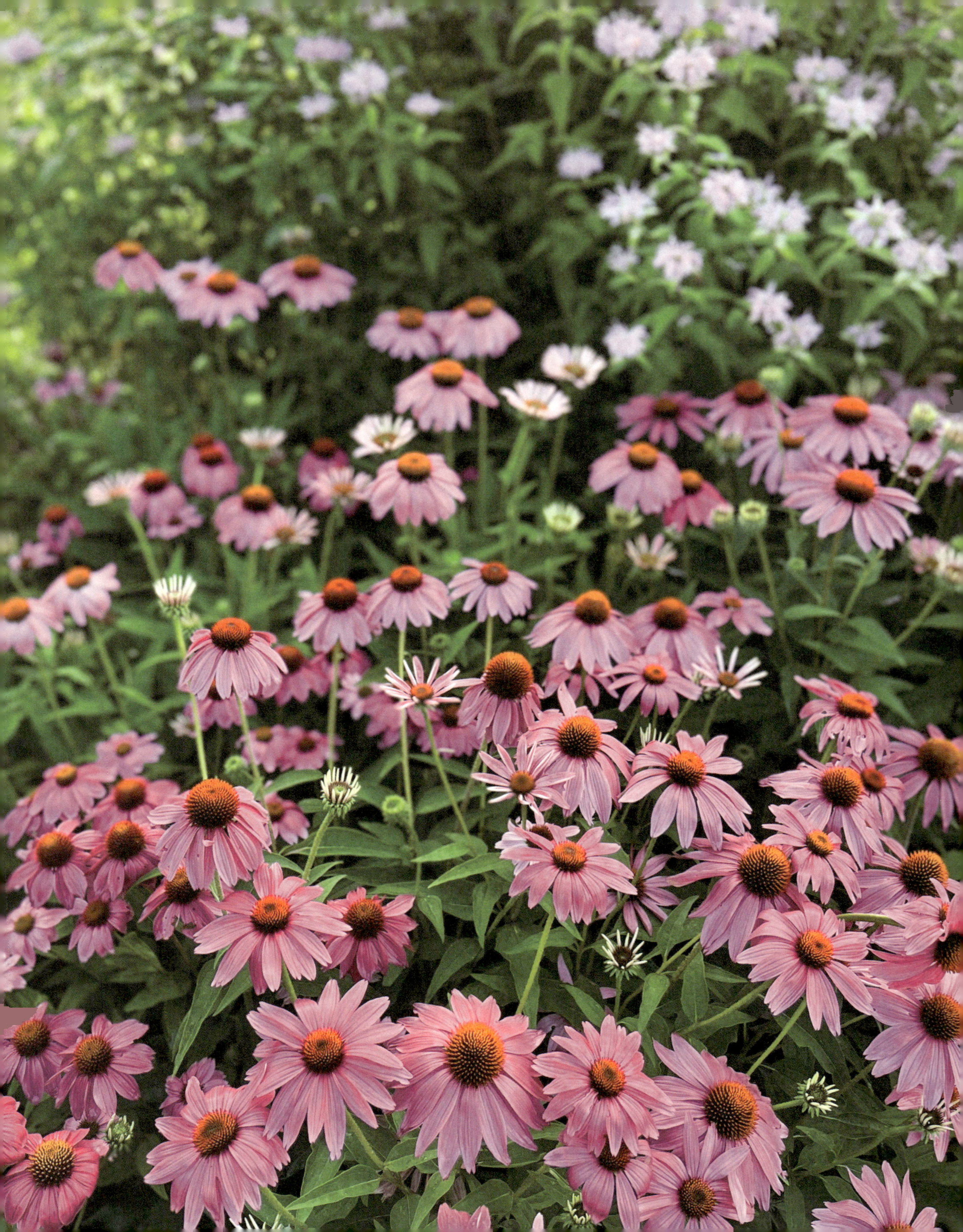

appendix

You can access the Appendix, which contains a number of recommendations and resources, using this QR code:

references

Why This Book is Worth Your Time

Hansen, M. M., Jones, R., & Tocchini, K. (2017). Shinrin-yoku (forest bathing) and nature therapy: A state-of-the-art review. *International Journal of Environmental Research and Public Health, 14*(8), 851. https://doi.org/10.3390/ijerph14080851

Park, B. J., Tsunetsugu, Y., Kasetani, T., Kagawa, T., & Miyazaki, Y. (2010). The physiological effects of shinrin-yoku (taking in the forest atmosphere or forest bathing): Evidence from field experiments in 24 forests across Japan. *Environmental Health and Preventive Medicine, 15*(1), 18–26. https://doi.org/10.1007/s12199-009-0086-9

Rook, G. A. W., Adams, V., Palmer, R., Brunet, L. R., Hunt, J., & Martinelli, R. (2004). Mycobacteria and other environmental organisms as immunomodulators for immunoregulatory disorders. *Springer Seminars in Immunopathology, 25*(3–4), 237–255. https://doi.org/10.1007/s00281-003-0148-9

Rook, G. A. W., & Lowry, C. A. (2008). The hygiene hypothesis and psychiatric disorders. *Trends in Immunology, 29*(4), 150–158. https://doi.org/10.1016/j.it.2008.01.002

This Book is My Act of Reciprocity

DeWoody, J., Rowe, C. A., Hipkins, V. D., & Mock, K. E. (2008). "Pando" lives: Molecular genetic evidence of a giant aspen clone in central Utah. *Western North American Naturalist, 68*(4), 493–497. https://doi.org/10.3398/1527-0904-68.4.493

Kimmerer, R. W. (2013). *Braiding sweetgrass: Indigenous wisdom, scientific knowledge and the teachings of plants* (First paperback edition). Milkweed Editions.

Section 1: Four Fun Essays About Healthy Natural Systems

James C. Finley Center for Private Forests. (2020, January 7). For water quality: Creating woods instead of lawns. Penn State College of Agricultural Sciences. https://ecosystems.psu.edu/research/centers/private-forests/news/for-water-quality-creating-woods-instead-of-lawns

Ch 1: Trees Build Soil

Anthony, M. A., Bender, S. F., & van der Heijden, M. G. A. (2023). Enumerating soil biodiversity. *Proceedings of the National Academy of Sciences, 120*(33), e2304663120. https://doi.org/10.1073/pnas.2304663120

Chen, J., Blume, H.-P., & Beyer, L. (2000). Weathering of rocks induced by lichen colonization: A review. *CATENA, 39*(2), 121–146. https://doi.org/10.1016/S0341-8162(99)00085-5

Harrison, E. (2000). *Cosmology: The science of the universe*. Cambridge University Press.

Heckman, D. S., Geiser, D. M., Eidell, B. R., Stauffer, R. L., Kardos, N. L., & Hedges, S. B. (2001). Molecular evidence for the early colonization of land by fungi and plants. *Science, 293*(5532), 1129–1133. https://doi.org/10.1126/science.1061457

Jackson, T. A. (2015). Weathering, secondary mineral genesis, and soil formation caused by lichens and mosses growing on granitic gneiss in a boreal forest environment. *Geoderma, 251–252*, 78–91. https://doi.org/10.1016/j.geoderma.2015.03.012

Jones, D. L., Nguyen, C., & Finlay, R. D. (2009). Carbon flow in the rhizosphere: Carbon trading at the soil–root interface. *Plant and Soil, 321*(1), 5–33. https://doi.org/10.1007/s11104-009-9925-0

Lavelle, P., & Spain, A. V. (2005). *Soil ecology* (2nd print. with corr). Springer.

Lynch, J. M., & Whipps, J. M. (1990). Substrate flow in the rhizosphere. *Plant and Soil, 129*(1), 1–10. https://doi.org/10.1007/BF00011685

Mergelov, N., Mueller, C. W., Prater, I., Shorkunov, I., Dolgikh, A., Zazovskaya, E., Shishkov, V., Krupskaya, V., Abrosimov, K., Cherkinsky, A., & Goryachkin, S. (2018). Alteration of rocks by endolithic organisms is one of the pathways for the beginning of soils on Earth. *Scientific Reports, 8*(1), Article 1. https://doi.org/10.1038/s41598-018-21682-6

Sagan, C. (1977). *The dragons of Eden: Speculations on the evolution of human intelligence*. Random House.

Tugel, A. J., Lewandowski, A. M., & Happe-vonArb, D. (Eds.). (2000). *Soil biology primer*. Soil and Water Conservation Society.

references

Ch 2: Soil Stores Fresh Water & Trees Move It

Agnihotri, R., Sharma, M. P., Prakash, A., Ramesh, A., Bhattacharjya, S., Patra, A. K., Manna, M. C., Kurganova, I., & Kuzyakov, Y. (2022). Glycoproteins of arbuscular mycorrhiza for soil carbon sequestration: Review of mechanisms and controls. *Science of The Total Environment, 806*, 150571. https://doi.org/10.1016/j.scitotenv.2021.150571

Ellison, D., Morris, C. E., Locatelli, B., Sheil, D., Cohen, J., Murdiyarso, D., Gutierrez, V., Noordwijk, M. van, Creed, I. F., Pokorny, J., Gaveau, D., Spracklen, D. V., Tobella, A. B., Ilstedt, U., Teuling, A. J., Gebrehiwot, S. G., Sands, D. C., Muys, B., Verbist, B., … Sullivan, C. A. (2017). Trees, forests and water: Cool insights for a hot world. *Global Environmental Change, 43*, 51–61. https://doi.org/10.1016/j.gloenvcha.2017.01.002

Harris, R. W., Clark, J. R., & Matheny, N. P. (2004). *Arboriculture: Integrated management of landscape trees, shrubs, and vines* (4th ed.). Prentice Hall.

Nobre, A. D. (2014). *The future climate of Amazonia: Scientific assessment report*. Articulación Regional Amazônica.

Phelan, P. E., Kaloush, K., Miner, M., Golden, J., Phelan, B., Silva, H., & Taylor, R. A. (2015). Urban heat island: Mechanisms, implications, and possible remedies. *Annual Review of Environment and Resources, 40*(1), 285–307. https://doi.org/10.1146/annurev-environ-102014-021155

Pöhlker, C., Wiedemann, K. T., Sinha, B., Shiraiwa, M., Gunthe, S. S., Smith, M., Su, H., Artaxo, P., Chen, Q., Cheng, Y., Elbert, W., Gilles, M. K., Kilcoyne, A. L. D., Moffet, R. C., Weigand, M., Martin, S. T., Pöschl, U., & Andreae, M. O. (2012). Biogenic potassium salt particles as seeds for secondary organic aerosol in the Amazon. *Science, 337*(6098), 1075–1078. https://doi.org/10.1126/science.1223264

Pöschl, U., Martin, S. T., Sinha, B., Chen, Q., Gunthe, S. S., Huffman, J. A., Borrmann, S., Farmer, D. K., Garland, R. M., Helas, G., Jimenez, J. L., King, S. M., Manzi, A., Mikhailov, E., Pauliquevis, T., Petters, M. D., Prenni, A. J., Roldin, P., Rose, D., … Andreae, M. O. (2010). Rainforest aerosols as biogenic nuclei of clouds and precipitation in the Amazon. *Science, 329*(5998), 1513–1516. https://doi.org/10.1126/science.1191056

Sheil, D. (2018). Forests, atmospheric water and an uncertain future: The new biology of the global water cycle. *Forest Ecosystems, 5*(1), 19. https://doi.org/10.1186/s40663-018-0138-y

United States Environmental Protection Agency. (2008). Trees and vegetation. In *Reducing urban heat islands: Compendium of strategies*. https://www.epa.gov/heat-islands/heat-island-compendium

Water Science School. (2018, June 12). *Evapotranspiration and the water cycle*. United States Geological Survey. https://www.usgs.gov/special-topics/water-science-school/science/evapotranspiration-and-water-cycle

Watson, G. W., & Himelick, E. B. (2013). *The practical science of planting trees*. International Society of Arboriculture.

Weil, R. R., & Brady, N. C. (2017). *The nature and properties of soils* (15th ed., global ed.). Pearson.

Ch 3: Trees Feed & Shelter Terrestrial Life

Beerling, D. J. (2017). *The emerald planet: How plants changed Earth's history* (1st ed.). Oxford University Press.

Cragg, G. M., Newman, D. J., & Snader, K. M. (1997). Natural products in drug discovery and development. *Journal of Natural Products, 60*(1), 52–60. https://doi.org/10.1021/np9604893

Donlan, C. J., & Martin, P. S. (2004). Role of ecological history in invasive species management and conservation. *Conservation Biology, 18*(1), 267–269. https://doi.org/10.1111/j.1523-1739.2004.00101.x

Eberhard, I., Mcnamara, J., Pearse, R., & Southwell, I. (1975). Ingestion and excretion of *Eucalyptus punctata* D. C. and its essential oil by the koala, *Phascolarctos cinereus* (Goldfuss). *Australian Journal of Zoology, 23*(2), 169. https://doi.org/10.1071/ZO9750169

Energy Institute. (2023). *Statistical review of world energy* (72nd ed.). Energy Institute.

Johnson, S. (1994). Evidence for Batesian mimicry in a butterfly-pollinated orchid. *Biological Journal of the Linnean Society, 53*(1), 91–104. https://doi.org/10.1006/bijl.1994.1062

MacKinnon, J. B. (2013). *The once and future world: Finding wilderness in the nature we've made*. Houghton Mifflin Harcourt.

Onaga, L. (2001). Cashing in on nature's pharmacy: Bioprospecting and protection of biodiversity could go hand in hand. *EMBO Reports, 2*(4), 263–265. https://doi.org/10.1093/embo-reports/kve077

Probst, J. R., & Weinrich, J. (1993). Relating Kirtland's warbler population to changing landscape composition and structure. *Landscape Ecology, 8*(4), 257–271. https://doi.org/10.1007/BF00125132

Veeresham, C. (2012). Natural products derived from plants as a source of drugs. *Journal of Advanced Pharmaceutical Technology & Research, 3*(4), 200. https://doi.org/10.4103/2231-4040.104709

Wei, J., Wang, L., Zhu, J., Zhang, S., Nandi, O. I., & Kang, L. (2007). Plants attract parasitic wasps to defend themselves against insect pests by releasing hexenol. *PLoS ONE, 2*(9), e852. https://doi.org/10.1371/journal.pone.0000852

Ch 4: Trees Pump CO2 From the Atmosphere & Sequester it Within Life

Chami, R., Cosimano, T., Fullenkamp, C., & Oztosun, S. (2019). Nature's solution to climate change. *Finance and Development, 56*(4), 34–38.

Christensen, L. B. (2006). *Marine mammal populations: Reconstructing historical abundances at the global scale*. https://doi.org/10.14288/1.0074757

Feulner, G. (2017). Formation of most of our coal brought Earth close to global glaciation. *Proceedings of the National Academy of Sciences, 114*(43), 11333–11337. https://doi.org/10.1073/pnas.1712062114

Lal, R. (2008). Carbon sequestration. *Philosophical Transactions of the Royal Society B: Biological Sciences, 363*(1492), 815–830. https://doi.org/10.1098/rstb.2007.2185

McCann, T., Skompski, S., Poty, E., Dusar, M., Vozarova, A., Schneider, J., Wetzel, A., Krainer, K., Kornpihl, K., Schafer, A., Krings, M., Oplustil, S., & Tait, J. (2008). Carboniferous. In T. McCann (Ed.), *The geology of Central Europe* (1st ed., Vol. 1, pp. 411–529). The Geological Society of London. https://doi.org/10.1144/CEV1P.9

Montañez, I. P., McElwain, J. C., Poulsen, C. J., White, J. D., DiMichele, W. A., Wilson, J. P., Griggs, G., & Hren, M. T. (2016). Climate, p_{CO2} and terrestrial carbon cycle linkages during late Palaeozoic glacial–interglacial cycles. *Nature Geoscience, 9*(11), 824–828. https://doi.org/10.1038/ngeo2822

National Ocean Service. (2023, August 24). *What are plankton?* National Oceanic and Atmospheric Administration. https://oceanservice.noaa.gov/facts/plankton.html

Ontl, T. A., & Schulte, L. A. (2012). Soil carbon storage. *Nature Education Knowledge, 3*(10).

Pershing, A. J., Christensen, L. B., Record, N. R., Sherwood, G. D., & Stetson, P. B. (2010). The impact of whaling on the ocean carbon cycle: Why bigger was better. *PLoS ONE, 5*(8), e12444. https://doi.org/10.1371/journal.pone.0012444

Roman, J., & McCarthy, J. J. (2010). The whale pump: Marine mammals enhance primary productivity in a coastal basin. *PLOS ONE, 5*(10), e13255. https://doi.org/10.1371/journal.pone.0013255

Wilmers, C. C., Estes, J. A., Edwards, M., Laidre, K. L., & Konar, B. (2012). Do trophic cascades affect the storage and flux of atmospheric carbon? An analysis of sea otters and kelp forests. *Frontiers in Ecology and the Environment, 10*(8), 409–415. https://doi.org/10.1890/110176

Section 2: Four Not-So-Fun Essays About Broken Natural Systems

Ch 5: We Are Destroying Forests & Grasslands

Campbell, J. E., Lobell, D. B., Genova, R. C., & Field, C. B. (2008). The global potential of bioenergy on abandoned agriculture lands. *Environmental Science & Technology, 42*(15), 5791–5794. https://doi.org/10.1021/es800052w

Food and Agriculture Organization of the United Nations. (2020). *Global forest resources assessment 2020: Key findings.* https://doi.org/10.4060/ca8753en

Food and Agriculture Organization of the United Nations, & United Nations Environment Programme. (2020). *The state of the world's forests 2020: Forests, biodiversity and people.* https://doi.org/10.4060/ca8642en

Hill, R. S. (1990). The fossil history of Tasmania's rainforest tree species. *Tasforests, 2*(1), 5–12.

Holmes, J. (2009). Losing 25,000 to hunger every day. *UN Chronicle, 45*(3), 14–20. https://doi.org/10.18356/a54cde0d-en

MacKinnon, J. B. (2013). *The once and future world: Finding wilderness in the nature we've made.* Houghton Mifflin Harcourt.

Mersmann, K. (2019, June 12). *NASA explores our changing freshwater world.* National Aeronautics and Space Administration. https://www.nasa.gov/missions/gpm/nasa-explores-our-changing-freshwater-world/

Milesi, C., Elvidge, C. D., Dietz, J. B., Tuttle, B. T., Nemani, R. R., & Running, S. W. (2005). A strategy for mapping and modeling the ecological effects of US lawns. *J. Turfgrass Manage, 1*(1), 83–97.

National Park Service. (n.d.). *A complex prairie ecosystem.* Retrieved November 20, 2023, from https://www.nps.gov/tapr/learn/nature/a-complex-prairie-ecosystem.htm

Rabalais, N. N., & Turner, R. E. (2019). Gulf of Mexico hypoxia: Past, present, and future. *Limnology and Oceanography Bulletin, 28*(4), 117–124. https://doi.org/10.1002/lob.10351

Ritchie, H. (2019, November 11). *Half of the world's habitable land is used for agriculture.* Our World in Data. https://ourworldindata.org/global-land-for-agriculture

Ritchie, H. (2021, February 9). *The world has lost one-third of its forest, but an end of deforestation is possible.* Our World in Data. https://ourworldindata.org/world-lost-one-third-forests

Rivers, M., Newton, A. C., Oldfield, S., & Contributors, G. T. A. (2023). Scientists' warning to humanity on tree extinctions. *Plants, People, Planet, 5*(4), 466–482. https://doi.org/10.1002/ppp3.10314

Samson, F. B., Knopf, F. L., & Ostlie, W. R. (2004). Great Plains ecosystems: Past, present, and future. *Wildlife Society Bulletin, 32*(1), 6–15. https://doi.org/10.2193/0091-7648(2004)32[6:GPEPPA]2.0.CO;2

Samson, F., & Knopf, F. (1994). Prairie conservation in North America. *BioScience, 44*(6), 418–421. https://doi.org/10.2307/1312365

Scholtz, R., & Twidwell, D. (2022). The last continuous grasslands on Earth: Identification and conservation importance. *Conservation Science and Practice, 4*(3), e626. https://doi.org/10.1111/csp2.626

Shepard, M. (2013). *Restoration agriculture: Real-world permaculture for farmers.* Acres U.S.A.

Smil, V. (1997). *Cycles of life: Civilization and the biosphere.* Scientific American Library.

United Nations Environment Programme. (2021). *Food waste index report 2021.* United Nations Environment Programme. https://www.unep.org/resources/report/unep-food-waste-index-report-2021

United States Environmental Protection Agency. (2017, February 14). *Outdoor water use in the United States.* https://19january2017snapshot.epa.gov/www3/watersense/pubs/outdoor.html

references

Vermeulen, S. J., Campbell, B. M., & Ingram, J. S. I. (2012). Climate change and food systems. *Annual Review of Environment and Resources, 37*(1), 195–222. https://doi.org/10.1146/annurev-environ-020411-130608

Weisse, M., Goldman, E., & Carter, S. (2023). *How much forest was lost in 2022?* World Resources Institute. https://research.wri.org/gfr/latest-analysis-deforestation-trends

Ch 6: We Are Turning Soil into Dirt & Running Out of Fresh Water

Food and Agriculture Organization of the United Nations. (2022). *The state of the world's land and water resources for food and agriculture 2021: Systems at breaking point.* https://doi.org/10.4060/cb9910en

Konikow, L. F. (2015). Long-term groundwater depletion in the United States. *Groundwater, 53*(1), 2–9. https://doi.org/10.1111/gwat.12306

Lund, J., Medellin-Azuara, J., Durand, J., & Stone, K. (2018). Lessons from California's 2012–2016 drought. *Journal of Water Resources Planning and Management, 144*(10), 04018067. https://doi.org/10.1061/(ASCE)WR.1943-5452.0000984

Makarieva, A. M., Nefiodov, A. V., Nobre, A. D., Sheil, D., Nobre, P., Pokorný, J., Hesslerová, P., & Li, B.-L. (2022). Vegetation impact on atmospheric moisture transport under increasing land-ocean temperature contrasts. *Heliyon, 8*(10), e11173. https://doi.org/10.1016/j.heliyon.2022.e11173

Mekonnen, M. M., & Hoekstra, A. Y. (2016). Four billion people facing severe water scarcity. *Science Advances, 2*(2), e1500323. https://doi.org/10.1126/sciadv.1500323

National Environmental Satellite, Data, and Information Service. (2023, June 30). *Extreme heat and severe weather plague parts of North America.* National Oceanic and Atmospheric Administration. https://www.nesdis.noaa.gov/news/extreme-heat-and-severe-weather-plague-parts-of-north-america

Richey, A. S., Thomas, B. F., Lo, M., Reager, J. T., Famiglietti, J. S., Voss, K., Swenson, S., & Rodell, M. (2015). Quantifying renewable groundwater stress with GRACE. *Water Resources Research, 51*(7), 5217–5238. https://doi.org/10.1002/2015WR017349

Rodina, L. (2019). Water resilience lessons from Cape Town's water crisis. *WIREs Water, 6*(6), e1376. https://doi.org/10.1002/wat2.1376

Savory Institute. (2023). *Savory Institute: Regenerating the world's grasslands.* https://savory.global/

Sofia, G., Roder, G., Dalla Fontana, G., & Tarolli, P. (2017). Flood dynamics in urbanised landscapes: 100 years of climate and humans' interaction. *Scientific Reports, 7*(1), 40527. https://doi.org/10.1038/srep40527

Tsegai, D., Augenstein, P., Huang, Z., Voigt, C., Lipton, G., Howard, J., Minelli, S., Alexander, S., & Liu, S. (2023). *Global drought snapshot 2023: The need for proactive action.* United Nations Convention to Combat Desertification.

United States Environmental Protection Agency. (2017, February 14). *Outdoor water use in the United States.* https://19january2017snapshot.epa.gov/www3/watersense/pubs/outdoor.html

Wake County Government, & Davey Resource Group, Inc. (2023). *Wake County land cover analysis and tree canopy assessment.* Wake County, North Carolina. https://s3.us-west-1.amazonaws.com/wakegov.com.if-us-west-1/s3fs-public/documents/2023-09/Wake%20County_FINAL_pages_R_0.pdf

Wilson, E. O. (2016). *Half-Earth: Our planet's fight for life* (1st ed.). Liveright Publishing Corporation.

Ch 7: We Are Killing Life

Baillie, J., Hilton-Taylor, C., & Stuart, S. N. (Eds.). (2004). *2004 IUCN red list of threatened species: A global species assessment.* International Union for the Conservation of Nature.

Benton, T. G., Bieg, C., Harwatt, H., Pudasaini, R., & Wellesley, L. (2021). *Food system impacts on biodiversity loss* (pp. 02–03). Chatham House.

Ceballos, G., Ehrlich, P. R., & Dirzo, R. (2017). Biological annihilation via the ongoing sixth mass extinction signaled by vertebrate population losses and declines. *Proceedings of the National Academy of Sciences, 114*(30), E6089–E6096. https://doi.org/10.1073/pnas.1704949114

Davidson, A. D., Boyer, A. G., Kim, H., Pompa-Mansilla, S., Hamilton, M. J., Costa, D. P., Ceballos, G., & Brown, J. H. (2012). Drivers and hotspots of extinction risk in marine mammals. *Proceedings of the National Academy of Sciences, 109*(9), 3395–3400. https://doi.org/10.1073/pnas.1121469109

Davies, R. W. D., Cripps, S. J., Nickson, A., & Porter, G. (2009). Defining and estimating global marine fisheries bycatch. *Marine Policy, 33*(4), 661–672. https://doi.org/10.1016/j.marpol.2009.01.003

Egler, F. (1970). *The way of science: A philosophy of ecology for the layman.* Hafner Publishing Company.

Flores, D. (2023). *Wild new world: The epic story of animals and people in America.* W. W. Norton and Company, Incorporated.

Food and Agriculture Organization of the United Nations. (2020). *The state of world fisheries and aquaculture 2020: Sustainability in action.* https://doi.org/10.4060/ca9229en

Hedrick, P. W. (2009). Conservation genetics and North American bison (*Bison bison*). *Journal of Heredity, 100*(4), 411–420. https://doi.org/10.1093/jhered/esp024

Hulme, P. E. (2009). Trade, transport and trouble: Managing invasive species pathways in an era of globalization. *Journal of Applied Ecology, 46*(1), 10–18. https://doi.org/10.1111/j.1365-2664.2008.01600.x

Johnson, R., Crafton, R. E., & Upton, H. F. (2017). *Invasive species: Major laws and the role of selected federal agencies.* Congressional Research Service.

Lewison, R. L., Freeman, S. A., & Crowder, L. B. (2004). Quantifying the effects of fisheries on threatened species: The impact of pelagic longlines on loggerhead and leatherback sea turtles. *Ecology Letters, 7*(3), 221–231. https://doi.org/10.1111/j.1461-0248.2004.00573.x

MacKinnon, J. B. (2013). *The once and future world: Finding wilderness in the nature we've made*. Houghton Mifflin Harcourt.

Martin, P. S. (2005). *Twilight of the mammoths: Ice age extinctions and the rewilding of America*. University of California Press.

McKinney, R., Gibbon, J., Wozniak, E., & Galland, G. (2020). *Netting billions 2020: A global tuna valuation*.

Mills, L. S., & Doak, D. F. (1993). The keystone-species concept in ecology and conservation. *BioScience, 43*(4), 219–224. https://doi.org/10.2307/1312122

Pacific Bluefin Tuna Working Group. (2016). *2016 Pacific bluefin tuna stock assessment: Executive summary*. International Scientific Committee for Tuna and Tuna-Like Species in the North Pacific Ocean. https://isc.fra.go.jp/pdf/Stock_assessment/EXECUTIVE_SUMMARY_ISC_2016_Pacific_Bluefin_Tuna_Stock_Assessment.pdf

Rigling, D., & Prospero, S. (2018). *Cryphonectria parasitica*, the causal agent of chestnut blight: Invasion history, population biology and disease control. *Molecular Plant Pathology, 19*(1), 7–20. https://doi.org/10.1111/mpp.12542

Ripple, W. J., & Beschta, R. L. (2012). Trophic cascades in Yellowstone: The first 15 years after wolf reintroduction. *Biological Conservation, 145*(1), 205–213. https://doi.org/10.1016/j.biocon.2011.11.005

Shamshak, G. L., Anderson, J. L., Asche, F., Garlock, T., & Love, D. C. (2019). U.S. seafood consumption. *Journal of the World Aquaculture Society, 50*(4), 715–727. https://doi.org/10.1111/jwas.12619

United States Fish and Wildlife Service. (n.d.). *Red wolf (Canis rufus)*. Retrieved November 30, 2023, from https://www.fws.gov/species/red-wolf-canis-rufus

United States Fish and Wildlife Service. (2023, October). *Red wolf recovery program*. https://www.fws.gov/project/red-wolf-recovery-program

Wagner, D. L. (2007). Cascading consequences of introduced and invasive species on imperiled invertebrates. In K. W. Gottschalk (Ed.), *Proceedings, 18th U.S. Department of Agriculture interagency research forum on gypsy moth and other invasive species 2007* (pp. 1–5). USDA Forest Service.

Weaver, J. (1978). *The wolves of Yellowstone* (Natural Resources Report 14). Department of the Interior, National Park Service.

World Wildlife Fund. (2018). *Living planet report 2018: Aiming higher*.

Ch 8: In Terms of CO_2, We Are Returning to the Carboniferous Period

Friedlingstein, P., O'Sullivan, M., Jones, M. W., Andrew, R. M., Gregor, L., Hauck, J., Le Quéré, C., Luijkx, I. T., Olsen, A., Peters, G. P., Peters, W., Pongratz, J., Schwingshackl, C., Sitch, S., Canadell, J. G., Ciais, P., Jackson, R. B., Alin, S. R., Alkama, R., … Zheng, B. (2022). Global carbon budget 2022. *Earth System Science Data, 14*(11), 4811–4900. https://doi.org/10.5194/essd-14-4811-2022

Gruber, N., Bakker, D. C. E., DeVries, T., Gregor, L., Hauck, J., Landschützer, P., McKinley, G. A., & Müller, J. D. (2023). Trends and variability in the ocean carbon sink. *Nature Reviews Earth & Environment, 4*(2), 119–134. https://doi.org/10.1038/s43017-022-00381-x

Keeling, C. D. (1960). The concentration and isotopic abundances of carbon dioxide in the atmosphere. *Tellus, 12*(2), 200–203. https://doi.org/10.3402/tellusa.v12i2.9366

Le Treut, H., Sommerville, R., Cubasch, U., Ding, Y., Mauritzen, C., Mokssit, A., Peterson, T., & Prather, M. (2007). Historical overview of climate change science. In S. Solomon, D. Qin, M. Manning, Z. Chen, M. Marquis, K. B. Averyt, M. Tignor, & H. L. Miller (Eds.), *Climate change 2007: The physical science basis. Contribution of Working Group I to the fourth assessment report of the Intergovernmental Panel on Climate Change*. Cambridge University Press.

Lindsey, R. (2023, May 12). *Climate change: Atmospheric carbon dioxide*. Climate.gov. http://www.climate.gov/news-features/understanding-climate/climate-change-atmospheric-carbon-dioxide

National Aeronautics and Space Administration. (2023, November 30). *Carbon dioxide concentration*. Global Climate Change: Vital Signs of the Planet. https://climate.nasa.gov/vital-signs/carbon-dioxide

Neftel, A., Moor, E., Oeschger, H., & Stauffer, B. (1985). Evidence from polar ice cores for the increase in atmospheric CO_2 in the past two centuries. *Nature, 315*(6014), 45–47. https://doi.org/10.1038/315045a0

Smil, V. (1997). *Cycles of life: Civilization and the biosphere*. Scientific American Library.

Taleb, N. N. (2010). *The black swan: The impact of the highly improbable* (2nd ed., Random trade pbk. ed). Random House Trade Paperbacks.

Tripati, A. K., Roberts, C. D., & Eagle, R. A. (2009). Coupling of CO_2 and ice sheet stability over major climate transitions of the last 20 million years. *Science, 326*(5958), 1394–1397. https://doi.org/10.1126/science.1178296

United States Environmental Protection Agency. (2023, February 15). *Global greenhouse gas emissions data* [Overviews and Factsheets]. https://www.epa.gov/ghgemissions/global-greenhouse-gas-emissions-data

Vallis, G. K. (2012). *Climate and the oceans*. Princeton University Press.

references

Section 3: Fast & Easy Ways to Help Heal Earth

Dodd, M. (Director). (2010). *The man who stopped the desert* [Film]. 1080 Film & Television.
Phillips, M. (2017). *Mycorrhizal planet: How symbiotic fungi work with roots to support plant health and build soil fertility.* Chelsea Green Publishing.

Ch 9: Some Important Notes Before we Begin

Licht, M. (2022, April 8). *Soil temperature map can help guide farmers' planting decisions.* Iowa State University Extension and Outreach. https://www.extension.iastate.edu/news/soil-temperature-map-can-help-guide-farmers-planting-decisions
North Carolina State Climate Office. (2023). *Station scout.* North Carolina State University. https://products.climate.ncsu.edu/cardinal/scout/
The Ohio State University College of Food, Agricultural, and Environmental Sciences. (2023). *The Ohio State phenology calendar.* https://weather.cfaes.osu.edu/gdd/

Ch 10: Start with Planting Trees–One of The Most Important Things We Can Do

Carrero, C., Jerome, D., Beckman, E., Byrne, A., Coombes, A. J., Deng, M., Rodríguez, A. G., Van Sam, H., Khoo, E., & Nguyen, N. (2020). *The red list of oaks 2020.*
Gilman, E. F. (2020, January 24). *Establishment period for trees.* University of Florida Institute of Food and Agricultural Sciences. https://hort.ifas.ufl.edu/woody/establishment-period.shtml
Kimmerer, R. W. (2003). *Gathering moss: A natural and cultural history of mosses* (1st ed). Oregon State University Press.
Lewington, A., & Parker, E. (2012). *Ancient trees: Trees that live for a thousand years.* Batsford.
Licht, M. (2022, April 8). *Soil temperature map can help guide farmers' planting decisions.* Iowa State University Extension and Outreach. https://www.extension.iastate.edu/news/soil-temperature-map-can-help-guide-farmers-planting-decisions
North Carolina State Climate Office. (2023). *Station scout.* North Carolina State University. https://products.climate.ncsu.edu/cardinal/scout/
Roman, L. A., & Scatena, F. N. (2011). Street tree survival rates: Meta-analysis of previous studies and application to a field survey in Philadelphia, PA, USA. *Urban Forestry & Urban Greening, 10*(4), 269–274. https://doi.org/10.1016/j.ufug.2011.05.008
Struve, D. (2009). Tree establishment: A review of some of the factors affecting transplant survival and establishment. *Arboriculture & Urban Forestry, 35*(1), 10–13. https://doi.org/10.48044/jauf.2009.003
Tallamy, D. W. (2021). *The nature of oaks: The rich ecology of our most essential native trees.* Timber Press.
The Ohio State University College of Food, Agricultural, and Environmental Sciences. (2023). *The Ohio State phenology calendar.* https://weather.cfaes.osu.edu/gdd/
Watson, G. W., & Himelick, E. B. (2013). *The practical science of planting trees.* International Society of Arboriculture.
Watson, W. T. (2005). Influence of tree size on transplant establishment and growth. *HortTechnology, 15*(1), 118–122. https://doi.org/10.21273/HORTTECH.15.1.0118

Ch 11: Save Existing Trees–They Rarely Need to be Removed

Baker, J. B., & Langdon, O. G. (1990). *Pinus taeda* L.: Loblolly pine. *Silvics of North America, 1,* 497–512.
Brockway, D. G., Outcalt, K. W., Tomczak, D. J., & Johnson, E. E. (2005). *Restoration of longleaf pine ecosystems* (GTR-SRS-83). USDA Forest Service, Southern Research Station.
Centers for Disease Control and Prevention. (2023, June 1). *Drowning data.* https://www.cdc.gov/drowning/data/index.html
Costello, L., Watson, G., Smiley, E. T., & Hauer, R. (2023). Best practices for root pruning. *Arborist News, 32*(3), 10–14.
Crick, J. (2017, March 30). *Wind is essential to natural processes.* Michigan State University Extension. https://www.canr.msu.edu/news/wind_is_essential_to_natural_processes
Godman, R. M., Yawney, H. W., & Tubbs, C. H. (1990). *Acer saccharum* Marsh.: Sugar maple. *Silvics of North America, 2*(654), 78.
Harris, R. W., Clark, J. R., & Matheny, N. P. (2004). *Arboriculture: Integrated management of landscape trees, shrubs, and vines* (4th ed). Prentice Hall.
Kushla, J. D., & Wilson, J. (2021). *Tree health assessment and risk management* (P3717). Mississippi State University Extension Service. http://extension.msstate.edu/publications/tree-health-assessment-and-risk-management
Lewington, A., & Parker, E. (2012). *Ancient trees: Trees that live for a thousand years.* Batsford.
Perry, T. (1982). The ecology of tree roots and the practical significance thereof. *Arboriculture & Urban Forestry, 8*(8), 197–211. https://doi.org/10.48044/jauf.1982.047
Pickens, B. (2015). Silvics of shortleaf pine. *Silvics of North America, 1,* 31–32.
Roberts, J., Jackson, N., & Smith, M. (2013). *Tree roots in the built environment.* Arboricultural Association.
Schmidlin, T. W. (2009). Human fatalities from wind-related tree failures in the United States, 1995–2007. *Natural Hazards, 50*(1), 13–25. https://doi.org/10.1007/s11069-008-9314-7
Tallamy, D. W. (2009). *Bringing nature home: How you can sustain wildlife with native plants* (Updated and expanded pbk. ed). Timber Press.

Tallamy, D. W., & Shropshire, K. J. (2009). Ranking lepidopteran use of native versus introduced plants. *Conservation Biology, 23*(4), 941–947. https://doi.org/10.1111/j.1523-1739.2009.01202.x

Thomas, J. W., Anderson, R. G., Maser, C., & Bull, E. L. (1979). Snags. *Wildlife Habitats in Managed Forests: The Blue Mountains of Oregon and Washington*. Portland, OR: USDA Forest Service, 60–77.

Vogel, S. (1996). Blowing in the wind: Storm-resisting features of the design of trees. *Journal of Arboriculture, 22*, 92–98.

Wendel, G. W., & Smith, H. C. (1990). *Pinus strobus* L.: Eastern white pine. *Silvics of North America, 1*.

Wray, A. K., Jusino, M. A., Banik, M. T., Palmer, J. M., Kaarakka, H., White, J. P., Lindner, D. L., Gratton, C., & Peery, M. Z. (2018). Incidence and taxonomic richness of mosquitoes in the diets of little brown and big brown bats. *Journal of Mammalogy, 99*(3), 668–674. https://doi.org/10.1093/jmammal/gyy044

Yellman, M. A., & Sauber-Schatz, E. K. (2022). Motor vehicle crash deaths: United States and 28 other high-income countries, 2015 and 2019. *MMWR. Morbidity and Mortality Weekly Report, 71*(26), 837–843. https://doi.org/10.15585/mmwr.mm7126a1

Ch 12: Perform Structural Pruning to Increase Strength–It's the Only Pruning That Matters

Harris, R. W., Clark, J. R., & Matheny, N. P. (2004). *Arboriculture: Integrated management of landscape trees, shrubs, and vines* (4th ed). Prentice Hall.

Hirons, A. D., & Thomas, P. (2018). *Applied tree biology*. Wiley Blackwell.

Ch 13: A Very Short Diversion on Pruning Shrubs

Banks, J. L., & McConnell, R. (2015, April). *National emissions from lawn and garden equipment*. 2015 International Emissions Inventory Conference, San Diego, CA. https://www.epa.gov/sites/default/files/2015-09/documents/banks.pdf

Leaf blower's emissions dirtier than high-performance pick-up truck's, says Edmunds' Insideline.com. (2011, December 6). Edmunds. https://www.edmunds.com/about/press/leaf-blowers-emissions-dirtier-than-high-performance-pick-up-trucks-says-edmunds-insidelinecom.html

Turnbull, C. (2012). *Cass Turnbull's guide to pruning: What, when, where and how to prune for a more beautiful garden* (3rd edition). Sasquatch Books.

Ch 14: Promote Soil Bursting with Life

Bates, A. K. (2010). *The biochar solution: Carbon farming and climate change*. New Society Publishers.

Bhakta, N. S., Morgan, D. L., & Borys, D. J. (2009). Copperhead (*Agkistrodon contortrix*) snakebites in the United States: 2000–2007. *Annals of Emergency Medicine, 54*(3), S19. https://doi.org/10.1016/j.annemergmed.2009.06.078

Brundrett, M. C. (2002). Coevolution of roots and mycorrhizas of land plants. *New Phytologist, 154*(2), 275–304. https://doi.org/10.1046/j.1469-8137.2002.00397.x

Chalker-Scott, L. (2007). Impact of mulches on landscape plants and the environment: A review. *Journal of Environmental Horticulture, 25*(4), 239–249.

Chalker-Scott, L. (2015). *Using arborist wood chips as a landscape mulch* (WSU Extension Fact Sheet FS160E). Washington State University Extension Publications.

Domínguez, J., Aira, M., Kolbe, A. R., Gómez-Brandón, M., & Pérez-Losada, M. (2019). Changes in the composition and function of bacterial communities during vermicomposting may explain beneficial properties of vermicompost. *Scientific Reports, 9*(1), 9657. https://doi.org/10.1038/s41598-019-46018-w

Enebe, M. C., & Erasmus, M. (2023). Mediators of biomass transformation – A focus on the enzyme composition of the vermicomposting process. *Environmental Challenges, 12*, 100732. https://doi.org/10.1016/j.envc.2023.100732

Feijen, F. A. A., Vos, R. A., Nuytinck, J., & Merckx, V. S. F. T. (2018). Evolutionary dynamics of mycorrhizal symbiosis in land plant diversification. *Scientific Reports, 8*(1), 10698. https://doi.org/10.1038/s41598-018-28920-x

Gao, Y., & Cabrera Serrenho, A. (2023). Greenhouse gas emissions from nitrogen fertilizers could be reduced by up to one-fifth of current levels by 2050 with combined interventions. *Nature Food, 4*(2), Article 2. https://doi.org/10.1038/s43016-023-00698-w

Greene, S. C., Folt, J., Wyatt, K., & Brandehoff, N. P. (2021). Epidemiology of fatal snakebites in the United States 1989–2018. *The American Journal of Emergency Medicine, 45*, 309–316. https://doi.org/10.1016/j.ajem.2020.08.083

Harris, R. W., Clark, J. R., & Matheny, N. P. (2004). *Arboriculture: Integrated management of landscape trees, shrubs, and vines* (4th ed). Prentice Hall.

Heckman, J. R., & Kluchinski, D. (1996). Chemical composition of municipal leaf waste and hand-collected urban leaf litter. *Journal of Environmental Quality, 25*(2), 355–362. https://doi.org/10.2134/jeq1996.00472425002500020021x

Insurance Institute for Highway Safety, & Highway Loss Data Institute. (2023). *Fatality facts 2021: State by state*. IIHS-HLDI. https://www.iihs.org/topics/fatality-statistics/detail/state-by-state

Joosten, H., Tapio-Biström, M.-L., & Tol, S. (2012). *Peatlands: Guidance for climate change mitigation through conservation, rehabilitation and sustainable use*. Food and Agriculture Organization of the United Nations.

Land, B. (2005, April). *Using Vitamin C to neutralize chlorine in water systems*. USDA Forest Service: Technology & Development Program. https://www.fs.usda.gov/t-d/pubs/html/05231301/05231301.html

references

Landeweert, R., Hoffland, E., Finlay, R. D., Kuyper, T. W., & Van Breemen, N. (2001). Linking plants to rocks: Ectomycorrhizal fungi mobilize nutrients from minerals. *Trends in Ecology & Evolution, 16*(5), 248–254. https://doi.org/10.1016/S0169-5347(01)02122-X

Lanterman, J., Reeher, P., Mitchell, R. J., & Goodell, K. (2019). Habitat preference and phenology of nest seeking and foraging spring bumble bee queens in northeastern North America (Hymenoptera: Apidae: *Bombus*). *The American Midland Naturalist, 182*(2), 131. https://doi.org/10.1674/0003-0031-182.2.131

Legal, L. (2022). "Lepidoptera flies", but not always…Interactions of caterpillars and chrysalis with soil. *Diversity, 15*(1), 27. https://doi.org/10.3390/d15010027

Lehman, R. M., Osborne, S., & Taheri, W. (2018, December 19). *Fall cover crops boost soil arbuscular mycorrhizal fungi which can lead to reduced inputs*. South Dakota State University Extension. https://extension.sdstate.edu/fall-cover-crops-boost-soil-arbuscular-mycorrhizal-fungi-which-can-lead-reduced-inputs

Menge, J. A., Steirle, D., Bagyaraj, D. J., Johnson, E. L. V., & Leonard, R. T. (1978). Phosphorus concentrations in plants responsible for inhibition of mycorrhizal infection. *New Phytologist, 80*(3), 575–578. https://doi.org/10.1111/j.1469-8137.1978.tb01589.x

Mulholland, P. J., Helton, A. M., Poole, G. C., Hall, R. O., Hamilton, S. K., Peterson, B. J., Tank, J. L., Ashkenas, L. R., Cooper, L. W., Dahm, C. N., Dodds, W. K., Findlay, S. E. G., Gregory, S. V., Grimm, N. B., Johnson, S. L., McDowell, W. H., Meyer, J. L., Valett, H. M., Webster, J. R., … Thomas, S. M. (2008). Stream denitrification across biomes and its response to anthropogenic nitrate loading. *Nature, 452*(7184), 202–205. https://doi.org/10.1038/nature06686

National Institute for Occupational Safety and Health. (2022, April 15). *Venomous snakes*. Centers for Disease Control and Prevention. https://www.cdc.gov/niosh/topics/snakes/default.html

Oder, T. (2015, March 30). *Redefining curb appeal*. National Wildlife Federation. https://www.nwf.org/Home/Magazines/National-Wildlife/2015/AprilMay/Gardening/Redefining-Curb-Appeal

Phillips, M. (2017). *Mycorrhizal planet: How symbiotic fungi work with roots to support plant health and build soil fertility*. Chelsea Green Publishing.

Simard, S. W. (2018). Mycorrhizal networks facilitate tree communication, learning, and memory. In F. Baluska, M. Gagliano, & G. Witzany (Eds.), *Memory and learning in plants* (pp. 191–213). Springer International Publishing. https://doi.org/10.1007/978-3-319-75596-0_10

Smil, V. (1997). *Cycles of life: Civilization and the biosphere*. Scientific American Library.

Strullu-Derrien, C., Selosse, M., Kenrick, P., & Martin, F. M. (2018). The origin and evolution of mycorrhizal symbioses: From palaeomycology to phylogenomics. *New Phytologist, 220*(4), 1012–1030. https://doi.org/10.1111/nph.15076

Trujillo, W. (2018, February 23). Can soil organic matter increase at an annual rate of 1%? *Sterling Journal-Advocate*. https://www.journal-advocate.com/ci_31690958/can-soil-organic-matter-increase-at-an-annual/

Tuckel, P. S., & Milczarski, W. (2020). The changing epidemiology of dog bite injuries in the United States, 2005–2018. *Injury Epidemiology, 7*(1), 57. https://doi.org/10.1186/s40621-020-00281-y

United States Environmental Protection Agency. (2015, April 22). *TENORM: Fertilizer and fertilizer production wastes* [Overviews and Factsheets]. https://www.epa.gov/radiation/tenorm-fertilizer-and-fertilizer-production-wastes

United States Environmental Protection Agency. (2018, November 28). *Radioactive material from fertilizer production* [Overviews and Factsheets]. https://www.epa.gov/radtown/radioactive-material-fertilizer-production

United States Environmental Protection Agency. (2023, November 30). *Where nutrient pollution occurs* [Collections and Lists]. https://www.epa.gov/nutrientpollution/where-nutrient-pollution-occurs

Vrinda Menon, K., & Deepa, J. (2020). Public health implications of rodent-borne zoonotic diseases. *Journal of Food and Animal Sciences, 1*(1), 13–21. https://doi.org/10.51128/jfas.2020.A003

Walling, E., & Vaneeckhaute, C. (2020). Greenhouse gas emissions from inorganic and organic fertilizer production and use: A review of emission factors and their variability. *Journal of Environmental Management, 276*, 111211. https://doi.org/10.1016/j.jenvman.2020.111211

Watson, G. W., & Himelick, E. B. (2013). *The practical science of planting trees*. International Society of Arboriculture.

West, D. A., & Hazel, W. N. (1979). Natural pupation sites of swallowtail butterflies (Lepidoptera: Papilioninae): *Papilio polyxenes* Fabr., *P.glaucus* L. and *Battus philenor* (L.). *Ecological Entomology, 4*(4), 387–392. https://doi.org/10.1111/j.1365-2311.1979.tb00598.x

Wheeler, J. (2017, October 6). *Leave the leaves!* Xerces Society. https://xerces.org/blog/leave-the-leaves

Ch 15: More Easy Ways to Promote Outrageous Diversity!

Bat Conservation and Management, Inc. (2024). *Bat conservation and management*. https://batmanagement.com

Boyles, J. G., Cryan, P. M., McCracken, G. F., & Kunz, T. H. (2011). Economic importance of bats in agriculture. *Science, 332*(6025), 41–42. https://doi.org/10.1126/science.1201366

Celley, C. (2021, June 11). *Bats are one of the most important misunderstood animals*. United States Fish and Wildlife Service. https://www.fws.gov/story/bats-are-one-most-important-misunderstood-animals

Centers for Disease Control and Prevention. (2021, September 22). *Human rabies*. https://www.cdc.gov/rabies/location/usa/surveillance/human_rabies.html

Centers for Disease Control and Prevention. (2022, November 16). *Plague: Maps and statistics*. https://www.cdc.gov/plague/maps/index.html

Cimino, A. M., Boyles, A. L., Thayer, K. A., & Perry, M. J. (2017). Effects of neonicotinoid pesticide exposure on human health: A systematic review. *Environmental Health Perspectives, 125*(2), 155–162. https://doi.org/10.1289/EHP515

Coe, S. T., Elmore, J. A., Elizondo, E. C., & Loss, S. R. (2021). Free-ranging domestic cat abundance and sterilization percentage following five years of a trap–neuter–return program. *Wildlife Biology*, *2021*(1). https://doi.org/10.2981/wlb.00799

Dutcher, A., Pias, K., Sizemore, G., & Vantassel, S. M. (2021). *Free-ranging and feral cats*.

Eid, A., Jaradat, N., & Elmarzugi, N. (2017). A review of chemical constituents and traditional usage of neem plant (*Azadirachta indica*). *Palestinian Medical and Pharmaceutical Journal*, *2*(2). https://doi.org/10.59049/2790-0231.1060

Fallon, C. E., Walker, A. C., Lewis, S., Cicero, J., Faust, L., Heckscher, C. M., Pérez-Hernández, C. X., Pfeiffer, B., & Jepsen, S. (2021). Evaluating firefly extinction risk: Initial red list assessments for North America. *PLOS ONE*, *16*(11), e0259379. https://doi.org/10.1371/journal.pone.0259379

Fernandes Mendonça Mota, T., Lima Oliveira, W., Gonçalves, S., Wust Vasconcelos, M., Silvia Beatriz Miglioranza, K., & Castilhos Ghisi, N. (2023). Are the issues involving acephate already resolved? A scientometric review. *Environmental Research*, *237*, 117034. https://doi.org/10.1016/j.envres.2023.117034

Fouet, C., Atkinson, P., & Kamdem, C. (2018). Human interventions: Driving forces of mosquito evolution. *Trends in Parasitology*, *34*(2), 127–139. https://doi.org/10.1016/j.pt.2017.10.012

Gehrt, S. D., Wilson, E. C., Brown, J. L., & Anchor, C. (2013). Population ecology of free-roaming cats and interference competition by coyotes in urban parks. *PLoS ONE*, *8*(9), e75718. https://doi.org/10.1371/journal.pone.0075718

Gonsalves, L., Bicknell, B., Law, B., Webb, C., & Monamy, V. (2013). Mosquito consumption by insectivorous bats: Does size matter? *PLoS ONE*, *8*(10), e77183. https://doi.org/10.1371/journal.pone.0077183

Griffin, D. R., Webster, F. A., & Michael, C. R. (1960). The echolocation of flying insects by bats. *Animal Behaviour*, *8*(3–4), 141–154. https://doi.org/10.1016/0003-3472(60)90022-1

Gunther, I., Hawlena, H., Azriel, L., Gibor, D., Berke, O., & Klement, E. (2022). Reduction of free-roaming cat population requires high-intensity neutering in spatial contiguity to mitigate compensatory effects. *Proceedings of the National Academy of Sciences*, *119*(15), e2119000119. https://doi.org/10.1073/pnas.2119000119

Gupta, P. K. (2018). Toxicity of fungicides. In *Veterinary toxicology* (pp. 569–580). Elsevier. https://doi.org/10.1016/B978-0-12-811410-0.00045-3

Health Resources and Services Administration. (n.d.). *Hansen's disease data and statistics*. Retrieved December 11, 2023, from https://www.hrsa.gov/hansens-disease/data-and-statistics

Jensen, M. B., Willson, S. K., & Powell, A. N. (2022). How effective is the Birdsbesafe® cat collar at reducing bird mortality by domestic cats? *Journal of Fish and Wildlife Management*, *13*(1), 182–191. https://doi.org/10.3996/JFWM-21-055

Jones, R. (2018). *Beetles*. William Collins.

Lee-Mäder, E., Hopwood, J., Vaughan, M., & Black, S. H. (2014). *Farming with native beneficial insects: Ecological pest control solutions*. Storey Publishing.

Longcore, T., & Rich, C. (2004). Ecological light pollution. *Frontiers in Ecology and the Environment*, *2*(4), 191–198.

Loss, S. R., Will, T., & Marra, P. P. (2013). The impact of free-ranging domestic cats on wildlife of the United States. *Nature Communications*, *4*(1), 1396. https://doi.org/10.1038/ncomms2380

Narango, D. L., Tallamy, D. W., & Marra, P. P. (2018). Nonnative plants reduce population growth of an insectivorous bird. *Proceedings of the National Academy of Sciences*, *115*(45), 11549–11554. https://doi.org/10.1073/pnas.1809259115

Nile, A. S., Kwon, Y. D., & Nile, S. H. (2019). Horticultural oils: Possible alternatives to chemical pesticides and insecticides. *Environmental Science and Pollution Research*, *26*(21), 21127–21139. https://doi.org/10.1007/s11356-019-05509-z

Owens, A. C. S., Cochard, P., Durrant, J., Farnworth, B., Perkin, E. K., & Seymoure, B. (2020). Light pollution is a driver of insect declines. *Biological Conservation*, *241*, 108259. https://doi.org/10.1016/j.biocon.2019.108259

Rosenberg, K. V., Dokter, A. M., Blancher, P. J., Sauer, J. R., Smith, A. C., Smith, P. A., Stanton, J. C., Panjabi, A., Helft, L., Parr, M., & Marra, P. P. (2019). Decline of the North American avifauna. *Science*, *366*(6461), 120–124. https://doi.org/10.1126/science.aaw1313

Sanahuja, G., Banakar, R., Twyman, R. M., Capell, T., & Christou, P. (2011). *Bacillus thuringiensis*: A century of research, development and commercial applications. *Plant Biotechnology Journal*, *9*(3), 283–300. https://doi.org/10.1111/j.1467-7652.2011.00595.x

Skelly, J. (2013). *Horticultural oils: What a gardener needs to know*. Extension | University of Nevada, Reno. https://extension.unr.edu/publication.aspx?PubID=3029

Tallamy, D. W. (2019). *Nature's best hope: A new approach to conservation that starts in your yard*. Timber Press.

Wagner, D. L., Grames, E. M., Forister, M. L., Berenbaum, M. R., & Stopak, D. (2021). Insect decline in the Anthropocene: Death by a thousand cuts. *Proceedings of the National Academy of Sciences*, *118*(2), e2023989118. https://doi.org/10.1073/pnas.2023989118

Wray, A. K., Jusino, M. A., Banik, M. T., Palmer, J. M., Kaarakka, H., White, J. P., Lindner, D. L., Gratton, C., & Peery, M. Z. (2018). Incidence and taxonomic richness of mosquitoes in the diets of little brown and big brown bats. *Journal of Mammalogy*, *99*(3), 668–674. https://doi.org/10.1093/jmammal/gyy044

Section 4: More Powerful Ways to Help Heal Earth

Thogmartin, W. E., Wiederholt, R., Oberhauser, K., Drum, R. G., Diffendorfer, J. E., Altizer, S., Taylor, O. R., Pleasants, J., Semmens, D., Semmens, B., Erickson, R., Libby, K., & Lopez-Hoffman, L. (2017). Monarch butterfly population decline in North America: Identifying the threatening processes. *Royal Society Open Science*, *4*(9), 170760. https://doi.org/10.1098/rsos.170760

Ch 16: Lawns are Ecological Disasters–Replace them with Meadows from Seed

Anderson, R. C. (2006). Evolution and origin of the central grassland of North America: Climate, fire, and mammalian grazers. *The Journal of the Torrey Botanical Society*, *133*(4), 626–647. https://doi.org/10.3159/1095-5674(2006)133[626:EAOOTC]2.0.CO;2

Atwood, D., & Paisley-Jones, C. (2017). *Pesticides industry sales and usage: 2008-2012 market estimates*. United States Environmental Protection Agency. https://www.epa.gov/sites/default/files/2017-01/documents/pesticides-industry-sales-usage-2016_0.pdf

Barden, L. S. (1997). Historic prairies in the Piedmont of North and South Carolina, USA. *Natural Areas Journal*, 149–152.

California Air Resources Board. (2021, December 15). *SORE: Small engine fact sheet*. https://ww2.arb.ca.gov/resources/fact-sheets/sore-small-engine-fact-sheet

Duke, S. O., & Powles, S. B. (2008). Glyphosate: A once-in-a-century herbicide. *Pest Management Science*, *64*(4), 319–325. https://doi.org/10.1002/ps.1518

Falcone, J. A. (2021). *Estimates of county-level nitrogen and phosphorus from fertilizer and manure from 1950 through 2017 in the conterminous United States* (Open-File Report 2020–1153). United States Geological Survey. https://pubs.usgs.gov/of/2020/1153/ofr20201153.pdf

Flores, D. (2023). *Wild new world: The epic story of animals and people in America*. W.W. Norton and Company, Incorporated.

James C. Finley Center for Private Forests. (2020, January 7). For water quality: Creating woods instead of lawns. Penn State College of Agricultural Sciences. https://ecosystems.psu.edu/research/centers/private-forests/news/for-water-quality-creating-woods-instead-of-lawns

Klepeis, N. E., Nelson, W. C., Ott, W. R., Robinson, J. P., Tsang, A. M., Switzer, P., Behar, J. V., Hern, S. C., & Engelmann, W. H. (2001). The National Human Activity Pattern Survey (NHAPS): A resource for assessing exposure to environmental pollutants. *Journal of Exposure Science & Environmental Epidemiology*, *11*(3), 231–252. https://doi.org/10.1038/sj.jea.7500165

Libbey, K., & Hernández, D. L. (2021). Depth profile of soil carbon and nitrogen accumulation over two decades in a prairie restoration experiment. *Ecosystems*, *24*(6), 1348–1360. https://doi.org/10.1007/s10021-020-00588-3

Mallinger, R. E., Gaines-Day, H. R., & Gratton, C. (2017). Do managed bees have negative effects on wild bees?: A systematic review of the literature. *PLOS ONE*, *12*(12), e0189268. https://doi.org/10.1371/journal.pone.0189268

Milesi, C., Elvidge, C. D., Dietz, J. B., Tuttle, B. T., Nemani, R. R., & Running, S. W. (2005). A strategy for mapping and modeling the ecological effects of US lawns. *J. Turfgrass Manage*, *1*(1), 83–97.

Page, M. L., & Williams, N. M. (2023). Evidence of exploitative competition between honey bees and native bees in two California landscapes. *Journal of Animal Ecology*, *92*(9), 1802–1814. https://doi.org/10.1111/1365-2656.13973

Sturm, A., & Frischie, S. (2020). *Mid-Atlantic native meadows: Guidelines for planning, preparation, design, installation, and maintenance*. Xerces Society for Invertebrate Conservation. https://xerces.org/sites/default/files/publications/19-052_MidAtlantic_Meadow_guidelines_web.pdf

Tallamy, D. W. (2019). *Nature's best hope: A new approach to conservation that starts in your yard*. Timber Press.

United States Department of Energy. (2011). *Clean cities guide to alternative fuel commercial lawn equipment*. https://afdc.energy.gov/files/pdfs/52423.pdf

United States Environmental Protection Agency. (2017a, February 14). *Outdoor water use in the United States*. https://19january2017snapshot.epa.gov/www3/watersense/pubs/outdoor.html

United States Environmental Protection Agency. (2017b, November 2). *Indoor air quality* [Reports and Assessments]. https://www.epa.gov/report-environment/indoor-air-quality

United States Environmental Protection Agency. (2023, November 22). *Yard trimmings: Material-specific data* [Overviews and Factsheets]. https://www.epa.gov/facts-and-figures-about-materials-waste-and-recycling/yard-trimmings-material-specific-data

Ch 17: Pocket Forests–A Better Way to Plant Trees

Byers, J. A. (1992). Attraction of bark beetles, *Tomicus piniperda, Hylurgops palliatus,* and *Trypodendron domesticum* and other insects to short-chain alcohols and monoterpenes. *Journal of Chemical Ecology, 18*(12), 2385–2402. https://doi.org/10.1007/BF00984957

Holl, K. D., Reid, J. L., Cole, R. J., Oviedo-Brenes, F., Rosales, J. A., & Zahawi, R. A. (2020). Applied nucleation facilitates tropical forest recovery: Lessons learned from a 15-year study. *Journal of Applied Ecology, 57*(12), 2316–2328. https://doi.org/10.1111/1365-2664.13684

Miller, K. M., Perles, S. J., Schmit, J. P., Matthews, E. R., Weed, A. S., Comiskey, J. A., Marshall, M. R., Nelson, P., & Fisichelli, N. A. (2023). Overabundant deer and invasive plants drive widespread regeneration debt in eastern United States national parks. *Ecological Applications, 33*(4), e2837. https://doi.org/10.1002/eap.2837

Ranger, C. M., Reding, M. E., Persad, A. B., & Herms, D. A. (2010). Ability of stress-related volatiles to attract and induce attacks by *Xylosandrus germanus* and other ambrosia beetles. *Agricultural and Forest Entomology, 12*(2), 177–185. https://doi.org/10.1111/j.1461-9563.2009.00469.x

Rodriguez-Saona, C., Poland, T. M., Miller, J. R., Stelinski, L. L., Grant, G. G., Groot, P. de, Buchan, L., & MacDonald, L. (2006). Behavioral and electrophysiological responses of the emerald ash borer, *Agrilus planipennis*, to induced volatiles of Manchurian ash, *Fraxinus mandshurica. Chemoecology, 16,* 75–86.

Vinogradov, D. D., Smagin, A. S., Belova, O. A., Tsurikov, S. M., Karganova, G. G., Tiunov, A. V. (2024). Identification of soil-dwelling predators of tick nymphs (Acari: Ixodidae) by stable isotope labeling. *Journal of Medical Entomology, 61*(2), 512–516. https://doi.org/10.1093/jme/tjad160

Section 5: Lead & Inspire Communities to Help Heal Earth

Clark, P. W., D'Amato, A. W., Palik, B. J., Woodall, C. W., Dubuque, P. A., Edge, G. J., Hartman, J. P., Fitts, L. A., Janowiak, M. K., Harris, L. B., Montgomery, R. A., Reinikainen, M. R., & Zimmerman, C. L. (2023). A lack of ecological diversity in forest nurseries limits the achievement of tree-planting objectives in response to global change. *BioScience, 73*(8), 575–586. https://doi.org/10.1093/biosci/biad049

Devine, W. D., Harrington, C. A., & Southworth, D. (2009). Improving root growth and morphology of containerized Oregon white oak seedlings. *Tree Planters' Notes,* 53(2), 29–34.

Feng, Z., Yang, X., Liang, H., Kong, Y., Hui, D., Zhao, J., Guo, E., & Fan, B. (2018). Improvements in the root morphology, physiology, and anatomy of *Platycladus orientalis* seedlings from air-root pruning. *HortScience, 53*(12), 1750–1756. https://doi.org/10.21273/HORTSCI13375-18

Koenig, W. D. (2021). A brief history of masting research. *Philosophical Transactions of the Royal Society B: Biological Sciences, 376*(1839), 20200423. https://doi.org/10.1098/rstb.2020.0423

Meadows, D. H. (2008). *Thinking in systems: A primer* (D. Wright, Ed.). Chelsea Green Pub.

Miller, B., & Bassuk, N. (2018). The effects of air-root pruning on seedlings of species with taproots. *Proc. of the 2018 Ann. Mtg. Eastern Region of North America IPPS.*

In Closing

Thích Nhất Hạnh. (2013). *Love letter to the Earth.* Parallax Press.

about the author

When you ask Basil what he thinks about himself, he'll tell you he is incredibly lucky. He has family he loves dearly, friends and colleagues who inspire him, and every day he gets to care for trees, soil, and flowers. Helping life flourish brings him so much joy. This includes turning a lawn into a thriving Piedmont Prairie, raising saplings from seeds, teaching his two boys how to find purpose, building an organization that brings good to an increasingly chaotic world, and creating new paradigms that leave life better off than it was yesterday.

He pursues his purpose and passions as the co-founder of Leaf & Limb, a tree care company in Raleigh, NC, and Project Pando, a non-profit that aims to connect people to trees. He is a Treecologist, ISA Board Certified Master Arborist, Duke graduate, and Wizard of Things. He sits on some boards and has won some awards, but he still feels most accomplished when he causes his incredible wife (the real brains behind all of this) to fall into fits of uncontrollable laughter. When he's not having fun at work, he likes to pull invasive plants from his pocket forests, contemplate on his front porch, and go hiking with his family.

Some random facts about Basil: sometimes he dreams about chocolate-filled taiyaki from Hiroshima. One of his favorite memories is celebrating Winter's Solstice with his boys on a mountain top in Linville Gorge under a sea of glittering stars. He is a brown belt in Brazilian Jiu-Jitsu. If you aren't familiar with Jiu-Jitsu, it's an activity where mostly dudes go to a gym in pajamas to attack each other. A week without plenty of reading, intense exercise, and blazing hot peppers is a sad week for Basil. He really, really likes garlic. Basil's favorite birthday breakfast tradition is to eat one of every type of French pastry at Lucettegrace in downtown Raleigh. And it probably goes without saying, he is not a fan of stuffy bios.

a note about type

The text of *From Wasteland to Wonder* is set in Avenir, a font designed by Adrian Frutiger and published by Linotype. The type is set larger to ensure accessibility and encourage you to bring it outside while you work. This book was designed by Miel Creative Studio and printed by Friesens on Sustana 30% post-consumer waste recycled paper.

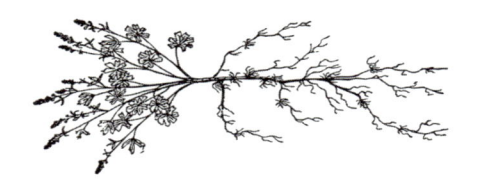